Business *by* Faith

A Journey of Integrating the Four D's of Success

Buried Treasures

Linda L. Smith

ZOE LIFE Publications, Inc.
Riverside, CA

Volume II: Buried Treasures of Faith

ISBN 13: 978-1-934556-73-3

Library of Congress Control Number: 2015901718

Published by: **Zoe Life Publications, Inc.**
Post Office Box 310096
Fontana, CA 92331

Editor: Linda L. Smith

Cover Design: Jiong Li and Amanda Johnson

Printed in the United States of America

Table of Contents

Introduction

Now, hopefully it's safe to assume you have read the first volume, *A Modern Day Example of Unwavering Faith.* I trust you were able to identify with my experiences and inspired to begin integrating the Four D's of Success into your own life, family, and business journey.

In this volume, *Buried Treasures of Faith*, it is my hope that you are still enlightened by my journey, one that has been full of ups and downs. The stories are real, and the results are what keep me going.

Life is full of uncertainty, and all we can do is press through the circumstances. This volume reveals many of those uncertainties and remains a testament to that Faith.

Within Volume I, and now in Volume II, the journal entries are very personal as it relates to business and family matters. *Why be so transparent you may ask?* Well, my intention is to provide some clear insight as to what it really takes to balance a successful business, family and, most importantly, a dynamic relationship with the Lord. It's a journey of faith always!

I share the intimate details of my life's story because, in reality, no one is immune to the cares of life and matters of the heart — it's how one responds that's key. Hopefully, my openness will be a ray of hope and light that leads you in the direction of passion and purpose in your life, one that will require you to dig deep within yourself and move with faith.

With Love,

Linda Lee Smith

Business by Faith

Journal 3 (continued)

Begins: July 2, 1997 ~ 8:25 p.m.

Ends: April 26, 1998 ~ 7:05 a.m.

7/2/97 ~ 8:25 p.m.

I started not to come to Choir rehearsal, but I'm glad I did. We are singing, *'It will work out for the good of them who love the Lord.'* Whatever I am going through, it will work out. The Lord will work it ALL out!

I have not taken the time to appreciate all that God has given me. I go from one project to another.

As I began to pray today before leaving for work, I began to cry as I thought of my marriage, work, mother, and home. Lord, I know You will guide and protect me through this coming storm.

Lord, I love You.

7/5/97 ~ 6:30 a.m.

Yesterday was the 4th of July, Independence Day. The girls and I went to visit Momma Julie, Grandma Russ, and Momma Vivian. While at my mother's house, I shared with the girls what my mother had done for me. She had taken a second loan out on her house for $37,000 to help me and the school.

As I explained things to them, I told them I had something to seriously inform them about. I told them that their dad and I were going to divorce. I was shocked at their reaction. They were calm! I told them I had seen an attorney. More calm! They said they were older and understood. I told them I was very concerned about their feelings. I was open to discussion. Both reiterated they were okay and understood what was going on. They both felt that this was between their dad and me, and as long as he/they maintained contact and communication, they were fine with what was to happen between their parents.

I have prayed and cried. I know I do not want to continue with this marriage. It's been a long time seeking affection and communication. For so long, I have felt alone. I know we will never change, and I don't want more years of this. I seek laughter, love, and expression of it with communication and touch.

I don't know what Ernell wants or needs. I sit and think have I ever asked? Has he ever said? Does he know? Will he ever say?

At times, I sit alone, wondering what it would be like without him, and I think it would be like now...okay. I sit alone, never having a conversation about a thing, NO issue of the kids, the house, our jobs, planned trips — nothing. Divorce would provide me a vehicle to openly seek active, verbal communication and joy.

Lord, I don't know what You will do with me, but I know You know my future. Guide me to safe ground. Continue to love me!

7/11/97 ~ 10:28 p.m.

Today, Theogene called to say HI! What a delight. Our call was cut short when he got a call from Kagali. It was great talking with him. Tomorrow is my 22nd anniversary. I sit here and think about my conversation today with an elementary school chum. She tells me her mother divorced her father after 27 years of marriage. She stayed to raise her children, to give them a better life, and after the youngest son graduated, she left. He was quite shocked. He thought she would never leave him. He asked her to stay, but she had another home. He helped her relocate. I thought of myself, ***22 years and I feel very strongly that it's time for me to go.***

I took the twins to see *Hercules* today. They enjoyed it. Afterward we went to McDonald's for them to play.

I ran into an old friend, Larry Ealy. We haven't seen each other for 20-25 years. We exchanged numbers. He is getting married in October 1998. I expect and requested an invitation. He said I looked like a model. What a compliment!

Time to do Bible study for Step Two. We made payroll, paid taxes and bills. God, thank You. I submitted a written response to ABHES for Christopher to review.

I pray it is acceptable.

Oh yes! 19 students graduated today. Lord, thank You. Bless their future.

7/6/97 ~ 9:57 p.m.

It will work out for those who love the Lord! Oh what a blessed day. Yesterday, all of the students passed the written exam for the CNA test. I am not sure on the skills portion, but all was going well.

I talked with a dear friend about my situation at home. The advice was to wait for an answer from God. Do not act on my own; do not try to orchestrate anything. Things will work out. I began to pray and ask God for guidance. It seems that everything that comes my way addresses marriage. To divorce or stay, I must pray to God. Today in class the teacher talked about being equally yoked. We were yoked in the beginning, maybe not in religion but equally yoked in love, sex, likeness, etc.

As I listen, they talk about a sister who saved a seat for her husband in church over a period of time. One day, he finally came and is now a deacon at Loveland. How long do we wait? What is God's intent for us? How should our life be? Are we to live together no matter what? I am truly empty and lonely in a house that is not a home of joy.

I don't know.

The word said God dislikes double mindedness. He is not like a wave. Our faith should be straight. Believe in Him, ask, and receive. We're not to ask in doubt!

I know He protects me. I am His child! I know Four-D is with Him and it will continue. He has blessed the school to be a foundation for prayer. The students prayed for each other before the test.

Today in class I gave a shout testimony. God brought us through 6/30/97. We made it. We are eligible for Financial Aid! In my class for the past five weeks, Keena sat next to me; today she gave me her business card. She is a Financial Aid officer at the University of Redlands. I grabbed her and screamed! The Lord delivers every time. He guides our path.

I was placing an ad to hire a Financial Aid manager in August. She is willing to assist us as needed. The Lord is good, ALL the time.

Tomorrow will be a blessed day. Love You, Lord.

7/8/97 ~ 6:20 p.m.

At 1:23 a.m., I received a call from Cherry. She received a fax from Dr. Biruta. He had a few questions about the plan, but indicated we could discuss those things when we returned to Rwanda.

We responded, requesting airline expenses for three people. We indicated we would leave on August 3rd or 5th.

I have felt that I would have something exciting happening around my birthday. This could be it.

I am truly excited about all of the wonderful things that are going to happen in 1997-1998 for the Academy, Cherry, and I.

We will offer CNA (300) Hr. program and the Pharmacy Tech program by October.

Lord, thank You for this wonderful blessing. I know You are our guide.

7/12/97 ~ 11:11 p.m.

Today is my 22nd anniversary. Neither I nor Ernell said anything about it. We solemnly attended the Pasadena Jazz Festival. I enjoyed the music. It is too bad that he and I have nothing to talk about. When I am alone with him, I feel alone. He continues to display his distant act, just like 20 years ago. I stopped going out with him due to how I feel when I'm alone with him. He sat across from me — silent. I observed other couples sitting close, embracing, and talking to one another; but as we sat at the table, my silent partner was across from me, few words were spoken...just emptiness. 22 years, what would the next 22 be like? Not like this, I hope. Should I expect any more fulfillment in my personal life? What a sad thought to be married and alone!

7/16/97 ~ 6:22 a.m.

Tuesday 7/15/97 was a very blessed day. I provided info for guardianship for the twins to the legal secretary.

Visited Allaiha at the Public Enterprise Center. She lifted my spirits as I did hers. We prayed. Oh what a joy. She said Satan tried to have me believe I was in a dark hole, but I wasn't. She sees the school as one of the "greatest" schools in the United States.

Busy at school, multiple interruptions, students, faculty, calls.

Van resigned effective 7/18/97. She gave 12 reasons. I kindly accepted, no painful loss.

I picked up my monitor after three months with a loaner.

I talked with Cherry last night for a long time. God, keep us going. We have much to do.

7/19/97 ~ 12:16 a.m.

This evening I was a judge at a Talent Show on End Time Ministries. I was invited by Geraldine, a graduate of the CNA Program. She told me Satan tried to stop the program because no one wanted to pay a registration fee so the coordinators dropped the fee.

What a blessing it was to see young people praising the Lord!

Minister Miller came to me. He looked at me and said, "I never met you before, but I seen you on T.V. God came to you about seven years ago and gave you a vision. I see you going forward doing good things, and what He will have you do is big." After church, I didn't get to see the minister, but I did meet his wife.

Tahira came to me last night to report a small bump behind her left ear. It is the size of a pea. She said she has headaches sometimes. It feels attached to bone, unmovable. Tonight she returned - no headaches, but the bump feels slightly larger in size. I referred her to MD Ross for exam in the morning.

I know my baby is fine. But she needs reassuring. She decided to wait until Finals are over on Wednesday.

God is good, all the time. Healed in the Name of Jesus.

7/19/97 ~ 11:21 p.m.

The preliminary financial report showed assets of $140,000 and liabilities at $94,000 liabilities. We met the 1:1 acid test. My capital contribution was $156,000. Only God knows where it came from! $37,500 E. Russ ... $ 23,000 S Sep... $11,000 on credit card... $10,000 on another credit card. The rest is unknown?

All taxes are current, all bills paid current, payroll current.

Keena came Friday to meet with Pam and Frankie about Financial Aid. She said we are doing well. She has talked with several lenders about loans for students. I know that August is going to be a great month for the school and me.

Cherry and I will be going to Boston in August. The twins and I to see Sadiq and, if possible, the Rwanda trip by mid-September.

I feel God is going to prepare us for a big growth. He has shaken me up. I have become a better manager. I love what I do. I receive peace and joy in serving the Lord through the school and students.

Today, Aisha and I attended our discipleship class. It was great. Tomorrow, we will perform our first lay ministry function. I know God will bless us. Greg Jordon, the class leader, said Aisha will be a leader for the youth. They have already seen her potential and how she works with the youth.

Tahira will be coming to church tomorrow. I spoke with her several months ago and she listened. God started a seed by introducing her to a young man who is studying to be a minister. She can see the difference in how he treats her versus how she has been treated by others – spiritually, personally, in conversation, etc. God is good.

Ernell and I have a cool environment. It has been on my heart to ask him what he wants, and if he will accept Jesus or want Him in his life. I fear his answer. I want to ask but the time is not right. God will guide this process. There is no joy here.

I attended the Jackie Robinson memorial at the San Bernardino Stadium. It is great. The history of his life, Black baseball players, etc. Tuesday I will be taking the boys. I know they will enjoy it.

Thank You, Lord, for this day!

Let me continue to walk each day with You.

Your Child, Linda

7/22/97 ~ 12:35

Oh what a day. I came in needing to pray. I asked Mary, Pam, and Frankie to pray for us, the school. We need to return to the premises on which we were founded. To spiritually acknowledge God in our daily walk and strive to make a difference in the lives of others.

We lift the name of Jesus. We thank Him for salvation, money, love, and guidance. Our first LVN student to pass the LVN Board, Bhavna Dinesh Potel, came in today to share her notice. Oh how proud I am of her and us! Things are going well.

I look at the suite within this building. It's a possible 2,600 sq. feet for additional training space. God is always with us.

Tonight, I will be taking my nephews and Jack to a baseball game.

7/23/97 ~ 10:24 p.m.

Today, while at lunch, Frankie and I started talking about life, our lives. As she spoke, I could hear the pain in her voice and see the change in her facial expression. She has been in an unhappy marriage for many years. She said, "I have been married 32 years. I'm 52. If I tell my husband I want to leave, I know what he will say. He will change. So why leave? I don't want the next 32 years to be like my first 32." I thought this was a profound statement. As she talked about her own unhappiness and loneliness, I saw myself in my 22 years of marriage. I decided I didn't want to be sitting in her seat in 10 years, feeling like her, talking to someone in my seat. I left work soon after and went to see my divorce attorney. I asked that she serve Ernell by August 1st. It is time to move beyond fear. Life holds so many uncertainties. I can't wait due to fear of being alone. God will not take the school from me. My children will be okay.

I will talk with Ernell on Tues. July 31, 1997.

Lord, guide us.

7/24/97 ~ 8:27

Yesterday was a blessed day. A young lady (student) named Tamika has missed four days of class. She has +1 over allowed for graduation. She had missed her last day in order to get her hair braided. I wanted to hurry her out of my office, but my spirit led me to ask her questions. She did not smile, seemed uncaring. Finally, she said, "Maybe I would smile if I went to church." I asked her if she had a church home, if she believed in God and His Son, Jesus Christ. I shared what I believed. I invited her to Loveland.

Aisha (my daughter) was at work. I asked her to join us. She shared info about time of services and we made arrangements to take her to church. Tamika lived in Rialto, we live in the opposite side of town, but I am thankful to God for the transportation He has given us.

Tamika does not have a car. She wants one and is considering her options. She thinks it's nude dancing. We discussed that! No nude dancing! Lord, I am so thankful that You are using me to help others. Guide me.

7/26/97 ~ 8:10 a.m.

Last night, a continued blessing. I picked up Tamika and her four-year-old cousin, James. We arrived at 7:35 p.m. Service started at 8:00 and Aisha, Michelle, and Sherry showed up at 8:30. After the service, the girls piled into Aisha's truck and went out for a meal. They had a good time with James. I am thankful to God to be in the place to help others. I feel as though Tamika is meant to be with me.

God will guide this relationship.

7/27/97 ~ 12:10

** Plant a seed. I would like to see Four-D Success Academy, Inc. develop into Russ University, a nationally recognized Educational Institution with an emphasis on Nursing and Health related academic development.

Plant a seed and it will bear fruit. God is the branch and we are the veins/fruit. God will guide us to this end.

7/29/97 ~ 11:30

I was scheduled to fly to Oakland yesterday, but the trip had to be cancelled. I had been disturbed in my spirit for several days, and I knew the time was upon me to talk with Ernell about the divorce. I have felt so uneasy. Last night, I arrived at home around t 9:30 p.m. I went into the bedroom, picked up the list, which was done to move "household" items. I asked Ernell to come to the dining room table. I calmly told him we were not happy and there was no need to carry on. I was divorcing him. He calmly agreed, stated he had felt the same way, and started to tell me about five months ago. He talked about differences of perception and how we had been affected. I told him I wanted the house. He told me, "You want the divorce. You leave."

"I have too much invested here," I calmly stated. We could both continue to live in the house, and the Judge would make the final decision.

He did not want to go over the list of household items. He agreed that he had his 'friends' and I had mine. He agreed that the marriage had been strained. By the time he tried to reconcile with me 2-3 years ago, I did not receive him. He felt a change in me 5 years ago. How odd. He acknowledged that he tried at different times, now he asks that we try together. We have been married for 22 years and I expressed that I did not/could not stay married for the sake of 'marriage'. I/we desired happiness in whatever form. I wanted someone who will see me, talk with me, and touch me affectionately. How much longer must I wait for him? How much longer must I wait on him? I should have known when I saw the pictures in his office of his friends, but none of the kids and me. After 17 years, he puts up pictures of the 'fellas'. His actions were a resounding statement to me. I had given him a picture of me in our 7th year of marriage and asked him to put it in his office. He said no, that he didn't need or want a picture of his wife/family in his office. I chose not to have one of him in my office, only the kids.

He called the girls down to inform them. Tahira asked, "After 23 years, can't you both put in effort to work on it?"

"When both or one is not willing to work together, then there's nothing to be done," he replied. This implies that I choose not to work on it.

Tahira needed reassurance that she would have access to both parents. She also felt comfortable in the fact that she would be moving out by the end of the year. I could see the sadness in her eyes.

Aisha seems to smile and say okay. Her focus was on the list. Her truck may be sold? Where are we going to live? Who is keeping the house? Will she have to live in an apartment? No expression of sadness, but concern of her shelter.

Ernell asked if my 'rings' were a part of the list and I said no. He had earlier asked if his WATCH was listed. How odd. Then, he wanted my rings; they could have $3,000-$5,000 value! The girls defended each of us and suggested we keep personal items.

He could keep the boat, van, Jet Ski, clothes, etc. I could keep my watch, rings, and personal items. I explained the list of household items. I could see the 'smirk' look on his face. He wanted the Oma Chima (Charles Bibbs) picture; he claims he bought it. I almost got frustrated with him. How could he say that? I earned the signature artwork. I worked on the Unity Coalition Committee and I had it framed. I was paying on it and now he was claiming it was his because he picked it up and paid the balance. It was needed for his meeting, he wanted to impress because the wall was empty. That's Ernell. I rose, went to the bathroom, and pulled off my ring. This may be the position needed to have a favorable outcome.

I slept okay. Tossed and turned some, rose at 8:00 a.m. and washed my hair. I feel pretty good. I pray this morning about things: work, relations, peace, my children, Ernell to give his heart to God, my mother, in laws, brothers. I prayed for me.

If I walk in the light, then darkness is a lie. I have peace, love, and happiness in my relationship with Jesus. I am okay.

7/29/97 ~ 10:28 p.m.

I feel good. Tonight I completed enrollment into La Salle University for the Masters in Business Administration. I should be finished by August 1998. Then I will enroll into a PhD Program. Utilizing my time exceedingly well. Plans, goals, stay focused. Pray. Stay focused.

7/31/97 ~ 6:50 p.m.

Another day. Today, Cherry and I shared thoughts regarding Financial Aid issues. We need someone and we know God will send the right person.

I found myself crying today. I grieved over Ernell's comment that he began protecting himself over 2 years ago.' I could not/did not ask what he meant. There was a time that I was in need of financial assistance, and I knew I could not go to him. He has protected his funds. I thought about how often I wanted him to see me, talk with me. I am sad because I know that lonely feeling will not elude me. Sorry it could not occur (happiness, conversation, touch) with him. I love him, but am tired of being lonely.

I signed more papers today with the attorney. He will be served next week. Only God knows what will happen. Yesterday, Tahira had a dream that her dad stopped paying the bills. She said not to worry. She assured me that she had two jobs and would be working as a LVN soon. She is buying tickets for Patti Labelle for my 45th Birthday gift.

8/3/97 ~ 10:45

I sit in church listening to the word of God. Pastor Chuck preaching about calling on the name of Jesus, and how to get to the throne.

I cry inside. I am trying to get to the throne. I am going through a private, personal crisis. I sit and wonder how this all came about...a divorce. I follow Jesus. What happened?

I think of Ernell's words, "You changed five years ago." What happened 5 years ago? I told him Jesus had spoken to me. I was to open a school and teach Nursing. To this day, he doesn't understand. He thought I was 'holding' money from him. He started protecting himself 2-3 years ago. I sit in joy feeling God's presence with me. I cry with joy in knowing His Son Jesus. I cry in knowing that Ernell knows neither. I cry knowing our lives have not grown spiritually together. I call on Jesus. He knows my sorrow. He knows my desires. I pray that that which I long for from my husband comes about. I also pray that if he chooses not to change, that Jesus continues to bless me with a good, spirited life and that He allows me to work with Four-D Success.

Last night at 7:00 p.m. the April '98 students had their pinning and capping ceremony. I felt confident that Jesus would bring Four-D through. We will receive the Financial Aid Program. I know Jesus sees and hears our prayer. He guides us as a team. I thank Him for what He has given us. I know we will continue to be able to minister to others through the school. Lord, I thank You. Keena will not be the

Financial Aid Officer, but she and I will continue to work together. Jesus will cover us with His blessings.

Lord, thank You for hope, strength, peace, joy... Jesus, Jesus, Jesus, my hope when I am hopeless. My song when I cry, Jesus, Jesus, Jesus.

8/4/97 ~ 9:29 p.m.

Today, Frankie, Greg Sheets, CPA, and I met to review his Audit Report. 1997 was a good year. We are still here! We went from a -$76,000+ to a +$17,000. Greg faxed the report to Mr. Robert Smith, the Financial Aid evaluator. He will respond ASAP. I know Jesus has guided us through this financial obstacle. He alone carried me. I thank Him for all of the support He sends my way. I know we will be approved. God said don't wave like the sea.

I spoke to Theresa today and said this, "Double-minded man is unstable in all his ways" from James 1:8... I know God has connected us.

She will replace Keena. Keena is unable to assist us due to personal issues. God always has a plan that is guaranteed to succeed.

Frankie said I looked tired. At times, I am. Greg said or admitted he wasn't sure we would make it, but we did. He is very pleased. Being more aggressive turned a negative net loss of $76,000 to a positive net worth of $17,000.

Lord, I thank You. I cried sadness and joy. I await final report from Mr. Smith. I love You, Lord!

8/6/97 ~ 10:07 p.m.

Well, today I received a call from a young lady. She worked for The City of San Bernardino Employee Training. I was informed that Four-D Success Academy, Inc. has been selected for the 'School of the

Year.' The award will be presented in September/October. What an honor for the school. How ironic, as I anxiously want to hear from Mr. Robert Smith in Washington regarding our status on Financial Aid, and to inform him that the school has been recognized by SB Co and City as one of the best.

We received a call from a director in Riverside. She stated she fired a CNA trained by that other school I was complaining about and was seeking Four-D graduates. I requested she write a letter of support for the school to Mr. Craig's contacts in Riverside.

Rwanda responded. They expect Cherry and I to return the first week of September. I must address the needs of the school. Cherry may go alone. She called me at work to say we both had to go. How sweet to be thought of. I know this is going to be a big project. I know God will guide us.

Ernell and I only speak — but that's all we've ever done. Speak kindly to one another. Good morning, hello, goodnight. How strange to be married so long and to divorce without noticing a miniscule change in how we talk to one another. Divorce, although painful, might be a normal process for us. I think we will silently part as we silently came together.

I told my mother. I will talk with Mama Vivian this weekend.

I believe Ernell has been served his papers, but being quiet as he is, I don't know. He has been working on finances on the computer.

At times, I cry with grief. Then there are times like this. I am at peace and calm. I shall sleep well tonight. Tomorrow, I will be 45 years old.

Looking good, God's child.

8/7/97 ~ 2:35 p.m.

Well Happy 45th Birthday, Linda!

I sat in 95° temperatures in my car. Driving on the freeway from Ontario, the car popped its cork. Burning hot, I made it to Riverside and Valley. It's hot. The men at the Chevron don't have a clue about this Sterling car.

Ironically as I left the Ontario Hilton, I thought to myself, I must get info together on this car in case of an emergency. Well low and behold, it happened. I am here. Now! What does a girl do without a man!

Stay calm, call for a tow truck and a friend. Help.

Walter Jr. called at 5:50 a.m. to inquire if the rumor was true about the divorce and to say Happy Birthday.

I call R. Smith in Washington, no answer for Financial Aid. Stay calm. Stay cool.

8/8/97 ~ 12:50 a.m.

Last evening, Ernell informed me he cancelled my American Express Card. He is so very calm. But as he said, he's been preparing for two years. Aisha and Tahira surprised me with flowers, apple cider, cake, and four tickets to Patti Labelle.

My radiator blew up and will cost $600 to repair.

All considered, I removed my wedding set today. It had been on my finger for 22 years and 2 months. I feel okay, not great, but okay.

Cherry told me of the possibility of future work with The Consortium at Cal Poly Pomona. The contracts they receive lacked a Nursing Component. We might have an opportunity in the future.

Lord, guide me. Give me mercy. I spoke with Frankie today. She has Shingles. Fatal nerve wrecked. Concerned about spouse's unemployment. He's not! I ask God to strengthen her, I ask God to bless Four-D Success Academy. Grant us the Financial Aid package. Keep us financially sound and allow us to Grow! Be encouraged.

8/12/97 ~ 6:33 a.m.

I am at the office. It is quiet except for the low hum of the computer. It's still, I feel shallow. I prayed coming in as I do most of mornings on the road. I asked God to fill me with desire, to allow me to see Four-D grow so I can continue to help others. Yesterday, in the LVN class, Tonya had the students doing aerobics, their method of learning the muscles.

I know I have done well, but I can do better and more, I ask/pray that God allows me to continue. At times, I fear He will end all that He has given me, because I choose not to remain in this marriage. How can I think that? God knows all. He could have ended this school at any time. I have had financial trials for five years. Always in need of prayer.

I sit and wonder why I don't want to be married to Ernell anymore. Loneliness, crying, sadness, no communication, no emotional exchange, limited expressed affection, no terms of endearment, coldness, indifference, and silence. How long? I reached my breaking point. I cannot let my life with him end my joy or drain my spirit of life:

- ✓ I withdraw in his presence, for I have experienced years of emotional neglect.
- ✓ I go silent in his presence, for I know no response will come forth.
- ✓ I disappear from his sight, for I know he doesn't see me.
- ✓ I cry in my silence, for I know he doesn't feel me.
- ✓ I choose not to go on. If he wakes up, I will be gone.

Pastor Turner called yesterday. Ernell called him for help. Now, am I supposed to understand, is this what God wants? Why is it the burden of the brokenhearted to mend the fence, once the hammer loses his head? It's like an Alcoholic Anonymous family member seeking treatment to handle and live with a drunk who is being helped. Well the hammerhead may be broken, but I am ***not*** the repairwoman!

Why is it that counselors encourage (mostly women) to remain in a broken home? Who does it benefit? What pleases God? What pleases man? Why is it when a woman is broken, she can't fly, and then is told not to walk away because he (the male) will change.

I've been married for 22 years. When will the change come? Must I wait 5-10 more years? I pray that anger, rage, and BITTERNESS not enter me; for my sake, you must depart!

I've not received a response from Washington regarding Financial Aid. God knows the next step. I will wait for guidance.

Lord, I lift up Your name. Thank You for what You have given me. Forgive me of my sin. Guide me. Give me wisdom. Fill me with joy and hearty laughter. Put the twinkle back in my eyes and turn the corners of my mouth upward.

I pray for focus in my prayer time with You and study time in Your word.

I ask that You aid me as I pursue my Masters in Business Administration. I pray I complete the program by March of 1998. Then allow me to enter into a PhD program and be complete with the requirement by March 1999. Well it's 7:00 a.m. and I offer a silent prayer to lift the day. I love You, Lord.

In my deep sorrow, yesterday, Cherry gave me a gift, a beautiful card expressing the Lord's love and the New International Version of the Bible Promise Book. As I read, I underlined versus that comforted me.

Thanks, Cherry.

8/12/97 ~ 10:34 p.m.

Not too much accomplished today by me. I await my 6 p.m. appointment with Pastor Turner and Ernell. I sat and listened as Pastor Turner carefully selected his words.

I know Ernell and I are miles apart. As I sat and listened to Ernell, I knew he had not changed lanes in 17 years. He says he felt ignored the last five years, with me always working, driving toward my goals, and not needing him. He sought activity to keep himself busy. I spoke of loneliness, lack of verbal communication, active listening, no vacations or time alone with him in 20 years. I could not take crying any more. I rose and left. Kindly excusing myself, I walked out to freedom. I stopped by Borders and purchased *The Heart of a Woman* by Maya Angelou. It seemed fitting by the title to read.

When I arrived home, he was sitting in his chair, same position as always, his left leg hanging over the armrest. I had asked that he not do that when I first purchased the chair. His heavy leg would warp the arm. It did. Yet still, he hung his leg. I stopped saying something a long time ago.

He called his sister Genie. I heard him say, "Genie, It's going to be a bitter divorce." Aisha is concerned that he will make me look bad in everyone's eyes. He is trying and I am not. He called her! His sister. He is prepared for a bitter battle. I am not. I must let God handle this for me. I ask for peace, however it comes.

Aisha is encouraging. "Don't be sad, don't worry, stay prayerful. God will take care of you; don't worry about what people will say." All this is said with a smile. I listen.

Today, I picked up a check. I called Roberta and asked if the check was in the front office, and if it was for at least $5,000. She said $11,000. It was for $15,500. Thank You, Lord. 10 students enrolled into the DSD, $3,000 and four finished Saturday and paid $1,200.

Frankie, in Financial Aid, called to say God has control over all things. "What you do for God will last." She was totally encouraging. Even Pam said, "Why do you worry? That's why we pray here at school, God will take care of everything. God is good."

Cherry and I talked about Rwanda, her meeting with Dr. Hart at Loma Linda, my Masters Program. We laughed about her chosen 'future' title, Dean of Student Affairs. She's crazy. We laugh. I want Chancellor for her! I am crying. She selected V.P. of Operations, we really laugh. I say, "If you select your own title, what will I be?" She responds, "Well when you are the Pres./CEO, where do you go?" I laugh. It's good. All is good.

We love working for Four-D.

8/15/97 ~ 10:10 p.m.

Here in Vacaville with Anwar and Jaise, it has been a fun trip. I got only a glimpse of what my mother had done daily. I know the activity with them kept her alive and moving. On the flight here from Ontario, they talked ALL the way with the man sharing a sit in their row. Non-stop conversation. Yes, he was conversing with them.

They openly expressed their love with words of "Auntie Linda, I love you, Auntie Linda, we love you." While reading in the car or while watching T.V. the words of affection come forth. They are close and support each other more than they squabble over little things.

The visit with Sadiq went well. Today, he shared with them why he was incarcerated, the incident, and the murder. He was not in school, but in prison. He loved them, and they would always be friends. They listened, kissed him, and asked him when he would come home. He replied when they were about 18. Young men. They said okay. They expressed words of love, exchanged tight hugs, and kisses. Then they were off to play. Anwar ran to get a tissue for Sadiq's tears and returned to play.

Sadiq asked if I would be okay caring for the boys, and if Ernell was okay with it. I told him it didn't matter what Ernell thought. I was divorcing him.

We discussed the reasons, outcome, religion, Koran, Bible, beliefs, my life, fears, blessings, and the joy I seek.

I shared with him Jaise's question. On the way to see his dad, he asked me if the wind he felt was the North or East wind. I was stunned. I said, "Baby, I don't know." Quietly, I smiled to myself.

I called home and talked with Aisha. She tells me my sister in law 'Bunty' called my office to speak with me about the divorce and how it wasn't God's way. This sister has said as little to me as Ernell in 20 years. The first 7-10 years, she hardly said 10 sentences. Hi, bye, small talk.

Now she and her husband split up. He's not supportive, and she feels she must live apart and married. Lonely is fine for her, not me. I just don't understand. Why must women consume the burden or pain of loneliness? Rejection for the sake of being married to a man who doesn't acknowledge them?

I simply choose not to believe that is my path.

I hear Earl is so upset he may call off the scheduled family picnic. What has Ernell shared? How much has he accepted of his own part of silence and rejection?

WELL, I AM HERE. I will survive. God loves me! I breathe new life of living with joy and the Spirit of the Lord.

Thank You, Lord for this day!

8/18/97 ~ 9:36 p.m.

Last evening, Tahira treated me and three guests to a Patti La Belle Show at the Hollywood Bowl. Cherry, Donna, and Betty, my cousin, accompanied me. The show was quite different. We had a great time.

I sit here in my room thinking about my life. I felt ill this morning, like this was not going to be a good day. I took it as a sign to look into hotels. Be prepared.

1) I called Washington about Financial Aid. Mr. Smith is aloof. Things look good; we made 1:1 + profit. I will be receiving a letter in 2-3 days.

2) I called Sacramento about CNA re approval. Mr. Marlin hasn't received our program, which arrived 6/29 (3 weeks ago). There are nine programs in front of us.

Betty came into my office, we talked, and she prayed for the school, the faculty, and me. It's great to have God-loving women to work with. Prayer is always needed.

I feel so overwhelmed. I cry to release some of the pressure from the impending divorce and the Academy. I cry about the divorce. How aloof Ernell has been throughout our marriage. A man who can't embrace and caress. A man without a kiss of compassion. After 20 years of tension in my body, I look at my feet. I just don't remember them being swollen as a young child or even before I married Ernell. *Could the silent strain and well-kept loneliness cause moderate to severe pitting edema in my feet and lower extremities?* I just don't know. *Will the swelling subside when I divorce?* I just don't know. I try to see my feet from years ago. They are not swollen, 3" heels, miniskirts, no edema. My weight? I put on a size 12 pantsuit and it felt a little tight in the bust. I look at myself and think, *All my life with Ernell, I always thought I was big!* Ernell has never complimented my weight or size. I have been a size 3, 8, 10, and 12, and there's no change in his response to me. I have looked good all my life to me — not to Ernell. I look okay and coming down. My goal is a size 8 by the end of September 1997! Aisha is monitoring me and doing a good job.

Lord, lead me. Guide me along the way. Sing until I come out of it. There is nothing that can separate me from God. NOTHING.

Sunny days ahead guaranteed – for I am God's child!

8/21/1997 ~ 7:28

I believe it was Tuesday of this week that a knock was at our front door. It was about 6:45 a.m. I ask who it was, and the man replied DON or DAN! "I am to see Ernell." I returned to the bedroom to awaken Ernell. He rose and ascended the stairs. I could not hear the conversation. Ernell returned upstairs and went into the den to read the papers he had received. He didn't say a word to me. Therefore, I truly don't know what they were. Was he served the divorce papers? His actions and silence gives no indication. His behavior is that of usual.

I think of these words in the counseling session with Pastor Turner. "His resentment of me is from early in our marriage." Have I been emotionally and physically neglected because of 20 years of resentment? I have cried much and I suffered needlessly. Simple communication 20 years ago could have eased this pain today. I sit here empty as a hollow shell of what I have always wanted in my life, a loving husband. Punished for 20 years. I have served my time. I want to be released. Yesterday, at the praise sessions, I cried out the pain, the questions, of how I have been treated. He punished me the best way he could. He denied me himself. He cast me into a pit of sorrow and loneliness. All my scars are internal, never to be visibly seen. He is a good man by many standards. Only I know how this good man has treated me. Loneliness can divide you out of and into another.

As I sit here, I begin to understand myself better: my actions, my tears, my pain, and my desires.

I pray to God for peace, patience, understanding, forgiveness, guidance, love, and His continued love. I pray He lift me above the walls that try to hold Four-D at bay. I pray He touches the heart of Gary Martin. Set straight our need to continue to teach and pray with our students. Lift each staff member up. Guide us as a team. Lord, I need You.

8/22/97 ~ 12:28 a.m.

God's Woman Conference

Melodies from Heaven is playing on the tape. I sit alone in my room, being healed of hurt and pain. I prayed to God for peace. To be a better, wiser leader of Four-D. I ask that He fill me up, use me, and speak to me, as He did in July 1991. Guide me, remove evil forces that stand in the way and attack the school and me. I pray for unity of staff, support of the philosophy, and mission statement of the school. I pray for the continued opportunity to receive students and pray with them. Share the word of God with them. I cry for this blessing. I call out His name. I pray for deliverance from this marriage. I cry out with pain, as I bear Ernell's words of resentment towards me. He has punished me for 20 years. He deprived me of what I wanted most – him. Time with him. I ask God to set me free. To bring into my life a man who loves the Lord first, a man who will love me without conditions, who will support me, and allow me to support him. I thank God for healing me of fear of loneliness, fear of Ernell's reactions, fear of losing Four-D.

I cry until I can't breathe. God gave me new life. Today was a day of healing, at the seminar I was filled with God's presence. I received what I came for — to feel His touch. I pray for and I pause to listen to the tape. I am more than a conqueror. The songs are healing... ***Don't take your joy away.*** I have God to fill me with love and joy. I told Ernell I wasn't going to let him take my joy.

I pray that each and every lady has received more than what they have come for. Lord, I love You.

Thank You for putting me here alone in this room to worship You!

8/23/97 ~ 12:18 a.m.

Yesterday evening at 7:20, Tahira Ayanna Smith graduated from Citrus College Vocational Nurse Program. My baby...a nurse. As my life separates from Ernell, it becomes quite evident how distant we are. We sat separately at the Graduation. He, Aisha, and his mother sat together. His sister and her sons sat in the row above them. His brother, niece, and her husband sat two rows below me. As I sat alone, I smiled, for tonight I was to witness my girl achieve a milestone. She was to be a nurse. How proud of her I am. When she came into the audience to present me with a white carnation, I held her close to my bosom and whispered how proud of her I was, that this day filled me with joy.

We all went out to dinner. I was comfortable with Ernell. No matter how I tried to get a roommate at the God's Woman's Conference, God said He was to work with me. My scheduled roommate's radiator blew up. I truly don't know if she ever made it.

Last night (Thursday), alone in my room, I kneeled to pray. I prayed for momma, brothers, school, kids, and Ernell. When I began to pray for me, the tears began to flow rapidly and fully. I prayed for peace, and to be relieved of the pain. How could my husband of 22 years resent me for 20 years?

I ask God to release me of the marriage, to provide me with a man who loved the Lord. A man who could love ME unconditionally, a man to hold, to speak to me, and a man who would allow me to give all he needed from me, accepting me with open arms — my love.

I don't know what He has in store for me. I pray to be attentive and let Him do His plan — not mine.

I attended the seminars on Divorce, Dealing With Hurt, Life After Divorce, and How to Remain Whole. All addressed me, provided me with tools and understanding to make it. God knows I want to work for Him the best I can. The Lord filled me up with joy. I love the Lord.

8/25/97 ~ 10:25 p.m.

I just finished Maya Angelou's book, *The Heart of a Woman.* Excellent reading. Today I received a call from Liz in Washington D.C. She requested a copy of the business license. I faxed the Accreditation Certification and the letter from the Council BPPVE. She said the forms were needed to review the evaluation and final preparation of the application approval. I shared the information with Frankie.

She hugged me and cried. I returned the embrace and thanked her for staying with me and Four-D. I shared the info with Cherry. She gave a big smile and said she has already seen her new car, a Mercedes Benz, and that she gave the salesman her terms. I smiled and said I need to see the letter of approval. Ana K. from the funding agency called me and we talked briefly. She said things sounded good and to call with any questions.

I opened up with a dear friend, and he said something so profound. Hell is, having travelled through it. Through my hell now, I should never mention or reflect on Ernell's statement of resentment. I have too much work to do. What did the past have to do with my future? To remove 'Linda' and 'I' out of the way and let God control. I dearly love him for his support, wisdom, and guidance. He has done well in helping me to grow into a fine person.

I called Aisha to thank her for her love and support. Today is the first day of the rest of my life. I will live it to my fullest; I will let God guide me. I am healthy, whole, and loved. Goodnight.

8/30/97 ~ 8:30 a.m.

In my deepest sorrow, He sent His messenger, Aisha. Thursday night, I again felt a heavy burden. I didn't cry, just felt burdened. Our finances continue to paralyze me. I had to give notice to several employees. It is so disheartening not to be able to help others. To lay them off means they must seek another source of income. I pray that they return to FDSA. Aisha shared the word out of the Bible from 1 Corinthians. She shared God's love for me. His gift to me — FDSA is His powerful work. Her words reassured me. This is God and He chose me. I must not get down, for God knows everything. As I listened to her minster to my heart, He soothed me. She volunteered to work at the school in any area that she could. She heard my plea. I love her.

Last night, Tahira said we need to do more things together like going to plays, etc. We will go in the near future. I picked up the twins last night. We are going to the Church picnic at Red Hill Park in Alta Loma today. Sadiq called and spoke with me about his book. It's almost complete. We love each other. I must speak with someone to help get it published. God has a firm hand on him.

I pray for ALL my brothers. They walk down dark paths. They don't know what the light path is about. I continue to pray for them and me. Four-D will make it.

Cherry is ready to go to Rwanda next week, 10/3/97. I pray for her safe passage and success.

9/1/97 ~ 4:00 p.m.

Yesterday, Tahira and I went to the Jewish Museum of Tolerance in L.A. Another place I've always wanted to visit, but never have. Tahira said we didn't spend enough time together. She drove us there. The lecture was excellent and presented by a survivor of the Holocaust. She shared info about the gas chambers, in-house treatment, and separation of family. I learned that not only were Jews killed but homosexuals, midgets, gypsies, and supporters of Jews were exterminated too. Estimates of 5,600,000 people were killed. The question was WHY? I had the opportunity to speak: the answer — indifference. "When we become indifferent to our fellow man, we lose the ability or desire to care for that person or group's well-being." I shared that the indifference continues to repeat itself in this century with the Rwanda Genocide. The speaker acknowledged the Rwanda Genocide and included the Children of South America, Yugoslavia, etc. Life is not always precious to those who do not know God!

Today is Labor Day. I started on the Master of Science in Advisor Administration. I will be complete by March 1998. I sit here looking out of my window at the clouds, the trees, the mountains, and think about tomorrow. What does it hold for me?

God is good. Friday night, Princess Diana died at the age of 36 in a car accident. Life is precious. Her children will grieve for the love and touch — never to be felt again. I value my life, my life to live. All that I have done will not compare to what I am to do in the future. God is guiding me to great things. I must prepare.

Thank You, Jesus! I thank the Lord. The treasures of His are mine, for I inherit what my Father has: love, peace, joy, and happiness, the eternal love of God.

9/4/97 ~ 7:17 a.m.

After reading, I felt too tired to write. I had such a restless night. My mind is plagued with issues. I took Cherry to the Airport in Ontario. Her flight was at 12:50 to New York to Brussels to Kigali. She was off to close our deal, to negotiate the contract for the Rwanda Health Education Project.

I had a telephone interview by The Business Press – Don Berton on Tuesday. Yesterday, Wednesday, I had a long telephone interview with Anina at West side Story. On Friday 9/5, I have a TV interview Channel 3.

I am seeking public awareness of FDSA. The State Consultant has not sent our signed approval to continue the CNA Program; and it's been 5 weeks since Gary Marlin received the minor revisions. I pray for God's intervention. As I tossed and turned, I could see a side of me that every man has — anger and revenge. Even through death. How thoughtless of him to stop my work, the Program. I have laid staff off and he seems so indifferent to our needs. My thoughts are not my own, but of the evil spirit that tries to raise its ugly head. I pray to God. I seek relief.

My left shoulder often disturbs me. I know it's nothing serious. I refuse to think of it being more than a pain in the butt.

We, I must go to work. I ask God what I do now.

9/4/97 ~ 10:30

I feel as though I am falling. Anxiety is too great. Left arm tingling, I warded off a stroke/heart attack. God is my source.

I call Washington to speak with Mr. Smith. He said he signed off the letter. We would be getting our approval for Financial Aid! I cry. Frankie and Pam came in for hugs.

I have a 4:00 Appointment with Cal Poly Assistant Dean to discuss Teacher Credentials. Ms. Lee refused to write a letter of explanation. I press on. I place another call to Gary Marlin for status of the CNA Program. Awaiting his call. I pray for Cherry's success.

9/8/97 ~ 10:10 p.m.

Today, Ruth died. I feel sorry for Charlie, not for her death, but for his loss. He loved his sister. I know he views death as part of life's chain and that's that, but I know he cries inside. I shall see him tomorrow.

We received the disk from Ed Tech, a letter from Crestor; approval from Bank One, and the Participation Agreement is coming from Washington in 7-10 days. Hopefully by 9-17-97, we will be connected.

Enrollment is quite low, possibly no class for Monday. Account low, bills high. God is in control! I shall rise up early and off to work.

9/11/97 ~ 10:25 p.m.

I spoke with Alexis in Rwanda yesterday; he is recovering from his car accident. He was sorry he was unable to see me. We look forward to seeing each other soon. He saw Cherry earlier that day.

I spoke with Cherry. Things are progressing well. She is meeting with Dr. Biruta today or tomorrow. Minor changes needed in the contract.

I met with a lender today to discuss the Financial Aid program. There is much to do. I hired a Financial Aid Officer; she will start on Wednesday 9/17. She is a good addition to the staff – a God-loving, spiritual woman. Thank You, Lord.

We may possibly receive five computers from SB Co JTPA. I submitted a letter to Keith today. Ironically, Frankie and I discussed the need for computers earlier in the day. On my way home, I stopped by Keith's office, had dinner and behold, my pick of computers…the rest is history.

As I proceed through this divorce, I pray for protection.

Lord, I love You!

9/12/97 ~ 11:45 p.m.

Well today, we received the letter granting us eligibility for the Financial Aid program. We are seeking a lender, submitting to Granting Agencies. Getting computers. OH HAPPY DAY!

I spoke with Gary Marlin about the CNA Program. More changes needed. Mary will correct the forms for him tomorrow. We have been quite slow, but things are going to get better. We have 13 students to date scheduled for the CNA class. Lord, guide us to the highest level of performance and productivity. Allow us to excel to excellence in the highest form.

9/13/97 ~ 9:47 p.m.

I have been feeling much better about myself. The swelling in my feet has been gone for a week. I remember rising up one morning last week, sitting on the side of my bed, and saying, "I love my feet." That's the first time I have acknowledged my feet in a good sense in 20 years. They really did feel great. My weight is gradually coming down. Aisha continues to prepare my daily lunches. I watch my intake and drink lots of H2O. I have more peace as I sit and write this than I have had in years. I guess making a decision about my future has given me strength. Oh yeah, I found Oprah on America On Line and wrote a letter to her noting our efforts in Rwanda. Who knows, she may write back.

Well I'm going to read a little, slowly progressing on the Masters Program.

9/18/97 ~ 7:44

Today is Tahira Ayanna Smith's 21st Birthday! Thank You, Lord for this day. She has graduated from a Nursing Program and is looking towards her state test and eventually living on her own. God will guide her.

Yesterday, Theresa did not report to work. She had back problems and was hospitalized. She will come in on Monday the 22nd.

I am working on setting up the Financial Department with supplies and computers. I know God is with us.

I am calm as I see the financial need, but God is the banker. After five years, I know God is all. Yesterday was Pamela Jackson's 5th year with the school. We must celebrate.

Lord, I pray for my mother's peace. I pray that You remove those from her life that bring her grief. Give my brothers, Donnie, Zachary, Gregory, a new place to reside. Strengthen her Lord. Put joy in her voice, love in her heart, and peace in her mind.

Guide me throughout the day. Love Your Child, Linda

9/18/97 ~ 10:37 p.m.

The end of the day for me.

Anna came today to talk with the NELA Agency; she is very positive. There are some things I must do for the student catalog. I will work on it this weekend. I met with Walter Jr. and momma to discuss our twin's behavior in school. Walter will attend school two times a week. They cried more for sympathy, but it will straighten them up.

The LVN Students are graduating this Saturday, 9/20/97. It will be held at the Church of Christ in Redlands. It will be quite nice. I was touched by the Spirit. I went throughout my house claiming it in the name of Jesus. I touched everything: walls, furniture, floors, pictures, and dirty clothes. I cried, praying and claiming in the name of Jesus that I be allowed to stay in my home. Then I watched channel 40, the preacher was preaching on Faith, Hebrews 11... ***"The evidence of things not seen."*** I listened, cried, and prayed. My faith must be deeper. I must be steadfast. I must know the power of God's blessings, my will to receive without doubt. God is my shield, my provider, my anchor, my food, my father, my clothes, my shelter, my finances, my lover, my life, my happiness, my all and all. God is all; I am His number one. I have all. I will not be without, I will not go hungry, I will not be without shelter, I will not be without funds to pay all my bills, I will not be without transportation, I will not be without His love, shelter, food, clothes, spiritual supper, faith, salvation, mercy, grace, His all and all. I will not be removed from Jesus, the Son of God. I will not be separated from Him. I will be blessed. I will be happy and full of His riches. I will not be shaken by evil, by anger, by malice, by people. I will not be distracted by Satan. He has no power over my life!

God is in control. I am with God; Satan, Ernell, anger, and bitterness will not prevail while I stand, walk, breathe, touch, feel, see, and smell —Satan and nothing evil can withstand the power of God. I am His child. Lord, keep my heart calm, patient, and keep me in prayer. Keep me, keep me. Lord, keep me! Keep me from all harm.

9/19/97 ~ 10:58 p.m.

Oh what a day. Nancy, Toy, Tonya, Tony, and I, along with approximately 15-20 students, attended the VN Board review in Burbank. We have excellent standings and were approved to enroll 30 VN students for September 29th. We had a 100% pass rate on VN Boards. We are to be watched as a school 'model,' and this was noted in writing. This will be placed in our school newsletter.

We may obtain five computers from SB Co. JTPA. The proposal is due 10/6 for the City of SB. Cherry is due to arrive Sunday at 9:30 p.m. She has not indicated the outcome of the visit. I don't know what to expect, but whatever the outcome, we will move forward. My feet are not swollen; it has been about three weeks. I truly do believe it is the result of my ability to let go of the trapped anxiety I have had for 20 years. I feel better and I sleep better.

Thank God!

9/21/97 ~ 6:15 a.m.

Yesterday, we had 12 Financial Aid students attend the workshop at the school. After it was done, Frankie, the bookkeeper, gave her verbal resignation. Due to personal home life issues with her husband and the growth of the school, she said the pressure was too great. I have empathy with the 'pressure at home.' I too am going through a separation and it is painful, but the growth of the school is what I strive to do. I told her I couldn't stop the growth of the school.

Unable to work out an alternate plan, we hugged. I know God will see her through her situation. I prayed for her last night and this morning.

Ironically, Ernell has been going out, coming in after I am sleep. This morning, I went to the bathroom at 3:45, the garage door was going up. This man would not take me out and allow me to enjoy private time with him. I marvel at how behavior changes and presentations appear. I found myself praying for Ernell's space, safety, and that he establish a relationship with God. As I prayed, I realized my peace. I had no anger...another step toward healing. I can pray for him sincerely. I thank God for my presence of mind.

The second class of LVN students graduated. The ceremony was held at the Church of Christ in Redlands. It was lovely. Everyone missed Cherry. I pick her up tonight at 9:30; she's returning from Rwanda.

I am proud of all the students; I know God is proud of US.

I pray He sends Four-D a mature, skilled, knowledgeable, analytical bookkeeper who can handle the growth of the school. One who has knowledge of Financial Aid. I pray, I pray for support from the Heavenly Father, that I continue to be guided and stay focused on the mission!

9/24/97 ~ 11:08 p.m.

I was exhausted last evening, just too tired to make an entry of the exciting day. Yesterday, I interviewed Ms. Chow for the bookkeeper's position. She will be an excellent addition to the Academy. She's cheerful, intelligent, positive, spiritual, friendly, seeking a challenge, and fine quality.

I received four computers from SB Co. JTPA. Oh what a blessing! One for the Financial Aid Officer, one for a second desk, and one for each staff office – free use for a year. Cherry completed a proposal to do Dental School to California Endorsement.

I know that God has a total hand in my life.

Ernell listened to the message from the legal secretary regarding the guardianship on the twins. I was stunned by his line of questioning. He wanted me to stop the proceeding because he would be implicated. When I asked, "How?" he could not answer. His attorney told him I should stop. His selfishness gave him concern that if my mother died, he would be legally responsible to assist me. How awful. What would make him or his attorney think that I need the court's permission to care for my nephews? How narrow-minded. How selfish. He says he can't wait to get out of this. I did not let his comments disturb my spirit. I was calm and peaceful. I know God has healed a part of me and there's more to come.

Today, I was busy focusing on billing, intake, applying for Ed Tech. and I introduced Theresa to the staff.

Lord, give us a breakthrough. I picked Cherry up on Sunday night 9/21/97 at 10:00. Things with the Rwanda Proposal look very positive. Wait on the Lord.

9/28/97 ~ 7:08 a.m.

God answered prayers. When Frankie resigned on the 20th, I asked God to send a specific person and He did. On the 22nd (Monday), Cherry gave me the phone number of Ms. Chow, a bookkeeper. She and I met Tuesday evening, the 23rd. A cheerful, knowledgeable, mature, challenge-seeking lady. She met with Greg Sheets on

Friday, the 26th. He felt she would be great for the direction Four-D is going.

Ms. Chow met with Frankie on Saturday. They covered the details of her job. I am concerned that Ms. Chow left without saying anything to me.

Frankie said she (Ms. Chow) said she has trouble getting up early. I don't know if Frankie is picking a way to create a negative environment before we even start.

Pam's attitude has not been pleasant. She is upset over the loss of one-day of pay. Yet others have been laid off and cut four days. She said, "I don't care about anybody else, I am talking about me!" How selfish, I am saddened, but I will move on.

Last night, oh what a blessing at Temple with Karen Wiggins and Dr. Margaret Douroux. The concert was uplifting, the message in song, *'It's already done,'* was for me. *The Storm is Over,* sung at Loveland today, filled with the presence of God, the Spirit. I shouted and cried. Today's message was about sowing seed and reaping the harvest.

Lord, I sow. I await the harvest.

I ask God to bless FDSA so that it may be a blessing to the 'Gospel House' Shrine by Dr. Margaret Douroux.

10/1/97 ~ 9:44 p.m.

Today, we received a Guaranty Agency, Northwest Education Loan Association (NELA). Next, we need a California Student Aid Commission (CSAC) connection. Then we are set to go! I am working on the San Bernardino Employment and Training Agency (SBETA) and Greater Avenues for Independence (GAIN) program proposal. God willing, we'll receive the contract.

Tahira has mailed off her National Council Licensure Examination (NCLEX). Aisha has started back at Cal Poly and I expect a great year out of her. God, grant me the wisdom to make wise decisions. My feet have swollen back up. I don't know why. I know I need new shoes, but I don't think the shoes are the cause of the swelling. God, heal me!

10/5/97 ~ 5:35 p.m.

God is good, all the time. Payroll was made by His grace. $17,000 paid. We have been blessed with an excellent accountant and Financial Aid Director. We are moving forward.

God is preparing us for a bright future. We are submitting a contract to the City for GAIN. I pray for acceptance.

God is giving me such peace as we proceed through this divorce. I feel good; I know God is my guide. I feel better than I have in five years...my spirit, my glow, my smile, my attitude, my walk, my joy, my PEACE. I feel great! I feel beautiful. I am free of fear; I am free of the unknown. I pray for Ernell, his direction, and his safety. I pray he establishes a relationship with Jesus Christ. That he seeks peace and not revenge; that anger will not consume him. Although he has not said a word, his actions tell so much. I wonder where we will be 12 months from today. Life will be good for both of us.

My girls are fine. I am pleased.

Thank You, Lord for keeping me, for protecting me with Your hedge. I look forward to tomorrow.

10/10/97 ~ 11:23

Oh what a blessed day. Today I met McGee, a referral for the Pharmacy Tech Program. We discussed the program, needs, philosophy, and goals. Rescheduled a second appointment for 10/21/97.

Considering a new contract for additional space of 1,400 sq. ft. for the LVN class, a room for the store with office space, and a small classroom.

Theresa sent off seven names to Washington, need E. Pin #. I had said the 10th was a deadline date for us and the Lord saw fit to send up the names.

While at the annual Wine/Vendor session at the Orange Show, I met Tony, a Pharmacist at SB Community Hospital. He will be the consultant for the Pharmacy Tech Program.

Thelma Bledsoe had good news for us regarding a possible facility agreement with Riverside Community Hospital. God is good. We have a bright future! Thank You, Lord!

Stay wise. Be humble.

10/15/97 ~ 7:45 a.m.

In Las Vegas for an Accrediting Bureau of Health Education Schools (ABHES) Workshop, I have quiet time with the Lord. The last couple of days have been wonderfully moving and spiritually uplifting.

On Sunday, the 12th, Tahira, Aisha, Anwan, Jaise, Tahira's boyfriend, and I went to the SB Stampede Park to hear Mrs. Coretta Scott King speak. She spoke on social issues focusing on all Americans, alcohol and drug use, the need for truth and fairness to the American Indians, their social land, affirmative action or lack of it and its effect on the drastic low enrollment of Minorities in Medical and Law School, Dr. Martin Luther King Jr., dreams, and keeping the goals alive. I feel it was an opportunity of a lifetime for me. I thank God for it.

Charlie introduced me to Chris Apoder O'Riordan-Adjah from Ghana, Africa, a lecturer in the Church of Christ Science. On Friday the 10th, we attended the Orange Show 4th Annual Jazz and Wine activity. I had the opportunity to share my work (FDSA) with him and he informed me of his work, healing sickle cell anemia. How marvelous it was to be in his presence.

On Monday evening, Charlie and I drove to Laguna Beach to hear him lecture on 'Understanding that Heals.' I was so lifted in spirit to hear this man speak of undying love, and trust in God and in the Christ Jesus. His elevated level of the truth was almost hard to comprehend as he told the story of his son...the invalid who could not walk, the doctors who wanted to do surgery, and his belief in the Christ's power. He saw his son as perfect in the spirit of love. He knew that his son was God's creation and God is perfect, that what He creates is perfect. What others saw was not the spirit of the child.

Through the course of time, he prayed not that his son's legs would straighten and that he would walk, but that the doctor could see the Spirit of God through his son. One day, his small son stood up and his legs straightened. He walked around the table. He (Chris) ran to the kitchen to get his wife. When they entered the room, the son ran to his mother's arms. God revealed Himself. The lecture spoke on unconditional love for another to look for the spirit. Even those who do wrong have the spirit of goodness in them. It takes a truly understanding person of God to achieve a depth of truth and live it daily, freely. I pray to reach such a level, especially in weak moments as I am now.

I don't have the money to pay bills, and salary, but the Christ Jesus has provided all. He will produce that which we need. I anguish as a child, lost, searching for answers to my life. My husband who has resented me for so many years. I cry in pain. I think of all the times I have been denied his time, his touch, and his company. Was he punishing me? Why for so long?

I know that God will bring me through. I ask for understanding, wisdom, knowledge, peace, love, and joy. I ask for a man, to grow with, who first loves the Lord, attends Church, and is active. A man who will hold a conversation with me about daily events, world events, life, children, people, jobs, likes, and dislikes. His joy, pain, and sorrow. A man who can effectively communicate. I desire a man of love, who can tenderly express himself in touch, looks, and words. A man to call my own. One that will call me "Baby" and not be ashamed. I seek a man of enterprise who seeks my support in his work ventures, a man who can equally support me or motivate me to strive for higher heights, as I would encourage him.

The Lord has heard my prayers and felt my tears. He will deliver.

Washington has not signed the application I returned around September 11th-15th. It's now October 14th, and I am told once it is signed, it could take 2-3 weeks for money to become available. All I can do is call on Him and pray that He hears. Lord, please pay the staff on Friday, PLEASE!

The verses that come to me are… *Trust in the Lord with all thy heart, with all thy might. Lean not unto thy own understanding. In all thy ways, acknowledge him and he will guide thy path.* As I read through the Bible, I seek the chapter of the TRUST verse. I come across Hebrews 12:1-2. 'Jesus, Our example of Endurance.' He endured the Cross and the shame, and sits on the right hand of the throne of God. Endurance – run but not get weary, do not faint. Lord, carry me. Strengthen me. Faith overcomes all – Hebrews.

Well it's 8:45 a.m., I'll read Maya Angelou for an hour, then prepare for my 12:30 meeting. Lord, I love You.

Your Child, Linda

10/18/97 ~ 9:15 a.m.

Well here I am in Modesto, California at my friend's home, the Quarles'. I have had a wonderfully, relaxed time. I arrived on Thursday around 3:30 p.m. I flew in from Las Vegas to Sacramento, rented a car, and drove to Modesto. They have a lovely (large) house in the Country Club. The dog, Simba, is constantly at my toes.

Linda and I have had a lot of time to talk, laugh, and relax. She is still in Volunteer services. I laugh when she says she has gotten tough, only 3 clubs instead of 10. She's in school, working on her Masters. She has taught school, but schoolwork takes up too much time.

Bubba, the Modesto Bee Publisher, is still Bubba to me. I have engaged his conversation. Last night, we sat out on the patio, sipping white wine, talking about my divorce. Bubba wanted to know what happened. He gave words of advice and caution. After dinner, he and Linda showed me a 30-minute film on their trip to South Africa. I must say it was impressive. There they were in the company of Nelson Mandela and Desmond Tu Tu. Hallelujah!

Alicia, their daughter, is a beautiful young lady. Like many (most) teens, she is sometimes sassy, and then, "Mommy, I need!" Kids don't know which way to go. Linda showed me some of Alicia's artwork. She is quite talented. I will request a piece before she becomes famous.

Today we are going to an Auction given by the YMCA, which Linda is a board member of. It shall be interesting. Local artists have donated some of their art. Individuals with large money (hopefully) are going to be there. That's what the board is hoping for.

Well I am going to get clean and dressed, I look forward to a great day. Tomorrow, I head south. Love, Linda... Oh yeah, God paid the salaries with staff. Money comes in time, Thank You, Lord. ☺

10/19/97 ~ 11:00 p.m.

Well, what an evening and day. I arrived at the Ontario Airport at 9:30. I went straight to Church. What a blessing. The class is on 'Experiencing God,' and today's lesson was God pursuing a loving relationship with us. Oh what a great joy in knowing that God pursues us for love so that we may love Him. He is omnipresent and omniloveable. He loves us individually.

Tonight, Aisha graduated from her training class and Step Two. I graduated from Step Two as well. I was introduced to a young man named Carl that lives in Walnut. He has met with Rudasinga to discuss Computer Technology and something (I must pursue) about Nursing School or a hospital for Rwanda in conjunction with the Azusa Pacific. I must call Theogene.

I feel so blessed today after visiting the Quarles'. I appreciated God's abundance; it is okay to have what the heart desires. I do my work for God. He has shown His love by keeping Four-D going. It's fine for me to have a nice chair and a new home and car. I give in love. I shall receive in love.

I met Rev. Jesse Jackson again tonight for the 2nd or 3rd time.

10/20/97 ~ 8:18 p.m.

I (we) received a fax from Pretoria, South Africa from Dr. Ntuli regarding training Four-D does. Cherry will head the project. I signed the lease on the additional space. Construction will start by Friday. We are scheduled to move in between November 16-20th.

I feel free in knowing God's plan for me. In class yesterday, we discussed God's love for us, His blessings. I am so thrilled in knowing that it's okay to have the abundance He has for me. I look forward to the newness of my life. I can openly and willingly (AISHA) receive all that God has for me.

I will call Gary (Mayor of Saginaw) in Nigeria. Is there still interest in Nursing? I thank God for paying the salaries and rent. He has always come through. I must refocus on the VNA Program. I set March as my completion date.

Lord, I love You.

10/21/97 ~ 7:15 a.m.

I read until 12:05 a.m., *C Cooper's Family*. Upon waking, I ponder Ernell's statement of resentment towards me. I have not fully nor clearly understood it. I realized FEAR had prevented me from seeking further clarification. This morning, I asked him, "What is it that you have resented about me all these years?"

His typical response was, "I told you many times." After several requests for him to explain it one more time in a complete sentence, he said he told me many times that he resented me being away from home. Work and school — always doing something.

Not quite stunned, I replied, "But I did everything. I cooked, cleaned, and cared for you and the kids. I went everywhere you wanted to go." I looked at him and felt peace and calmness within me. Where would I be if I didn't walk my own path? ***My life will continue.***

I drove to work thinking of my horizon of experiences: my work, my pursuit of education for myself and the kids, reading books, helping with homework, teacher/parent conferences, spiritual growth, emotional growth, physical understanding. I did it all, the best I could. I loved my man, tried to encourage him to follow his desires and dreams. He chose not to. I followed mine. I have no regrets.

At work at 7:15 a.m., I smile. I feel peaceful, no turmoil in my spirit.

I thank the Lord for this day!

10/24/97 ~ 7:26 a.m.

Oh what a day yesterday. We received our final approval from Washington's Department of Ed for the Federal Financial Aid Program! Lord, when I saw the letter, I cried with many thoughts going through my mind. I thought of being able to pay off my mother's house. Paying off the $250,000 debt. Paying back all bills, paying staff with raises. I was filled with joy.

Cherry and I had spoken earlier; I said we were going to have a great 1998-year. She said we would leave 1997 with a BIG BANG. We were both right.

I met with Frank D. Smith of Press Enterprise. He will be working with me on how to market Four-D. He is preparing a press release. He has very good ideas. I think we will develop a deep business relationship.

Lord, my mother quit smoking after 60 years. She is 74, started smoking (lightly) at the age of 12 or 13. She said she felt 'heaviness' in her chest. She went to the doctor and they discussed family issues, her smoking, and diet. She quit on the spot and gave her cigarettes to my brother who needs to quit. She has not had the desire since October 19th, 1997.

I know she will live to see the twins graduate. She said, "I guess I will live to see Wilbert home." That is my prayer; see Sadiq home.

Lord, thank You for such a big blessing.

10/25/97 ~ 9:53 p.m.

Today, I attended the annual Bethune Recognition Luncheon. I had the privilege of introducing Dr. Mildred Dalton Henry to the guests. It was a wonderful feeling to be involved, to be around black women of substance. I have the opportunity of going to Washington Dec. 6th-11th for the National Convention if Carolyn does not go. I met Barbara Perkins of Paramount. She has been closely connected to Dr. Height in Washington. I spoke briefly of the Rwanda Education Project and Dr. Theogene's desire to meet Dr. Height.

Yesterday, I went clothes shopping at Macy's after my presentation of the Community Service Agency in S.B. I feel good and deserving to treat myself better. Suits and sweaters. I should (will) do this more often.

God is all and perfect. I am His child, I have all that He has for my perfect life, I learn, live, and enjoy His blessings and work.

Linda, Your Child

10/28/97 ~ 10:18 p.m.

God is love, God is spirit, and God's love transcends all. This is what I hear today, this is what I needed to hear. Yesterday evening, Ernell said I could drop his health insurance since he had received his own. Remembering what my lawyer had said, "No changes during divorce proceeding," I asked that he put it in writing. He became his obnoxious self, staring at me as though he had won a challenge. He refused. I requested one sentence. He refused. He said he needed to speak to his attorney.

At that moment, I understood his selfishness and stupidity. He would rather cause a disturbance for his PRIDE rather than write one sentence. His resentment runs deep. We exchange words. I know I have no desire to remain with such a selfish and stupid man. I told him he has never known how to give love or to receive it. He wasted 22 years being stupid. I meant every word.

Aisha slept with me; she was determined to keep us apart. My girls witnessed our worst and last moments together.

Lord, forgive me. See me through.

10/31/97 ~ 11:04

Well today, my mother, Eula Russ, and I went in the SB Superior Court. We were granted co-guardianship of the twins. I thank God for this day. I will let Sadiq know. He will be pleased.

Payday was made, Thank You, Lord. Tomorrow is a busy day. 9-12 at work, 12-4 practiced for the Fashion Show, 7-9 sing at Chaffey High School with Loveland mass choir. Afterwards, I took the twins to Loveland's Halloween party. They had fun.

I am tired. Lord, goodnight.

11/3/97 ~ 11:15 p.m.

Yesterday, I spent time with Christine at Emmanuel's in Loma Linda. She had come to California to see Cherry, me, and the Rwanda family. Today she returned to the airport, heading back to Washington D.C. and then to Rwanda.

Gary contacted Cherry. He informed us of his upcoming trip to Nigeria on November 15th. I plan on going to see Nigeria and Uganda to seek opportunities for Nursing Services.

My home has been calm. I think it's because I have completely resolved/dissolved my marriage. I know Ernell will not know how to love me or allow me to love him. I am empty of him. I am free.

I continually thank God for my peace. I seek Him for protection as I proceed with my life. Tahira is anxiously awaiting the results of her State test. I know she will pass.

Thank You, Lord.

11/5/97 ~ 10:03 p.m.

I have moments of grandeur, and then I have moments of sadness and wonder. Today, employee taxes were due. The checking account is at $2,000. Taxes are $5,000. I thank God for my personal credit cards. I transferred $4,900 to the school's account. I continue to give what I can, all that I have to the school; but it's God who provides the avenue to achieve the outcome. I feel solemn driving home and I cried out to God to show me what to do. He has provided for FDSA and me. I need to know if I am doing the right thing for the school.

Marketing Strategies, Development Strategies. Do I go to Nigeria or not? Will the Financial Aid come to us by Friday? Payday will come from JTPA.

At times, my spirit is at peace, and then it is stirred up and shaken. I have to refocus on God, His guidance, and my first night with Him. We will make it. My joy outweighs my sadness.

Thank You, Lord.

11/16/97 ~ 11:55 p.m.

Well it's been a while since my last entry. Much has happened. We finally received the Financial Aid approval and connection. Theresa has diligently worked on policies to ensure we are aligned with the Federal Education Standards. Ms. Chow has worked with Pam on Receivables and Pam has improved greatly in this area with the computer. God continues to show Himself and His blessings to all of us. The school still stands; we have good plans for the future.

My mother-in-law called for me last week. She purchased the tapes, *Women are from Venus and Men are from Mars*. She expressed how much Ernell loves me and that he is so hurt by my divorce action. It amazes me how she and others can speak for Ernell. He is in this house with me and says nothing. I inform her she does not know the man I know and live with.

The class 'Experiencing God' is great. I am learning His love for me! What freedom and joy in knowing He loves me NO matter what.

I am working with the twins on their schoolwork. They need positive reinforcement and praise for doing a great job. This past week, they did very well on their spelling tests. They earned a dollar each.

Momma is doing fine. The four sons are back. Ronnie on the couch, Donnie in robe, Greg drunk, Zack sleeps (he's the only one who lives there). It is 12:30 p.m. and they are in PJ's, oh what a sad and disappointing sight. Life moves on.

I established a 'Management Team' last week on Thursday 11/13/97. Ms. Chow, Theresa, Cherry, and I met to discuss goals and issues for the growth of the Academy. We have much to do, but we have the time and desire to achieve all that we set out to do.

I was in a fashion show for Helen Smith. I will audition in January for the over 40 group. I will make it. I had fun and met some nice ladies. I bought a gorgeous black evening gown. Even Aisha liked it, she told me to buy it. Helen is giving me the pantsuit I liked for free. Oh, I am a happy camper.

God is working through me and for me and He allows us to make payroll. He guides me to the extra money on the credit cards. I know it all will be paid back soon.

I had an allergic reaction to something I ate at Helen's. Whelps on my face and upper torso. This morning, my feet and legs itch a great deal. Tonight, I continue to itch. In the morning, I will be healed.

Goodnight, Lord.

I visited Shirley at Upland Community Hospital. She is as beautiful as ever. Surgery went well; she is going home on Tuesday. I look forward to her return to Four-D.

11/17/97 ~ 1:30 p.m.

I received a call from Rwanda. We deposited $29,000, no bounced checks, Thank You, Lord. I am working on my assignments for the Masters Program.

11/18/97 ~ 10:16

Sunday, I visited Shirley at the hospital where she is recuperating from knee surgery. We had a wonderful visit. She is doing excellent. She was discharged yesterday; she is planning to return to Four-D as an instructor in June or July. I miss her and truly look forward to her return.

This morning, I was overwhelmed with the spirit of God's presence. I prayed and was compelled to kneel and give Him thanks. He has brought me through the valley. I know that my personal life will continue to be good. God's plan for my future is exciting. No fear of not having a home, no fear of loneliness, no fear of being unable to make it. No fear of Ernell's actions. I know God has not given me the fear of anything. He is my provider, protector, guider, Savior, and my Lord!

The school still stands for Jesus. Payroll has been met again, but only by the grace of Jesus.

I am praying for the Pharmacy Tech class to be successful. I do know (and believe) that David will be a good addition to the faculty. Lord, thank You for keeping us together.

My girls are healthy, happy, and focused. I pray for their continued blessing by You. I pray that they grow to know You and establish a love relationship with You.

Guide me. Make me a better person. I love You, Lord.

Thank you for all. The Financial Aid is coming, stay tuned!

11/23/97 ~ 1:20 p.m.

Well I just walked out of my 'Experiencing God' class with Aisha. She reminded me that I always needed to prepare for her at Christmas and we laughed. It was good to spend time with her at Church.

Today, in class, I heard her openly pray for the first time. Tears came to my eyes. My baby loves the Lord. I could feel our love for one another and God's love for all of us.

I swell with tears as we sing. ***He's able. God is*** able. We sing, ***Stand no matter what.*** I cry for I know that God is able to help me stand. Nothing will put me down; I give thanks for my life, and my journey, the school, His love for me, and momma's support. I stand for Jesus.

I am on my way home, but I'll be back tonight at 7:00 p.m. to sing to Jesus. I love You.

11/24/97 ~ 10:41 p.m.

Oh what a blessed day, an extension of yesterday. The message at church was great. Pastor Chuck returned home safely home from Nigeria. There were 70,000 or as much as 200,000 people who waited four days to hear him preach. Oh what a blessing.

Last night, at the evening services, Pastor Starks continued his ministry on 'Financial Freedom'. Matthew 6:19 says, "Don't worry. God is in control." He provides how to save, and exercise prudence.

Today, I felt the Lord around me. I arrived at work at 8:15 and asked the ladies to pray. Theresa informed me that Ms. Chow slammed the telephone down and yelled, "Alright." The money from the Financial Aid $39,000 had been deposited into our account. We prayed and hugged, and I cried and thanked God. Five years, believing and praying and today, it all came together. Lord, thank You! David accepted the position as Pharmacy Tech instructor. I know this program will do great. I am thankful to God for all that He is providing us. Yesterday, my cousin Alma Lou died in Arkansas of cancer. Even in joy, there is sorrow.

I talked to Ernell this evening about the divorce. I had requested we sell the house and property in San Bernardino, pay the line of credit off, and separate. He said no, that he wanted it all — the house and property. I am at peace with this. The outcome, only God knows.

I have an early rise. Ms. Chow and I will attend the Colton Chamber of Commerce. Time to market Four-D. Goodnight, Lord!

Oh yes, my baby, Tahira Ayanna Smith, passed the Boards. She is a Licensed Vocational Nurse. She's looking for her own place; she will be working at Foothill Presbyterian Hospital in West Covina.

11/27/97 ~ 9:26 a.m.

I was with Jesus on my mind. I give thanks and prayers to Him for His guidance and love for me. I pray for safe passage for my mother, brothers, cousins, and nephews as they journey to Arkansas for the funeral of my cousin Alma Lou. I spoke with Aunt Nancy yesterday, how sad to call regarding the loss of her daughter. We had a good conversation. God is strengthening her; her kids will be with her.

Last night, I attended the Thanksgiving prayer service at Loveland. Testimonies were given and songs were sung by the Prison Ministry. Margie Hill delivered the word from Exodus 16:19 "God

Got Your Back Covered." He protected the children of Israel as they left Egypt. As they traveled through the desert, He provided water passage through the Red Sea. – Deliverance. God had them covered, and He has me covered too!

I was starting to think of how I could protect my school, God's school, from Ernell. He (Ernell) wants to find out what the 'Assets' are. I wanted to lay a plan, but God has me covered. I don't need a plan. I don't need a scheme. Ernell can't take what God has given. My spirit rests, and I move on!

As I lay in bed this morning, praying and giving thanks, this was placed on my heart and placed in my spirit to operate a Skilled Nursing Facility. I think of how it should run. It's called 'My Best' Skilled Nursing Facility. My best work, my best laundry room, my best dietary department. Our employees would perform their best, the best care to the residents. They would work at my best job. The philosophy would be, "I provide my best to God's best." For He alone is the best provider of all my needs.

My best care to those who deserve the best that God has to offer. My best attitude and approach to others is to bring out the best in them.

My best is what God will give me. One day, I will operate a Skilled Nursing Facility where My Best will provide its best service to those in need. My best will be God's best time.

Cherry and I are collecting clothes for her store. My mother has donated as well. We are storing things in Riverside until we are able to open a location. It's coming. God is good.

Today, I will have dinner at my mother-in-law's. I pray for a peaceful time, love, and joy. God is good.

Linda loves the Lord. He hears my cry, He dries my tears, He guides my path, He forgives, and He continues to love me. I am His Child. He is my FATHER!

11/28/97 ~ 4:05 p.m.

Well it's the Sunday after Thanksgiving. I had a relaxing time; I visited Temecula with a friend, went to Tijuana and had a taco and a margarita, and window-shopped. Returned to Temecula for dinner and had a joyful, relaxing evening.

It's raining and cold outside today. Tahira is out shopping, Aisha is asleep, and Ernell is out. I am home sitting on my bed looking out the window at the winter grey skies. I am thankful to be shielded and warm.

God will grant my family a safe passage home. I pray for my brother, Greg, who can't make home his home. He chooses to be on the streets living a hard life. At the age of 34, he has nothing. His face reveals the deep tracks of his life. I must call Roshann, my sister, tomorrow or when my telephone is fixed.

Sometimes I wonder about things. What will I be doing a year from now? Will I be healthier, look better, feel better, have an open, loving relationship? I think of what Ernell has given me: shelter, a home, things. Do I value physical love and affection more than shelter? What if I had a man who did not work, but was great on the compassion end...would I settler for that? The answer is no. There is someone who is capable of working, sharing, and loving. God, direct him to me.

What would life be like if we did not settle for anything less than what God wanted us to have?

11/29/97 ~ 8:10 a.m.

Last night, Ernell came to talk to me. He said he didn't want a divorce. He had been listening to the tapes his mother had given him, *Men are from Mars and Women are from Venus*. He learned that men and women do communicate differently. He expressed his love by doing for me (not touching me). I discussed his inability to kiss and hug and to speak terms of endearment, the $64,000 taxes. He said he would not have signed the line of credit if he weren't concerned. The line was signed a year before the tax bill. Strangely enough, he never said he was sorry about anything. I told him he couldn't change. He does not do what I need, and I don't do what he needs, and it's okay.

Yesterday's teaching by Pastor Chuck was 'Forgiveness.' I woke this morning thinking about that. Do I forgive or do I not forgive? Things haunt me, for I repeat them over verbally and in my mind.

I think I should move out, seek a legal separation. I'll talk with Ernell in the morning.

12/3/97 ~ 8:10

Monday 12/1/97 was the first time in a year Ernell and I spoke to each other peacefully. He has been listening to the tapes from his Mom. He could identify with his actions, behaviors, my responses, and my need for affection. For the first time in my 22 years of marriage, I believe he was beginning to understand me and hear what I had been saying. He said he never knew I wasn't happy. That I didn't want our bed set from Steven (the temp) even though I had voiced it repeatedly. He sees it as furniture; I saw it as a whore's bed. He offered to get me another set.

I cry out with much hurt and pain. How sad it is when people drift apart and then leave each other due to small things.

Ernell recalled Bishop Ruffin's statement at Ernest Dowdy's banquet, "If a marriage starts out with love, it should end with love." That stayed with Ernell. Our marriage should end with love. Charlie told me to love my way through it. I didn't understand that. He said it's like praying my way through it. Monday night, I began to pray my way through it. Last night, Ernell asked me to listen to a tape with him. I did. The author clearly identifies the differences between men and women: their likes, hearing, responses, and needs. As I listened, I could see both of us in our situation.

After we listened to the tape, Ernell initiated the conversation. He talked about staying together and replacing the bed set. I told him I could not replace the bed because I didn't have the money to pay for it and I didn't want to charge it. I don't know the outcome of our marriage. He said we needed to start somewhere and he is no longer concerned about saving money; he wants to spend and enjoy it.

We agreed to listen to another tape tonight. I asked for a hug and whispered, "I love you, Ernell." After our embrace, I left his bedroom and entered mine. I thank God for intervening. This is hope for our survival. We both want to make it and stay together.

This morning, I called Cherry. She is $3,500 behind on the house note. I called Ms. Chow and told her to cut a check for net $3,500. Cherry has sacrificed much to help me stay in business. It is a blessing to be able to repay some of what she has given.

12/4/97 ~ 7:59 p.m.

Last evening, Ernell and I listened to another tape on communication. It truly spelled out our problems. It identified the levels of misunderstanding we had. It provided clarity as to why I was feeling so sorrowful; it helped me to see years of pain and sadness and how my wedding set was forced upon me. I wanted a gold band with a simple marquee. Ernell and the salesman selected a set with a small stone, and suggested I have the set soldered for the band look. I left the mall three times before I settled for less than I wanted. I shared this with Ernell and found myself crying out 22 years of hurt. He expressed how I had hurt him. When he redid the kitchen grout, I did not say anything nice or thank him. We both have hurts. We do love each other. I love Ernell. I am thankful to God for another chance. Ernell said things will be better, he will see to that, he guarantees it.

I called him at work today to ask if he still meant what he said. He reaffirmed his thoughts and said, "I love you." I do look forward to a blessed and loving marriage. Thank You, Lord.

12/6/97 ~ 2:12 p.m.

Last night, I slept with my husband. It has been a year since I have wanted to be in the same bed with him. There was no sex, just holding. He said, "I love you, Baby." Those words mean the world to me. We talked about starting over. Moving to a new home, learning from our mistakes, to make a better future for both of us and for our family.

We are going shopping. I love You, Lord. Thank You for giving us another chance.

12/8/97

Yesterday was Ernell's 48th Birthday. We went to Church at the 6:00 service with Aisha. Tahira was out shopping. It was wonderful sitting with him, holding his hand after I came from the choir. We went to Marie Calendar's (he and I) afterward for dinner. We discussed our past, but focused on the future. I pray to God that Ernell will receive Him. We prayed for a secure, loving, and everlasting marriage.

Lord, thank You.

12/10/97 ~ 8:48

Last night was the Academy's Christmas Party. It was held at Pomona Valley Mining Co. Approximately 30 guests were there. I was happy to be with my husband. I can see the difference and feel the difference in our relationship. There is great love. Thank You, Lord.

12/14/97 ~ 3:18 p.m.

All praises to the Lord. On December 12th, Ernell and I went to San Diego. He made reservations at The Heritage Park Bed and Breakfast in Old Town. We stayed in the Grandview room. Upon entry to our room, I saw the full sized four-post canopy bed, ceiling fan, Victorian sink, tub with Jacuzzi, a dozen roses, with a teddy bear, and card. Also, there was a box of delicious Godiva Chocolates. NO T.V. My husband treated me like his queen. Whatever I wanted was okay with him. We walked the streets of Old Town holding hands; I had him walk on the outside. I laughed and told him I was going to train him on what I wanted and how I wanted to be treated. He agreed. I also asked that he tell me what he wanted so I could be a better wife to him. Lovemaking was an exciting feeling and rewarding. God granted us another chance and we knew it.

We discussed our finances openly for the first time. We have about $13,000 in savings between the two of us. We agreed to establish a joint checking and savings account. Establish one checking and saving for the rental property. We discussed him closing his Credit Union checking and savings accounts. I assumed the responsibility of closing my checking account, taking care of all bills with the joint account. Our time together has been full of laughter, conversation, touching, passion, commitment, and love. We discussed moving to a new home, purchasing cars, trucks, and trips in the future. All was provided by God. I placed my hand in his lap, held his thigh. It felt good. While driving on the freeway, I told him how satisfied I was to simply be touched and to touch. Ernell guaranteed me my life would be better with him. His pride will never prevent him from being a caring and loving husband.

Today, we arrived back in time for me to attend my 'Experiencing God' Class. He went to LL Prime Time, but left after hearing the Gospel RAP. After my class, we drove home.

Mom Vivian called to say she was home from Hawaii. As Ernell talked with her, I could tell he was not going to share the good news. So I spoke with her and informed her of our reunion. She cried, "Thank God!" She was happy.

The atmosphere at home is better. We all are happy, including Tahira and Aisha. Lord, thank You for one more chance.

Your Child, Linda

12/15/97 ~ 7:48

Well, we're still in love. We call each other at work to say, "I love you". Ernell printed out the info on the property rentals and I deposited $1,000 into the joint account.

Today, when he called the office, Aisha answered the telephone. She told me the most important person in my life was on the phone. She is so right. Life is different and better.

Four-D is blessed. God allowed us to open a separate checking and savings general account. The B of A shows $118,000 in the checking account. My God, we are going up. I must focus on enrollment into the Continued Ed classes. We earned $93,000 between July 1, 1996 and June 30, 1997. Between June and December of '97 we have only earned $32,000. We are down $8,000 from previous years.

The students in the LVN Program and instructors are going to the Museum of Tolerance. They will have a great time. It is part of the Cultural Exchange Day. Mommy and kids are doing well. I sit here alone thanking God for all: friends, advisors, family, school, and His love for me. I have so much to be thankful for.

Lord, thank You. Your Child, Linda

P.S. Thank You for forgiving 70 x 7 (daily). I need them.

12/18/97 ~ 10:11 p.m.

I received a call from my husband. He checked into hotels for Vegas for New Years Eve. The cost would be $700, which is too much. He uses sweet words now, calls me Sweetheart, and Honey. Oh, the little things he does to make me happy.

He's happy too. Even the girls are happier, hanging around our room, laughing, and talking. Thank You, God.

12/22/97 ~ 11:04 p.m.

Oh what a difference! Ernell and I are in love with each other. This morning, we made love for the third time this week. This will not stop. We both have missed each other terribly. How sad, so much time lost in pain and silence. I ask God for 22 more years to enjoy.

As we were standing by our cars before I drove away to work, he smiled and said, "The difference is 'You wanted me' when we made love," and I did!

God has blessed us with $90,000 in the checking account. Payday made – oh what a feeling.

The CNA's graduated today, and a guest sang *I Want to Help Somebody*. This song brought tears to my eyes; it told me why Four-D exists. I asked God to allow me to help somebody. He did.

Lord, thank You.

Yesterday Ernell, Aisha, Cherry, and I attended a "Celebration of Life" for Madeline Seymour. It was quite nice. She has been an inspiration to many. Charlie, thank you for the invitation. Ernell and Tahira are out shopping for gifts; Aisha is cleaning out her closet. Her life has changed and so has her clothing style.

I am here...I am here!

12/24/97 ~ 1:07 a.m.

On Tuesday 12/23 we had a staff meeting, our last meeting for the year. God has brought us through. All bills are paid, payroll is made, and students in the LVN program are on break. CNA students graduated yesterday, and we leave for five days.

Tonya is off to see her boyfriend, and Cherry and the girls off to Michigan. I am home with my family where there is plenty of laughter, love, joy, and happiness. Ernell and I sat on the floor in the den wrapping gifts. It's a good time.

Tahira came in at 11:00 p.m. – out shopping for gifts and clothes for herself. She is happy. Aisha is looking for diamond earrings.

I talked with Donna a bit about marriage. She recommended the ***Conscious Love*** to read. Good spiritual therapy. Donna is always positive. She wants me to be happy; I love her.

The girls are downstairs, Ernell is asleep, and I am sitting. Goodnight, Lord.

Oh yeah Robert Rochelle and I talked. He called to say his greeting. We reminisce about our first meeting, me, and that purple suit. God sent him. Happy Holiday.

12/25/97 ~ 11:40 a.m.

Today is Christ's day! He was born for our sins, so that my family and me would have everlasting life in accepting Him as our Savior. Today, my family is together – Tahira, Aisha, Ernell, and me. Last evening, I cooked turkey, macaroni and cheese, green beans, potato salad, and four sweet potato pies. The fireplace burning, Ernell and the girls are wrapping gifts and laughing, the T.V. is on, and there is an aroma of good cooking. I am happy.

This morning at 8:30, we all rise to open gifts. We are grateful for everything. Sweats and diamond earrings for Aisha and me. A leather jacket for me, and lots of housewares. Tahira received sweats and a ski set. Ernell was given a sports coat, ties, and slacks.

We will be leaving for SB now, to visit everyone.

I called my family together and we prayed, giving thanks for God's grace. We are together and all hugged each other. Thank You, Lord!

12/25/97 ~ 11:17 p.m.

Well, here I am again, home in bed. Today was beautiful. We opened gifts here, and then headed for SB to momma's house. Walter, Genie, and kids, Ronnie, Greg, and Jack were there. Momma was so happy to see us. She grabbed Ernell, gave him a big hug, and left the room crying. I followed her to the bathroom and gave her a hug and said, "Thank you for everything. I love you." We then left the room to join the others. It was very pleasant and warm.

We picked up momma Julie. She didn't know I was in the backseat. Momma Julie and I have always had the relationship to laugh and joke; I love her.

At mom's house, Earl, Nikki, and kids were present. Walt, Genie, and kids joined us. I know mom was thrilled. Genie said seeing Ernell and I was the best Christmas gift she could have received. Family's love is very special. Tahira and Earl left first. Ernell and Aisha and I left at 8:15 heading home.

I practice patience. I got upset while talking with Ernell about his side of the closet. I had taken out a dozen or more ties and sweaters, straightened the back of the closet, then remembered and thought to myself, *He may not want this done.* What had I learned from the tapes? I talked with him, and when he said he wanted to keep some of the ties, I became upset. Ten-year-old ties need replacing. He had about 40 ties, but why was I so upset?!? Well this evening, he and I talked. I became upset. I apologized, he cleaned out the closets and discarded two bags of old items that were not being worn or were worn out. Again, I apologized. I refuse to make a mountain out of a molehill. I love this man.

I sit here thinking about the past year. Charlie says, "There is no power that can separate us from God." A lesson well-learned.

Thank You, God, for Jesus. Love, Linda... Daddy, I love you.

12/29/97 ~ 11:00 p.m.

Well, still in love. Ernell and I went shopping for a big screen T.V. He's looking for one before the Rose Bowl. It's nice being out with him. Talking and laughing, holding his thigh as he drives. He opens the door for me to enter and exit. I love it.

I talked about the 'new house' I am preparing for. He smiles and says okay. I look forward to a better life now.

Today, I visited Ms. Alice. She is a bit down with illness, but high in spirit. Ms. Alice talked about God and good things for an hour. I made lemon tea for her. She talked and sipped. What a pleasure. God has truly blessed me with very positive people in my life.

Lord, thank You.

1/1/98

Four-D Success Academy, Inc. bank balance is $124,428.86. Lord, thank You!

Happy New Year! Lord, thank You for bringing us through another year. I stop – to pray, to acknowledge God, and His son, Jesus. I thank Him for life, love, happiness, for financial blessings, for the spirit of FDSA, for the spirit of the staff, for the motivation of the staff, and for the students. I pray to help make a difference in their lives. Even by them hearing Your name. I thank Him for the Uniform Shop, for Cherry Closet (store), its prosperity and service to the community. I thank Him for my mother and her love and financial support.

I thank God for everything.

Cherry called – we talked about the love of God and His goodness for an hour. About His blessings and bringing us through 1997, our personal lives and situations, the joy we have.

I called my mother, crying. I thanked her for her love and support of Four-D. She understands, and said, "If you live long enough you will learn and understand." I do. Gregory is not feeling well...chest or stomach pain. I think he has the flu but will not go to the doctor. I suggest rest and lots of fluids. She tells Greg that if he died, he would be cremated.

She had a wonderful time with Betty and Jeanie in Laughlin last night on the turnaround trip.

I look forward to 1998.

Donna Bostic is cleaning up her room. This gave me a big laugh. I suggest she take things out this time. She has been cleaning for four years! What a laugh we had. I love her very much.

Aisha wants to move to a Mansion, a very big house, an Estate. We will go looking today; it must be in Claremont or North Upland or she will not move. Not a bad idea! I love my child. Aisha is the greatest.

1/3/98 ~ 5:07 p.m.

Well, I have been home all day. I still look the same with my PJ top, rollers, and scarf. It's overcast with light rain and I decided to stay in. Aisha went to dance practice, Ernell to mom's, Tahira and I stayed in. What a relaxed day. I am reading ***For Better or For Best, Understanding Your Man.*** Good stuff.

I am trying to program my telephone with absolutely no success. Gadgets and me do not mix well. I spoke with Charlie today; he and several men are setting up the computer. He is a true friend...God-sent. His guidance, love, advice, and support has aided in my success, at work and home.

My ankles have been normal for two days and my feet feel great. I think I've lost 3lbs. Only 37 to go. I will make it. Lord, thank You.

1/9/98 ~ 7:30 a.m.

God is good. Yesterday, my mother turned 75 years old. Her long life is God's gift to her children. Her strength, caring, compassion, love, tough skin, sharp tongue, gentleness, and forgiveness has shaped my life and supported my work. Saturday on 1/10, my brother Walter Jr. is having a surprise party for her at his house. My gift of appreciation – a cruise to St. Thomas.

My husband continues to express his love. He calls me at work using terms of endearment. "How is my Sweetheart doing?" I just smile, showing all my teeth! He has asked me to go to San Francisco for Valentine's Day. I will have a great time. I received my reports back from La Salle. I received credit for all classes, but disapproval on nine core cases. I must talk to Dr. Mortmon.

Lord, keep me focused. I have You in my life; therefore I know all is well.

1/13/98 ~ 7:37 a.m.

Saturday 1/10, Walter Russ Jr. had a surprise birthday party at his home for Eula Mae Russ, momma's 75th year of life. Oh what a surprise! I told her I wanted her to see a home in North San Bernardino that we were considering buying. I took the twins because it has a swimming pool. Well, when the door opened and she heard SURPRISE, and the song *Happy Birthday to You,* she couldn't say a thing. It was well attended by cousins and friends. I presented my cruise to St. Thomas gift and a poem — *A Mother's Unwavering Love.* Betty Alexander will accompany us. I will submit my poem to the paper for publishing. Lord, thank You for my life, my love, my job, my love for You, and my family.

Bless this day. Thank You.

1/15/98 ~ 1:00 a.m.

Well, the school's Newsletter, *The Lamp,* is out and it looks great to me. 1,000 will be mailed out to students, JTPA Caseworkers, agencies, etc. The school's logo sign and the new uniform shop were approved by the City of Colton. Both logo signs are up. We are moving forward.

Today, I was irritated with Ms. Chow. She has requested a third week for a vacation and Theresa, the financial aid director, comp issue did not sit well with me. Later, Theresa tried to joke with me about it.

Ernell and I are packed for the Utah ski trip. We will have a lovely time.

Lord, thank You.

1/20/98 ~ 8:46

Thursday, Ernell and I flew to Utah for a ski weekend. We joined the National Brotherhood Ski Club. My husband made sure I was well-prepared for the 30-degree chill. Clothing, food, heat, and comfort. I love the attention Ernell gave me. I found myself holding his hand, touching fingers. He voluntary embraced me openly. We had a wonderful time. I took ski lessons while he started on the big slopes.

We danced, laughed, cared for each other. We arrived home at 6:30 on Monday 1/19/98.

1/25/98 ~ 11:00 p.m.

Today was a wonderful, spirit-filled day. I got started at 7:00 a.m. for Church. Sung at the 7:30 and 9:15 Service. I donated $1,000 to the Telecast for Loveland Christian Program. I know that God has blessed us; we must give in return.

After Church, I went to Four-D to pray. I prayed through the building, every room, touched items in each office: chairs, furniture, carpet, and books. I prayed for peace, togetherness, and friendship. I prayed for quality, preparation and 100% placement.

For staff, I envisioned the Riverside site and prayed for staff and students' future. I prayed for my family, my kids, my husband, my friends, and me. I thanked God for all He has given. I thanked Him for my mother, and my love for my brothers. I just prayed. I cast Satan out of Four-D. I stepped on my enemies. I stood in the shield of God's protection.

I then went to Charles' to meet with Boise, Kahaled, and Madge, asking about a Computer Training Program. We met from 2-6 pm. Positive discussion about partnership. They have the programs; we have the credibility.

We will meet in a week or so. Boise will bring the computer program down in a week.

We will then meet at Four-D. I know God's plan is working. We are the tools. Lord, thank You for the opportunity.

2/2/98 ~ 10:00 p.m.

Well, this past weekend, I took Sadiq's four kids to see him. It was the special day of Ramadan – the end of the 30-day Muslim fast. It's all about body cleansing, spiritual cleaning, and focus. It was a wonderful time with Anwan, Jaise, Tacara, and Jamila. We flew to Sacramento and drove to Vacaville. Rainy days, dry nights. Sadiq is doing fine. He's in good spirits and health. He expressed his love for his kids verbally, and with embraces and kisses. I am thankful to be able to be a part of his life. I'm able to see him grow, regardless of his obstacles. His kids are happy to see him. Anticipation to leave the hotel after we arrived only let me know how much they love their dad.

Cherry made a wonderful presentation to the LVN Board for the upcoming LVN Class. Not knowing the direction of the board, she was nervous to start a new class once she witnessed several schools receiving denials. Well, God prevailed. She was approved. She presented data on why Four-D students failed the boards and provided recommendations for consideration. The entire board was pleased with her research and presentation. They approved Four-D Success Academy classes to start, and 29 students were registered.

I ask God to lead me. I sang the song all the way to work. I know He has His plan and Satan has his. Nothing can stop our progress. Obstacles will rise, but we will overcome. I pray for focus, wisdom, and finances.

Ernell and I discussed the possibility of moving. He wants the agent I met to work with Mike B. or split her commission fees. I don't agree. I would rather have one agent. Secondly, there is the down payment on a new loan. Do we keep this one, or rent out? Where will the money for the down payment come from? Will I/we attain another home? I began to think of Aisha. I must stay in faith. God can provide if I make my request known.

I look about me. I have much. Is it wrong for me to want to move? Isn't it okay to want a new car and home? I am not selfish. I simply desire a change. I do want another home. I still desire the Jaguar.

Thank You, Lord.

2/6/98 ~ 11:00 p.m.

Today, we had a surprise award ceremony for Pamela Jackson. She has been with the Academy since September of 1992. Five years of dedicated service. Her husband, Lavar, sisters, girlfriend, and stepfather-in-law were guests. Staff members attended, as well as Mary Ann Payne, Dawn Grimes, and Charlie Seymour – Advisory Board members. The event was catered by Al and Michelle. We had a wonderful time. Pam and I have grown. We have seen Four-D grow. I know she will always be with Four-D and me. I truly and sincerely care for her well-being and her future.

Ms. Chow resigned today. Juanita will be her replacement. God continues to send what we need.

Payroll was paid with $7,000 left in the general account. We show $121,000 plus in the federal account. We have come a long way with God. I met with Kenneth and Joseph regarding our computer problems. We must have better service. The staff desires to be productive. I must establish a much better means of processing their flow of work.

I thought of God's love, my father, my mother. I held my cry. I smiled.

Lord, thank You.

2/8/98 ~ 10:15 p.m.

Well, last night was a night of loving passion. An event of embrace and sensual exchange of kisses never before expressed with my husband. The freedom we have has unleashed our sexual spirits. We are in love.

I have asked to move. Ernell is okay with the ideal. He wants the rent to be $2,000 - we currently pay $1,730. The increase is insignificant. God provides abundantly. I pray that our business grows. I pray for the ability to purchase the house of our choice. I believe. I must believe God provides as we seek. He has given me so much. I accept all with open arms.

Tonight, Aisha and I graduated from the 'Experiencing God' Class. Lord, my God, thank You for this day. Thank You for my life, my home, family, and the school. I love You.

2/12/98 ~ 10:35 p.m.

Before I could leave my home, I prayed and cried. I felt God's spirit all over me. The presence of the Lord filled me, and all I could do was cry. I thought of my life, marriage, children, parents, and my brothers and their situation and my nephews. I feel like I have so much to do. I thought of Four-D and I prayed for wisdom. The Proverbs speak of wisdom. It says to pray for it, and I do. I pray for direction, a bright light to follow. I ask God to speak to me. Where do I go, Lord?

I had a 10:00 a.m. appointment with Dr. D. DeBruhl, PhD., the principal at Rio Vista. Sadiq has requested my assistance in getting his book out. She and I had met over a year ago at an Optimist meeting. I was reading the Black Voice and came across her picture. I knew I had to seek her out. Today was good. She was pleased with the book. There were some minor changes. She will purchase some for the children. She also advised me on marketing, starting a business within Four-D Success, business cards, etc. I sent letters to other principals. Sadiq will be pleased.

I obtained transfer papers to enroll Jaise and Anwar to Rio Vista. The waiting list is only five students. They may have to ride the bus out until July, and then they will be in Rio Vista on a year-round program.

After arriving back at the office, I asked Pam to call Margie. We need the help. Tomorrow, my honey and I are flying to San Francisco. Twenty-one years later, well, it's never too late. Happy Valentines, Ernell and Linda. We fly out at 8:00 a.m. on Friday and return Sunday evening. I am happy.

I spoke with Booker about T.V. commercials. We are scheduled on the 20th for taping – need to leave a memo for staff.

I was speaking with a client and she asked questions about Phlebotomy. I thought of BRN ad for blood withdraws. Leave a message to Health Staff for Judie. I feel great. Lord, thank You.

2/15/98 ~ 8:29 a.m.

Ernell and I arrived in San Francisco Friday morning. We had a wonderful time. Friday, we walked the Wharf sightseeing, and ate. Saturday, we had breakfast, toured the town, and then drove to Modesto to see the Quarles'. It rained. The drive, which took two hours, was nice. There was rain, touching, talking, and sleeping. It was nice to see Amber this time. She and Alysia are surely long legged and once again, Alysia is very tired. Last night, we had a wonderful dinner. We walked the Wharf, purchased luggage and an umbrella.

2/19/98 ~ 8:07 p.m.

I stand in my bedroom packed and ready to go to St. Thomas with my mother and cousin Betty. It's raining and the house is quiet except for the faint sounds from the T.V. downstairs. I pause and thank God for this journey. I am looking forward to the safe trip, fun times, and laughter.

Tomorrow, Booker will be on site to film. The staff has been prepped and they are ready.

I will miss my family. I know God will keep them safe for me.

2/24/98 ~ 9:25 p.m.

I chose not to take the diary on my trip to St. Thomas. My mother, Eula Russ, Cousin, Betty Alexander, and I flew from LAX to Atlanta to San Juan Puerto Rico. From Puerto Rico to the Nordic Express Cruise Ship, Room 4023, Deck A.

Momma loved St. Thomas. We were greeted by Mary – Betty's friend who lives in Tortola. We toured the island by Ray. The beach was white sand with blue water. We ate and ate, laughed, danced, ate, laughed, walked, and slept.

We visited St. Martin, not as pretty as St. Thomas. Blue sky and ocean. Life is so different on the island. The economy is supported by tourists.

I read *Sister 2 Sister,* and then I brought two books by Norman Vincent Peale: *The Positive Principle Today* and *Why Positive Thinking People Have Positive Results*. As I began to read the Positive Principle, I began to envision myself in my new house with my family. I realize that God has abundance and He will provide for what I will have. I prayed that Ernell's income triples, and that he seeks God's will for him and His blessing.

God will provide. Four-D is still doing well. God has shared His vision. We must simply do it. Lord, thank You.

2/26/98 ~ 9:15 p.m.

My God – today Four-D Success Academy, Inc. was awarded the honor of School of the Year, Outstanding Training Facility by the City of San Bernardino Employee and Training Agency. I can only remember parts of what I said. I speak from my heart. I first thanked God for His grace and generosity to the Academy and to me.

I give thanks to the staff, advisories, Mr. Dowdy and staff, and the students. We started out with two students in 9/92, and last year we trained over 1100 students. God is good. I thank my husband.

I don't know where God will take us next, but we are prepared and willing to do our best to do all that He has for us. Our future is bright and we are ready. Lord, thank You.

Today, I spoke with Sadiq. I shared with him the plans for the book. I will complete my assignment in two weeks.

Love You, Lord. And thanks!

2/28/98 ~ 9:45 p.m.

When I pause to reflect on my life, I cry and praise God. He has given me a legacy to leave. I strive to make a difference in someone's life and to have a foundation to stand and the wherewithal to say, "Through God, all things are possible." On Thursday, we received recognition as the School of the Year. Certificates were given from Congressman Brown, Assemblyman Joe Boca, Senator Ayala, and Senator Bill Lenard.

I had not taken one second to read the inscription. Friday morning, I was thinking of what to pursue next. I want to obtain contracts with insurance companies and Hospital Corporations to do training. I spoke with Roz Nolan for assistance. The seed has been planted.

Well, Friday after work, alone in the school, I began to walk the halls. I thanked God for the blessing. We are still here. As I passed the awards hanging, I thought of what we had received. A novel idea, why not read them! The first one I read brought me to tears. From Joe Boca was acknowledgment of 'The School of The Year' — but also the first and only African-American owned accredited school with an LVN Program. That notice was followed by a letter. It really hit me, the awesomeness of the level of achievement, ***the first and only***. I began to think, there must be 52,000 nurses in California, and there are 115 LVN schools. We are the first - the first. God chose us. I know God is pleased for we did not quit.

I cried, I cried, I cried, I cried. I (we) had accomplished something significant in my life. I cried, Lord, I cried. Thank You for choosing me, for not only hearing my prayer request, but for giving me this assignment.

Today I had a blessed and busy day. 7:30 at the Nordstrom Gallery for the Fashion Show featuring NCNW and Links. I left at 10:15 to drive to Sylmar to participate in the San Fernando Valley NCNW Block Festival. I shared info about the Rwanda Education Project and the blessings of the Academy. It was a good meeting ground. A young man named Mario Tate sung ***Faith That Can Conquer***. I immediately stood up and embraced him, and told him he must sing at our April graduation— he agreed. I felt the song was for me. Faith has kept me going. I left the program at 3:15 to drive to Redlands for the 6:00 capping and pinning ceremony for the LVN Students.

I was tired, but cheerful. Driving to San Bernardino, I was early, so I stopped at South Seas for dinner. I needed to eat and take off my shoes. I wanted to be in a quiet, comfortable restaurant with good tasty food. I indulged until I was full. At 5:30, I left to proceed to Redlands Church of Christ.

The ceremony was lovely. Family and friends were present. Students radiating, teachers beaming, Cherry and I reflected on where we are. We both left the graduation at 8:00 p.m. or so. I am home and sleepy.

Tomorrow, I sing at 7:30, 9:15, and 6:00. Goodnight.

3/2/98 ~ 7:35 a.m.

I listened to Ron Parsley's ***Breakthrough — Celebrate Jesus.*** Continued my praise with Jesus from Sunday. I began to praise Jesus and cry. Ernell is in the bathroom. I share with him about the spirit at Loveland's first services. Praises, high spirit, and joy totally fill members. There is crying, dancing in spirit, and running. I become so full, I began to cry and clap. I stopped my husband and hugged him. I wouldn't let go. I told him how God had interceded on our behalf. God saved our marriage; there is nothing God would not do for us. I prayed and tears flow as I write, for I know Him.

Today is the day the Lord has made. Yesterday, I read a note in the front of my Bible dated 8/24/98. I asked God for a mate who loved Him and studied His word. A mate who would love and touch me, a mate who would help me and let me love him, a mate I could talk business to and help each other.

Yesterday, on our way to the 7:30 a.m. Church service, Ernell and I began to talk about his business and how to grow it, maybe do a commercial. God, thank You. On our way to Church, each with our Bible, my husband who loves and touches me had a decision about business.

John 15:1-8 – Just ask. God is the vine who bears much fruit. I am ready for all changes. I think of God's work with FDSA. There is a pyramid. 52,000 nurses in California, several thousand black nurses, hundreds of accredited schools, 115 accredited Licensed Vocational Nurse Programs, and then there is Four-D Success Academy.

3/5/98 ~ 11:15 p.m.

Today, Cherry, Nancy, and I flew to Sacramento to meet with the new Nurse Consultant Jeannie M. It was important to have an official introduction, a 'personal' meeting. We wanted to introduce our spirit, philosophy, purpose, and work ethics. She needs to see the management team. We initially prayed prior to entering the building. We prayed for a positive reception and that the consultant finds favor with Four-D Success and us. Well, she herself had a degree in theology. She understood and admired the program. She was impressed with all that we do for our students: uniform, shoes, childcare, transportation, etc.

We discussed compliance to regulations. Reports she needed, the low pass rate of the last class. She was informed of the research we had complied and presented to the board earlier in the year. Due to the late request to start a class, we are unable to start in May. We will request 60 students in July. The 8-12 slots that are currently available will be filled. We made lemonade out of lemons. The delay for the May class provides us time to clarify issues and prepare for the future.

We parted with handshakes, smiles, and respect. We have her support. The day was blessed. On 3/3 Marilyn Johnson from the Colton School District and member of the Church of The Living God shadowed me. We discussed Four-D services, operations, etc. She sat in a LVN Class, met staff, and assessed the environment. We discussed Sadiq's work; she recommends I meet with Dr. Herbert Fisher, District Supervisor, who is running for County Sup. God is great.

On 3/4/98 Dr. Fisher was present at the SB Chamber of Commerce. I introduced myself. He accepted my card and said his secretary would be calling me for an appointment. He said he would bring his correction specialist to review the book. Margie will redo the work ASAP. God is good, and He is lighting the path.

We are planning to receive a large blessing. GROWTH.

Lord, thank You. Love, Linda and Four-D Advisors

3/8/98 ~ 10:45

Ernell has no desire to move. He says to pay off the 1st and 2nd is about $55,000. Why? He couldn't sell the house. When I stated we would not have any down payment, he looked as though he had not thought of that, or I get that blank look. I felt myself retrieving within. Am I being selfish? At Church, I saw him and lit up. I hugged him and said I was okay. I was hurt last night when I realized he had been putting me off. That's why he had no response when I showed him the houses.

3/10/98

Anger consumes me. Why? While my mother was on her dream vacation to St. Thomas, Zachary broke into the house. He cut open the locked windows. She had said she couldn't find her rings and some money before the trip. I thought she had misplaced them. But after the trip, she found the garage door open. I feel angry and trapped. I want to move into a larger house and move her in. Ernell is not willing to pay $3,000 a month. Although I do understand, I still feel angry and trapped. I spoke with Henry Horsley, Zack's counselor. He said what I needed to hear. "I can't do a thing as long as Ms. Russ keeps opening the door." He asked, "Are you going to move into her house? Then you can't do a darn thing!" We all need to hear the truth before we accept that which we cannot change. I have no control.

My anxiety spills over to my work. I am short-tempered with workers and the computer man. I feel my spirit shift. Lord, bring me back. Ernell is going to Canada for skiing. He will be back Sunday night. I miss him. I must apologize for my outburst taken with the computer man.

Life takes many twists and turns. Last night, I received a call from David Perry. He is putting a book together and asked if I would be in it. I am pleased – the book is called, ***What Momma Used to Say!***

I have been nominated for the Women of Achievement Award by Cherry to YMCA Pomona. Lord, guide me!

3/11/98 ~ 5:55 a.m.

God is great. Today I am listening to Reverend Hagee. He is teaching on the attitude of fortitude. He is teaching me. Yesterday I wrote about my attitude and how I was responding to others.

The attitude of life...nothing is impossible with Jesus Christ.

Prosperity is an attitude. There is struggle before success. Look at the stories of Joseph, Moses. God seeks warriors, not wimps. Our attitude is our fortitude, our confidence.

My attitude shapes my presentation for the day.

"I can't is the brother of I don't want to." Lord, thank You for this message.

Touch my heart. Change my attitude. Give me peace in my soul. Let me be kind to others. Remove me from me.

3/12/98 ~ 11:35 p.m.

Before a new day, I must express the joy of today. This morning, I listened to Pastor Hagee teaching on "attitude" again. I called Cherry and told her to turn to channel 40. Yesterday, he taught on attitude and it brought me to tears. I called Ken Booker and apologized about my negative attitude regarding the computers.

Today, Cherry and I are thinking about the K-Mart Building we looked at with Charlie Seymour. The 102,000 sq. ft. building has an additional 9,500 space for a garden. We can fill the space with classes, offices, Cherry's Hope Store, Child Care Center, Media Development Department, Financial Aid, Uniform Shop/Book Store, Conference Room, Pharmacy, Food Service, and Computer training.

I stand still and envision the school with corridors, large rooms, and students...a bustling academy. I envision the name of the school on the building and the parking lot is full. The Academy.

Today, Tonya was placed on the development of the BSN, Master Nursing Program. ABHES faxed the approval of the Pharmacy Tech Program. I spoke with J. Cavenznaa of the California Endowment. The Dental Program is still pending. The results will be determined by July. We will submit the CNA and LVN Program if applicable in August. I called several agencies for information regarding available funding for Community Health Initiatives.

We are receiving a Computer from SB County. It has two years paid Internet service. I spoke with Pastor Turner of Church of the Living God. He is an Adm. with the Veterans Administration. I shared what we needed: equipment, fax, and copier. I requested he not throw away a thing. Let me see it all. He was delighted, as I. The Lord guides us.

Tomorrow, I will be at the God's Woman Conference working the tape counter. Aisha will perform with the Praise team. Tahira is off. She has been assigned to CLEAN her room and the bathroom. The girl is on the go and her room shouldn't be.

My husband, Ernell, is in Canada on a Ski trip. He had a good day yesterday. I do miss him. That's wonderful.

Life is good.

P.S. Juanita is paying off bills. God is bringing in the money. We have $204,000 in the Federal Account and $30,000 in the General Account. This time last year, we were in debt with loans against the school.

We will grow and fill up the building. Cherry and I want to have a meeting with the President of K-Mart. We want the building given to us and renovated. You can't get if you don't ask.

3/15/98 ~ 12:01 a.m.

What a blessing the God's Woman Conference was! There were over 700 women being blessed. We praised the Lord. We danced for the joy of knowing Jesus. Dr. Shovell taught on being left dead, not accepting all that God has for us, how we think we are, knowing right from wrong. She taught us of God's power in us, not to be ashamed to praise Him, to dance, to move and dance. I moved from my spot for the first time in my love life for Jesus. Growing up as a child in Christ, I watched the adults at the Church of the Living God. Sister Overstreet and Sister Fulghan seldom, if ever, shouted much more than Amen. Never shouted loud, never danced with joy. I know they had a relationship with the Lord. They raised me! They set the pattern of my Christian life. I think of them and I thank God for them.

I worked the tape session. I paused and thought of Ernell. I miss him. We weren't too busy. This August at the GWC we expect 3,000-4,000 women. We will be quite busy. Lord, thank You.

Oh yes! My Aisha danced with the praise team. I am filled with God's love.

3/18/98 ~ 11:15 p.m.

The last three days have been extremely exciting. Last Thursday, we received the ABHES approval for the Pharmacy Technician Program. It is eligible for the Financial Aid Program.

Monday, I flew to Sacramento to a CAPPS Meeting. There, I met several individuals who will assist me in moving forward. Sandra Brown and Floyd provided me with information to seek international work with Senegal, Africa. Bruce Lee with Employment Training Panel (ETP), the VP at Coastline Community College who is involved with foreign training, the final with BPPVE, our Degree Program Vendor who supplies books. The possibilities are endless.

Saturday, I participated in the God's Women Conference. I was filled with the spirit of the Lord. What a blessing.

Today, I received notice that I have been selected as one of the Women of Achievement for Entrepreneurship by the YMCA 1998. My husband returned home from Canada. He had a wonderful ski trip with 18 other snow buffs. While on the slope, he had a revelation: I should have a Jaguar. He wants me to have it; his wife deserves it. I am so happy for his approval. It eases the effort in our discussion on transportation for me. He has started to look. I want a red one with white interior, license to read, Four-D SUCCESS.

Today, Chris and I participated in the Vista Heights Middle School Career Day Fair. It was interesting to speak to 6th-8th graders. I was effective. Several of the staff/faculty shook my hand and told me they like what I had to say, and that I was a good speaker. Theresa has been diagnosed with Diabetes. She had visual problems on Monday. She is okay. Tonight, I stood in intercessory prayer for her at choir rehearsal.

My Lord, my Jesus, thank You, and Satan we cast you out! I am God's child!

With a smile!

3/19/98 ~ 11:15 p.m.

Today, Theresa informed me we were approved for the SEOG Program by the Department of Education. We were assigned $121,000. The Student Work Program came to $60,000. These funds will allow students to receive funds, which will aid in decreasing their loan amount. Lord, thank You. I attended a meeting to discuss the Black Inventor Museum; a committee was pulled together by Al Twine and Linda Gray. I represented the NCNW. This will be a great event for all children and the community members.

I spoke with Judy White, Assistant Superintendent for SB County, regarding Sadiq's book. I will meet with her next week.

Things are moving along. This morning, I called Ms. Harrington and put her on administrative leave until Dr. Houston met with her on Tuesday at 10:00. As she leaves, we move forward.

3/22/98 ~ 2:30 p.m.

Moved by the spirit today, Ms. Young came up to me and said, "Ms. Smith, thank you. I don't know what I would do without you and the school. Sometimes we argue in class, but I know this is good. Sometimes, I am afraid. I don't know why, I am just afraid."

I took her into my arms. I embraced her as God embraced me. I prayed for her, holding her tight. I asked God to remove Satan from her presence. I prayed that He provides her the vision of His spirit for her. That she not be afraid of growth, that she not set limitation on herself. I told Ms. Young that I could see her as a nurse with a PhD Education. All she needed was time and faith, and it could be done.

She cried and said, "I wish I had your faith."

I replied, "I have seen what God can do. I believe in Him." I prayed that He remove all negative forces from her path, that she pay all of her bills, that He keeps the family healthy and strong, that her husband continues to give her encouragement and support.

I thought of July 31, 1991, the awakening, the bathroom, God's presence in me. I became filled.

As we finished praying, I knew God had done it all. He let me praise Him in the presence of others using Four-D Success Academy as the Foundation. I said, "Ms. Young, if I do nothing else, I have done God's work."

As I walked to the choir stand, God's love entered me. I could hardly walk because I wanted to praise Him. The choir began to sing, ***I am God.*** Overwhelmed by the spirit, I let God have His way. I cried and shouted out to Jesus, I thanked Him over and over. I cried for Him to use me. Help me be a tool to help shape the lives of others. Let me exemplify His goodness. Let me continue to pray and feel God. He cleans me, He frees me, He forgives me, He protects me, He loves me, He likes me, He is within me, and I am within Him.

Pastor Chuck preached on John 7:27, 'The river that flows through me. The river of God.' I am blessed. I pray that Four-D spreads to the four corners of the world. It will always be the foundation where we can stand and say, "Through God, all things are possible."

Lord, thank You for this day!

3/26/98 ~ 10:25 p.m.

This week has been a continued blessing from God. Let go and let God. Let God handle your problems. God can handle your heart pains, your debt, and your sorrow. He fills you with love, solutions, money, and happiness. Monday, Cherry asked for the insert from my diary dealing with my secret moment with my father — his death. I hadn't read September 26, 1994. I cried. I missed daddy. As I scan the next several days of the diary, I recall moments of pain, joy, sadness, sorrow and, finally, gladness and peace.

I gave her the diary, with pages tagged. She is writing a book, which will be a great success.

I had a miserable year with RAM Copier. They drove me to a point of rage. I asked God to take over – to remove my anger and let me see clearly.

I was able to contact the Regional Office. After talking calmly and expressing that I am an unsatisfied customer, and RAM was a dishonest vendor destroying the name of MITA, I got their attention. RAM Service has advised me of the parts needed to repair the machine.

Tomorrow, the Riverside CASE managers are coming to Colton. Now this is God's work. After two years of separation, we are going to be visited by 28 people. I wrote a letter to them on Tuesday requesting a visit of the Colton and Riverside site. On Wednesday, I got a call requesting a tour for Friday. They had not received my letter. God moves things — mountains. Margie has prepared a neat looking package for them. All staff has been notified. I expect a positive outcome.

The application to BP PVE was mailed to finalize the Pharmacy Tech Program. They approved Financial Aid. ABHES has already approved the program. I faxed a letter to Dr. Mali in South Africa, requesting a response to Cherry's letter from October '97. I wrote a letter to Dr. Thram in Senegal, Africa. I was referred to him by Sandra Brown, who I met in Sacramento at a CAPPS Conference.

I pause and think of the nightly Bible reading my father did when I was a child. He would call my brothers and me to our bedroom. 1450 Mt. Vernon Ave, San Bernardino, CA (it brings a smile to my face). We would sit on the bed and on the floor and listen to him read a chapter or two, or three, each night. He would answer questions and pray. Mom would be in the kitchen or her room. I don't know why she never read to us or sat in on the readings, but she was never too far. Sometimes she would correct the pronunciation if he asked. Daddy could pray, and he prayed from his soul to God.

Lord, we ask for favor at the Academy and in our personal lives. Grant us Your love and protect us against those who choose to stand against us. Provide us the professional and dedicated persons we need to produce the best quality programs possible. Allow Cherry, the other team members, and I to receive the rewards of a job well done. Guide me to be a better manager and a good steward of money. Keep my heart open to give with love. I know as I donate in Your name, You will multiply 10,000 fold. Keep my family safe and in good standing with each other.

Your loving child, Linda

3/27/98 ~ 11:38

What a day. We had an advisory meeting at 8:00 – 9:45. The Board was informed of financials, new programs, Medical Claim Examiners, Medical Billing, computer training, and a new facility.

We are looking at the K-Mart building at 116,000 sq. ft. Cherry has contacted the Corporate Office in Michigan. We want them to give us the building. He recommended we have a conference call. He thinks something can work out – favoring free rent. The upcoming LVN Program for July has 60 students. Cherry and her staff have a lot to prepare for. The Financial Aid is going well at 10-12. Theresa and I met with JTPA about Proposal and Financial Aid. She is quite capable of taking the program forward. We will be looking at all programs. I truly believe we will receive all contracts for fall services. I see God preparing us for intake, testing more students, and classes. I see Riverside being viewed for intake with seven student referrals. This is going to be another good year. The Riverside Case Manager visited Colton in groups of three; they were impressed. The presentation went very well. They toured the facility, presented, and all was good.

I hired an Administrative Secretary; finally, Barbara is able and willing. She was highly recommended by Theresa. She's skilled with the computer, organization, research for foundations, telephone skills, and is eager to be in a positive, spiritual, loving, and caring environment. She cried when I asked why she wanted to leave Cal Baptist College. I understand her reason; loving the job, but not the spirit in which things were done.

Ms. Harrington was given the opportunity to resign or be terminated. She has caused destructive flow in the business. She resigned. We talked. Cherry considered having her work out of the home on the BSN Program. Well, that girl called Dr. Long at Martin L. King and told him his services would not be needed for the April 17th graduation! She called this morning at 7:25, talked with Pam, and left the message. Too many questions. Why did Dr. Long call her, not his secretary? Why not call Dr. Houston? When did he call? We got in contact with Dr. Long. He said Tonya had been trying to contact him for several days. She told him his services were no longer needed! He need not speak – he will come and be the guest of honor speaker. God, work things out.

She will not return. All that she attempted to do to harm us – we are under God's protection.

No enemy should rise up against us.

Lord, thank You.

3/30/98 ~ 9:36 p.m.

Satan is on the move in the absence of his little helper. A VN Student, Paul, was disruptive in class. The instructor asked him to leave. He refused. I had to call him out. He announced to the class, "Ms. Harrington will be participating in the graduation." The instructor asked a question, and he replied in his condescending matter. I had to set him straight; neither he nor Ms. Harrington was in charge — I was. She would not be on the program. He asked if I needed to talk with his lawyer. I told him, "Forget your lawyer." He didn't have charge. I did.

How sad on my part. I must maintain control and present calmness. Lord, work on my temper. I need to have peace at my core when I feel that which I love is being attacked. Tomorrow will be a much better day. Lord, thanks again. Linda

Ernell and I went to look at Jaguars. I should get one soon.

4/1/98 ~ 11:05 p.m.

On Tuesday March 31, 1998, I attended a Bidders Conference for the SB County 1998-1999 year. The conference was for a few providers who wanted to offer a full service contract. We propose to provide intake, assessment, support services, and child care per client for $3,000. This also included the Vocational Training Component. The state is requesting more training and service for fewer dollars.

Based on the projected members of clients we can provide service to, I estimate at $3,000 x 300 = $900,000 for the CNA/HHA. I would guess a low of $600,000. I left the meeting thinking of all of the possibilities. We need more space. I called the Cooley Park Office to inquire about 930 Mt. Vernon. I have an appointment tomorrow to see the inside of the building.

Last evening after work, I went to visit my mother. As she unlocked the door, she began to whisper through the screen door. I could not make out what she was saying. Why was she whispering? I asked her to repeat what she had said. Her response sent chills through me. I felt sick to my stomach. My body felt as though a jagged spear had pierced me. My mind felt as though the cells ruptured, bombarding themselves against the inner membrane of the meninges. I became saddened. What did she say! Something about, I had to talk to him. Saying something about seeing his girlfriend? "Who? Donnie? Where is he? In the back room?"

As I passed the room without breaking my stride, I glanced at him. There he was, proud and clean. White pressed shirt, creased trousers, healthy, muscular, and ready for a night out. Fresh from the incarcerated walls of his home for the past 12-15 months. He was released from jail and back at momma's house. I continued my stride to her room only able to force out a civil greeting, "Hi, Donnie." As my nephews called out my name, "Hi, Auntie Linda," I became more ill. I thought of the negative influence of Donnie — his ways, smoking, vulgar mouth. I became disgusted with momma. After all we had discussed, to keep them out of her house, the stolen money, jewels, food, and so much disrespect. It had to end. Mr. Horsley had told me, "Ms. Russ will let them in. Unless you plan on moving in and standing at the door, you will have no control." My solution — move. Seek another home large enough for my family, mother, and nephews. I was looking for a 5-6-bedroom house! She let him in! I had to leave. As I leaned over to kiss her goodbye, I could only say, "I love you, but I am so disappointed."

I called her today to express clearly that she had control of her home. I could not emotionally become involved with her and the boys. But I would do all I could for her and the twins. We talked calmly. I sensed peace enter me. I said, "I love you."

She said, "Thanks for calling."

Today, Cherry and I met with Ronald Berggren, V.P. Educational Development, at Crestline Community College. What possibilities. Ronald freely discussed the programs offered via Tele course. He spoke of partnership, Four-D being able to offer an AA Degree, increase enrollment. We received a tour of the facility and a tape for review. We were introduced to his partner Peter. One thing that Cherry and I noticed was the eye contact and firm handshakes from both men – especially Ronald. He grasped his hands around each of our light hands, and we said our goodbye. He said we would meet again as soon as Cherry and I requested another meeting.

At lunch and through 6 p.m., we talked of growth, God's goodness, and possibilities. We began the review of the proposals. We are joyful about the work that lies ahead. God is opening doors and we will walk through! Cherry has been reading my diary. She thinks I should write a book – one day. I received a call from Joe. We discussed my progress. The response from Cherry had not been read. She called just to ask if I had any questions. I took total advantage of the opportunity to share my personal accomplishments. I told her with laughter, "I was good at what I did. I really had earned the MBA and was interested in the PhD Program." By the time I finished talking, she had to go and pull my file. I truly encouraged her and added if she could have a positive influence on the outcome to help herself. I felt elated. I reflected. Yes, I have earned the Master in Business.

Linda L Smith M.B.A, B.S.N, P.H.N., President & CEO.

4/3/98 ~ 7:15 p.m.

A troubled spirit. Yesterday, Cherry shared with me a fax she had received from Celestin in Rwanda. He wrote of the enormous opportunities in pharmaceuticals. He also wrote that Helen, Jeremy, and Charles were coming to Michigan.

He had met a young man who operated a business that dealt with pharmaceuticals and said we should fly to meet with them regarding a feasibly study. I responded with dullness. My thoughts were a conference call could be as effective for discussion and much less expensive. Her coolness set the tone of 'this is my project; I know what I want to do.' This response is not what I will subject myself to with an immediate response.

I know that if two people are in the well, it is difficult to get out. But if one of us remains outside of the well, God's hand will guide the person who is outside, the strength to pull the other out, not physical strength but spiritual strength. The well affects how we think. The deeper one goes, the more self-centered we become; the less open one is to the suggestions of others. Being outside the well keeps the mind, body, and soul open to the spirit of God. I will strive to remain outside the well, for I have been inside the well. I struggled to come out of the well, and it took years. I shall never return. The song, ***Hold on to God's Unchanging Hands,*** tells me that no matter where I am, His hands are there for me. Being in the well of darkness can cause one to forget that God's hands are always there.

Cherry's mood changes are because she forgets that God's unchanging hands will lead her. She need not try to make things happen. Sitting still to listen is good; it is good for the mind, body, and soul. Her desire for international education under her direction is done through God's will. He will (has) opened the door. He has given her more than she can handle.

Peace be still and let it multiply. Lord, thank You for my lessons of life. Thank You for Your love, for keeping me focused. Give me visions. Make me a good steward of Your money. Let me plant seeds of faith, love, joy, and prosperity to others.

I pray to receive the financial blessing through Four-D to give a 10 percent pledge offering to the God's Women's Conference. Lord I desire to give $10,000. Therefore, I seek your financial blessing of one hundred thousand dollars to Four-D Success Academy by July 31, 1998.

Keep the team together and strengthen it. In Your name, Jesus.

Your Child who knows what You can do. Your child who has seen what You have done. Your child who knows what You will do.

Your Child, Linda

4/5/98 ~ 10:01

Today, I put money down for a Red/Cream 1996 Jaguar from Rusnak in Pasadena. My husband took me to see different models, and I know he also went to negotiate. I can't barter in Tijuana. I can see Four-D, but as Ernell said, when I see something I like, I will pay for it.

I am tickled pink. I have my car! I will pick it up Wednesday. The manager said it will be extra clean and polished for me. I take that; I believe God gave it to me. I have been a good steward of His money. I sung the song, *Can't Nobody Do Me Like Jesus*. I am filled with joy. My life is filled with joy and happiness.

I was told on Saturday by Aisha that I was selected as the Business Person of the Year by The African-American Chamber. Only last Saturday did Charles suggest to Cherry that she nominate me. She submitted my name. On Wednesday, I got a call inquiring if I would be attending since I was nominated. I was surprised. No official notice by letter or telephone, only a lady asking me to purchase a ticket. I chose to attend choir rehearsal. We are preparing for a concert on May 2nd. I was more filled with praising God than I would have been receiving self-gratification and acknowledgment from others.

I know God has great things planned for me. I must let the river flow through me. I am a dam in the middle of the stream. Four-D Success Academy has the four corners of the world to reach. Tomorrow, Cherry and I will begin to write for the SB County JTPA Contract. I seek a minimal of $900,000 (300x3000) for CNA/HHA clients and $100,000 for the Pharmacy Tech.

Lenox Leach called today. Tyrone Daisy is dead. He died 30 days ago. Tyrone couldn't live without Michelle. She kept him alive. She died October 13th (I believe) 1992. It doesn't seem that it has been six years. Life goes on. No day is promised. Lord, thank You for this one.

4/7/98 ~ 9:12 a.m.

"FEAR — FALSE EVIDENCE APPEARING REAL."

Today, Rod Parsley spoke these words on his televised program. These are words Charlie repeated to me after I went through my self-inflicted torment over the finances of Four-D Success. Fear accelerates as a breakthrough comes. Last night, Cherry and I worked from 2:00 p.m. to 11:00 p.m. on the SB County proposal. I noticed how we support each other as we address each item. We alternate in our spirits and support.

I complain of so much. She keeps typing. She says, "We should have given this to the staff. We will never finish." I keep dictating passages and giving suggestions. I inform her we will write the proposal. We fuss a little and then laughter comes. We keep going until she turns off the computer and announces she can't go any further, "See you early in the morning." I am up at 6:00 a.m. and at 7:20 a.m. I am out the door. We will have a blessed day, for God has laid the path we walk and it is straight and leads to goodness. Love, Linda

Oh yes, yesterday at 1:00 p.m. Mr. Dowe brought me the Business Person of the Year Award. That's right – the African-American Chamber of Commerce selected me. I didn't attend the function. I was at choir rehearsal learning new songs for our Loveland Concert. I really didn't take the nomination seriously. I was submitted a week before the function, and thought surely they had already selected someone.

"Well, you never know who is watching you, so carry yourself well." These are words my daddy would say to me often. "Linda, people in the community are always watching. Carry yourself with respect. Don't shame me." My dad was right. I marvel at what God has done through me and for me. I was chosen out of all He has created to do this will of His. I see myself as less capable in so many ways, but God sees me differently. He has brought me hard workers, gifted people of excellence, love, and high positive spirit.

Linda Lee Russ, born August 7, 1952, started a school in March 1992. The first African-American owned and Accredited Vocational School in California. The first owned and Accredited Vocational Nursing Program in California – only through God. He sees me as I don't see myself. He guides me daily, carrying me all the way. Sometimes I cry just knowing all that He has done with me.

- Me, a child who thought death was better than life during a low point in my life.
- Me, a child who was told I had a "thick tongue" by Mr. Hall in Junior High School. He would not allow me to be a part of the Theatrical Team.
- Me, a fat child with dimples who found peace in being alone.
- Me, who found joy in knowing the Lord.

I can't express all that God and I have talked about. I know He is real because I have talked with Him, and I heard Him answer.

God is real. He's real to me.

4/10/98 ~ 2:11 a.m.

Well, what a day yesterday was. At approximately 8:30 a.m., Norman Jones with NTV San Bernardino arrived to begin filming for Comcast and Network T.V. Four-D Success Academy will be featured on April 14th, 15th, and 16th for 5-7 minute infomercials and 30-second commercials. The advertisement will be great for the school.

I received a call from the artist who designed the Business of the Year Award I received from the African-American Chamber of Commerce. It was a true pleasure speaking with him. The young lady assisting Norman (Doris) said she had a contact for Nigeria. I was sharing our Africa ventures. Her 'lights' went on; I expect to hear from her. She will also set us up for the American Business Expo in Ontario – June 19, 1998.

Well today, I received my gift from God. I truly believe that, for being a good steward of His money, I have been rewarded. My car arrived – red 1996 Jaguar with cream interior. It was delivered to Cherry's house. We were writing proposals. I signed the paper, received a quick info session, and returned to the house to work. From 3:30 p.m. to 2:00 a.m. I gave it little thought. Oh, I do appreciate it. I just needed to concentrate on the business at hand. We received a fax from Kahaled; he is still in the ball game with the computer program. This is good. A young man from Senegal interpreted the fax we received from Assone and Dr. Thian. They are interested in our desires to establish dialogue with training services.

I told Cherry when the doors open, we must walk through. That is all... be willing to walk through. Never let fear interfere. What is there to be afraid of if God is in control?

Well, tomorrow, the CNA students (5) will graduate. Monday, a class of 10 will start. God is good.

Goodnight...I do like my car.

4/12/98 ~ 11:45 p.m.

Easter Sunday, the day recognized as the day Jesus rose. He died for our sins and rose to give us a new life for us to see the power of God. He died to show favor to His children. I believe in the Lord Jesus Christ as the Son of God. I believe in everlasting life with Christ. I believe that I am a child of God. God is all and I deserve all that He has to give. My path is lit; the doors are opened, waiting for me to enter. I walk the path without fear, and I enter the doors to the great surprise and wonders of the Lord My God!

I am thankful for so many things. First, my family. My husband and I are together because God granted favor. He guided our hearts and we listened. We forgave each other as God forgives us. Our children and family are joyful. It was wonderful to sing praises to God from the choir and to look out into the congregation and see Ernell and Tahira. Aisha was with her Sunday school class children. Thank You, Lord. Yesterday, I visited my mother. I was at peace as I saw Donnie drive up in his new car. It is her choice to care for her sons. No one should expect a parent to close the door before his or her time. Her time may never come. So be it. I love her and the twins. I know God can do a much better job taking care of them than I can.

Yesterday, Cherry and I completed the SB Co Title II, a special needs proposal. It will be delivered tomorrow, one week ahead of the due date (4/30/98). Tomorrow we will begin the IR Proposal. She may have completed it already.

I feel God is going to open doors we never imagined — internationally and at home. I pray for staff and faculty who have a personal relationship with the Lord Jesus. I pray for those who are committed to quality work, those willing to put in the time to get the job done. God answers prayers.

The Jaguar is great. I thank God for this lovely gift. Lord, thank You. I pray for those who are ill. I ask God to heal their bodies and minds. Lift their spirit, move all pain and aches, clear vision, and move limbs. I pray for the growth of Four-D Success, its students that are present, and those to come. I thank God for the ministry to stand and say, "Through God, everything is possible." He has fulfilled my prayer; I can only continue to work for Him.

Lord, I thank You for doing for me. I thank You for my relationship with You.

Thank You. Thank You. Your Child, Linda. Thank You.

Praises to God.

4/15/98 ~ 6:05 a.m.

I had intended to write in the diary last night, but I worked until 1:10 this morning. I suddenly became very sleepy, so I retired. Well, good morning, World.

My conscience is bothering me. I know that I have been working at 50% capacity. I have not been making the best decisions for the Academy. I feel I'm not being the best manager of my time. I am not guiding Four-D properly.

One thing that I am referring to is Theresa's time. She has had more excessive time off for personal and sick needs in the last five months than any staff has had after one year of employment. I will monitor her for two more months. Then, I will make a sound and wise decision on her status. My spirit, which I will follow, has told me she should be an hourly employee, not salaried.

Cherry said she had noticed I was not myself for the past 2-3 weeks. I guess silence says a lot. I expressed my thoughts to her. I must do what is best for Four-D Success. There is much to do, and I must become a better manager of people and projects to move the Academy forward.

The Adm. Secretary is working out great thus far, two days on the job and she is accomplishing things. She assisted with the proposal completion, scheduled dinner appointments, handled the minutes, reviewed the Veteran's proposal, and set up a schedule for personal appointments. She came into my office, closed the door, and took notes. Yesterday, she gave me a tape and asked me to record letters for her to type. I need this help. I am pleased. I have told Cherry to be nice with her assertive self.

She has already performed over the telephone, and the new employee came into my office teary-eyed. I explained Dr. Houston to her and her approach. I could only say, "I will speak with her." I did. I told her she would meet with her on Wednesday or Thursday. Cherry does not realize how aggressive she sounds, even though she is simply processing through and verbally expressing herself in a loud voice. This girl is naturally loud, and her hand gestures add to her assertive presentation.

Barbara is not timid. They will get along fine, I expect. Juanita is a good bookkeeper who brings experience to the table of corporate management. She is guiding me with advice on current policy regarding vacations, sick time, and work hours.

Our personal taxes, Ernell's and mine, are due. We are looking at $20,000-$25,000. This will be $15,000 to IRS and $6,000 to the State from our saving plans. I am grateful to God that Four-D is able to assist us. Ernell and I had a calm discussion on how best to proceed. We listened to each other, and for the first time, he seriously listened to my financial advice regarding how to best proceed. We talked about the need to meet with a financial advisor, the need to log his mileage for business, and the difference between deductions for an employee and a self-employed individual. He is paying his American Express gas charges with his own income and not tracking miles. He should track miles for business deductions. Lord, thank You. I know all is well with You. In spite of my decision and the changes I go through, You are steady and grounded. Therefore, so is the Academy.

I am in need to continue to seek God for relief of the emotional anxiety I feel regarding my mother and her sons. I spoke with Charlie. Through wisdom, He guides the discussion. He will not let me drain myself on a pity party. I have too much to do. He says, "Turn it over to God. God is all." There is nothing God can't do. I just need to ask for His protection and that's it. He is right – turn it over. Come out of the well of despair. I can't think clearly, nor do I produce greatly whenever I am in the well. Daylight is on the horizon. The well will not hold me. I look high and see my Lord. As Ernell left for work, I said, "Call me. I'll see you at 3:00."

He responded, "This is a depressing day."

"Why?"

"Today is tax day."

I clarified with this response: "This is not a depressing day. A depressing day is owing $25,000 and not having it. Owing $25,000 and having it is not a depressed day. Owing $25,000 and knowing God has it is not a depressed day. God is all, You have to realize and understand that." As I speak these words, Charlie's statements come back to me. God is all.

God is all.

4/18/98 ~ 1:07 a.m.

Well, we have another LVN Graduation under our belt. We had guest speaker, Dr. William Long, Orthopedic Surgeon at Drew Medical Center. The ceremony was quite nice. Kim Pauley sang a song. She is such a lovely lady with a beautiful spiritual voice. God is blessing her.

Charlie Seymour was the MC. He was nice, no jokes. He moved the program right along. Two students received the Walter Russ Sr. Scholarship.

Although Ms. Harrington had been dismissed from the faculty, she showed up and received a certificate from the students. After the graduation, a woman, unknown to me, said she was Pablo's sister and began to question why he didn't receive the Perfect Attendance Award. I stated he did not have perfect attendance. I was somewhat taken back by her approach and line of questioning. I freely told her my stance. She then inquired what the situation was with Ms. Harrington. I firmly told her it was none of her business. I do not discuss Academy issues with students or her.

Her reply was, "I will ask Ms. Harrington. She will tell me."

I stated, "I guess she will."

Dr. Houston decided to give Paul the certificate at the reception. This woman stood next to me talking under her breath, so I turned to her and said, "Cut it out. You have no idea about any Four-D matter."

She was close to being slapped! I felt a quiet rage, but Mr. Seymour took my arm and removed me from her presence with some good advice, "Control."

We left for a pleasant dinner at The Hilton. Dr. Long, Dr. Houston, Clara, Katherine, Mr. and Ms. Seymour, and I had a lovely dinner with old and new friends. It's late. I am tired. My kids are asleep (Well, Tahira is at work!) and Ernell is asleep on the other side of the door. Lord, after all, through it all, I say thank You.

4/19/98 ~ 11:15 p.m.

This morning, my dear husband and I embraced and relaxed — this is quite new...Ernell, still quiet with me in his arms at 8:00 a.m. We rose together at our own pace.

Today, I worked on projects, drove to the park alone, and sat on a bench looking at the lake and ducks in Riverside. It was warm and pleasant. God is good. Ernell went to Steve's house to lift weights, and to Joe Pete's to visit. I returned home, talked with Tahira, and enjoyed a quiet dinner.

Tomorrow is a new day. God has already blessed it. The SB County proposal will be turned in.

I have tried to convince myself to lose weight. 25 pounds off would be good for me.

Goodnight all. Time for book #4, I am running out of writing space.

Cherry has # 2 for her book; I must get it back soon.

4/21/98 ~ 6:33 a.m.

Well, since I have not purchased another book, I must make one final entry.

Yesterday I met with Greg Sheets, CPA, and he shared the cost of the Jaguar for personal use. I told him to spread my cost over a year if he thought Four-D would be around. He said if Four-D didn't die last year over the finances, nothing would kill us.

I met with Theresa about her employment status (salary vs. hourly) and excessive absences. I stressed productivity, performance, and teamwork. She expressed her salary as a FA Director. She will list job tasks completions and projections for 1998 in our June meeting. Last night, I dreamed FDSA was awarded the contract from SB Co for Training 180 students. The kicker is that we were the only school awarded. I then realized we needed 30 computers. Lord, this is real!

4/22/98 ~ 1:15 a.m.

Well, yesterday the management meeting was held at Cherry's house. Pam and I attended. We covered Poly and Pasadena's manual needs, LVN Program, and more productivity of support staff.

Cherry and I met with Ron at Coastline. He gave us a tour of two sites. We were able to see two lecture halls, the computer lab, and the video room. We had further discussion regarding cost, partnership, and classes. We feel very positive that a great partnership and foundation for the future is being laid. Cherry and I talked about the K-Mart building — seeking redevelopment funds from the City of Colton or SB County. Ron spoke of how they (Coastline) acquired property and buildings, and we realized the process could be duplicated in Colton. I will contact Wesley Jefferson, Al Twine, and Dick with the Chamber for Guidance.

The ride in the Jaguar was nice.

I told Cherry and Pam about my dream last night. SB County had awarded the contract to Four-D Success Academy only. All the other presenters were trying to determine who 3211 was. The dream was so real. We must start collecting 15, no, 30 computers. After seeing the lab with 32 computers — the dream told the story.

As we drove home, I told Cherry I was trying to decide how to place the initials on my home badge. She told me the highest degree first: MBA, BSN, RN. We laughed, added more initials, PAN, AA, BPPVE. Little did I know, LaSalle had approved my courses and the mail had been in the kitchen for 2-3 days. I called Cherry at 12:15 to tell her. We laughed and reflected on where we are going, the workweek, and our positive relationship. God, put a good team together. I am sleepy now. I do thank the Lord for all. I get excited about the future.

4/26/98 ~ 7:05 a.m.

I awaken with a prayer on my mind, uttering the words from my lips, "Lord, forgive me for not taking care of Your temple. The temple You have given me." I felt a twinge in my left breast. I laid my right hand over my breast and prayed to the Lord. I asked for forgiveness. "Forgive me for consuming that which was neither good nor healthy for me: excess food, fat, alcohol, no exercise, and very little water." I was ashamed of my weight.

Yesterday, a young man and woman asked me and several others to participate in a ski survey. When I was asked my weight, I said 150 lbs., knowing I weigh closer to 175-180 lbs. If I must be ashamed and lie, then I ask God for strength to improve my status. I will return to the healthy, physical body I once had. I envision myself at the age of 24. Ernell and I have Tahira at the mountain park. I was in jeans, my arms were slim, and I looked and felt great. I was not ashamed. I had lost weight after having Tahira by running and eating properly. I will return to the Linda of old. Aisha has been talking to me and praying for me. She too has prayed that I take care of my temple. Her prayers will no longer be ignored by me.

As I lay here in Mammoth at Snow Creek. I am thankful for all that God has given me: my husband, our much-improved relationship, my kids, my life, and my job. I pray that each member of the Four-D Success Academy team contributes their best.

Looking Back …

- I will always trust in the Lord with my whole heart, and I will lean on His understanding, not my own.

- There is safety in a multitude of counsel. 'Don't move until you seek God for guidance first!'

- I know what it means to seek Him while He may be found! The Lord is available 24/7 and it's in our best interest to tap into His well of resources: love, wisdom, guidance, comfort, hope, courage, passion, purpose, and more – all of which are available when we look unto Him, the Author and Finisher of our Faith.

- It's always a blessing when the school is well spoken of and publicly acknowledged. It's like God's stamp of approval openly displayed.

- Leaders should always seek creative ways to inspire others, especially those that look to them for wisdom.

- You must decide on the four W's: **Where** will you give your attention, **What** will you give your attention to, **Why** you are giving it your attention, and **Who** will get your attention.

- Distractions are sure to come, but don't give your attention to anything you have no control over because there is too much work to get done!

- When it appears that your world is collapsing from under your feet, just know that there is a peace that surpasses all understanding, and God will endow that peace upon you if you desire it. If you have not, it's because you ask not. Seek peace and pursue it today so you can walk through troubled times unscathed.

- Perseverance requires one to Pray, Prepare, and Proceed without delay, for faith without works is nothing!

- It's important to have a 'secret place' to meet Him. It can be under a tree, by a water fountain, in your living room, or whenever you take time to journal. It matters not where or how you meet Him, just purpose to meet Him somewhere every day.

- I have learned through the highs and lows of life, that absolutely *Nothing* can separate me from the Love of Christ, for He loves me unconditionally.

- I came to understand what it meant to *stand still and see the salvation of the Lord.* He will be in the intimate details of our lives if we desire Him to be. All we have to do is *cast our cares on Him, for He cares for us.* He really does.

- Time really does heal all wounds. The balm of Gilead is there; you simply must reach out for it.

- I serve a God of second chances, and I am thankful for His goodness and mercy that follow me all the days of my life.

- How sweet it is! The family that prays together stays together. **I thank the good Lord for restoring my family!** The institution of family is important to Him and should be with each of us. I honor Him for keeping my family together and whole, even when I thought it was broken beyond repair. Our times are truly in His hands.

- When I lack wisdom, I simply ask God for more. He gives it liberally to those that seek it.

  That which I have *NO* control over will not have control over me. I am free by the grace of God!

- The Lord God is the only constant in our lives. He is the same yesterday, today, and tomorrow.

- Some friendships are really only meant to last for a season. I had to learn to let go.

- I have learned to trust Him to perfect all that concerns me. His thoughts are higher than mine, and His ways better than mine. Therefore, I surrender my ways and thoughts to Him every single time — especially when worry/fear would try to cloud my vision.

- You never know who is watching you, so carry yourself well. More importantly, the Lord is watching, and we should strive to make Him proud! The accolades will come, but stay grounded in your purpose.

- My dad's words still ring true today: "Linda, people in the community are always watching, carry yourself with respect."

- Staying true to the vision can be difficult sometimes, yet we are to hold on to the vision planted in our hearts. In time, it becomes our story and His glory.

Focus, focus, focus! Stay focused on the tasks that are before you. It will be challenging sometimes but you can do it. Do it with a smile in your heart because you know, as you remain diligently focused, in the end you win! As your vision opens up before you — you win! When opportunity supports the thoughts and plans you see for yourself — you win! When God places angels in your life that add value to your purpose — you win! When distractions come (and they will), and you realize you're able to press through those with a determination that far exceeds the fiery darts that try to impede your forward progress. Be clear about your goals and objectives and you will win!

Business by Faith

Journal 4

Begins: May 1, 1998 ~ 4:55 p.m.

Ends: September 23, 1998 ~ 7:26 a.m.

5/1/98 ~ 4:55 p.m.

What an unbelievable day. As a small child playing in dirt at 1450 Mt. Vernon Ave in San Bernardino, I knew at the age of five I wanted to become a nurse. I remember looking at the picture of the lady in a white uniform. She was a nurse. She took care of others. That was what I was to become.

Today I attended the YMCA 1998 Women of Achievement Award ceremony. I was selected to receive The Entrepreneurship for Outstanding Service Award. As I sat with my colleagues, I thought of God's goodness and favor. I was selected by God to do this work. I give my all without self-proclaiming our achievement. I seek God's guidance, asking the Lord, What do I do today? No great academic knowledge can I claim, but I do have an unwavering faith in God's love for me. As the presenter continued the reading for the Elizabeth S. Genne Lifetime Achievement Award, I thought about how Ms. Genne had worked to address injustice of others. I sat there thinking of this woman, her work, her dedication. What an honor to know that I was sitting among others as one of the nominees. To my astonishment, my name was announced, "Linda L. Smith is this year's Lifetime Achievement Award." Paralysis, I thought, *God that's me.* How? Me? Have I had such an effect in serving others to be recognized? Your little girl from 1450 Mt. Vernon Ave., the nurse who prayed to You to take the best of me to make a positive difference in someone's life. Me, He allowed me to work for Him. Words can never express my joy.

Fearful to dwell on certificates, honors, and awards, I accept them all humbly. I set them aside and keep on working. I was told once that if one began to believe all that is said of them, they would forget what they should be doing. I can't forget where my strength comes from, for it comes from the Lord.

Last week, I received a letter/resolution form the State Treasury. What a surprise, all of the 'Where As' for personal achievements. I placed it on top of many others behind me, enclosed in their respective folders.

I have earned nothing that God had not intended for me to receive. It is God's will because I have used what He has given me: compassion, love, desire, and a caring heart.

Although I do not know where God is leading me, I go without fear or question.

Lord, thank You. Protect the treasures You have given me.

5/2/98 ~ 7:20

I awake with yesterday's event on my mind, still in awe of the recognition given to all the women and myself. I am too moved to cry, shout, or laugh. I continue to sit still and wonder how...how was I selected for the Lifetime Award, at the tender age of 45? Doing what I love, what I asked God to allow me to do, to strive to make a positive difference in someone's life. For my true and genuine efforts, I receive honors. Words cannot be expressed.

I'm able to reach my mother Eula Russ this morning. She was out last evening when I called. No one was home. As I shared the events of yesterday, I could feel her smiles. When I mentioned the Lifetime Achievement Award, she replied, "You are not done yet. You are going to receive the Pulitzer Prize Award. You know the one King and Bethune received. He put all his money back into his business. You will see. I may be dead and gone by then. You are not through yet." Was she planting a seed? Linda Lee Russ Smith, recipient of a Pulitzer Prize? Possibly, yes. What would it mean to me? That God allowed me to continue my work.

I keep focused to help others with my drive, desire, determination, and deliverance. I called my dear friend, Donna Bostic, to share the wonderful news. She too is proud; she said I am an inspiration to her. She carries me with her. I become teary-eyed. What influences we have on people when we least expect it! Today is Aisha and Linda Day.

5/3/98 ~ 7:30 a.m.

Well Aisha and I had a nice, friendly, pleasant day at the mall. We shopped for clothes, shoes, purses, and we ate. Then, we returned home for the evening event — the Loveland Gospel Concert. Oh what a blessing from the anointing of the Lord to praise and worship in song. I was blessed. Thank the Lord for the spirit that flows through me. I am consumed with God's love for me. I know that He has spoken to me. Today, TD Jakes word was on how God is getting me ready for a big breakthrough. Even jealousy from others will not hold me back. Satan, move out of God's way, for He has made a journey for me. I am ready.

Last night, Debbie called to remind me of my appointments. She told me the K-Mart building bill was $14,000/month. Oh, what an electric bill! Well, we must get the building free. Today, I have an appointment with Delores Armstead to discuss redevelopment of the store. God has already blessed and set the outcome for us. He will send us to our new home. Yesterday, Aisha and I stopped at a construction site for new homes in Claremont. God will bless us with a new home.

5/4/98 ~ 10:56 p.m.

The "Inland Empire Educational Development Project" – the tag name for the K-Mart Building. We are claiming that building in Jesus name. We spoke with Stephen Zurrentla in Michigan. We will submit the proposal obtaining a letter of support. We are requesting free rent for 18 months. New loan payment of $10,000 per month with $2,000 increments per month, each year thereafter until $30,000 per month reached. The current monthly is about $68,000. The light bill history is $14,000 per month. I met with Delores Armstead, County Redevelopment, seeking info/guidance for funds. We spoke with Ron at Coastline. He will send financial projects to set up the computer lab, lecture hall, etc.

Tomorrow, I will attend the Colton Chamber Tea at 7:30 a.m. I am networking for support. Cherry and I don't think in terms of 'if or but.' We just do it! God is laying the sound foundation as we walk. We are secure in Him. I didn't take the time to hang up the award; I placed it along with the certificates along with the others. Actually, I was very busy and my time is valuable. Too many awards in my office.

It has been said that once you believe all that is written, you actually believe you are it. Well, I am in awe of all that has happened. Yet, I cannot stop too long to ponder the effects. I must stay focused on the mission at hand. Besides, all recognition and glory belongs to God. I appreciate His unselfishness, allowing me a glimpse of pride in what we're doing together.

I see the K-Mart building and all it can be, all those it can serve. Lord, remove all obstacles, direct our path. I feel peaceful and calm.

I am loved. I am happy. I am me. Thank You, Lord.

5/6/98 ~ 12:02 a.m.

I attended the Colton Chamber of Commerce meeting. I met with Richard, the V.P. He had convinced the board to support our effort to rent the K-Mart Building. He is going to meet with the redevelopment director to lay the groundwork for my meeting with him. I am pleased with the progress of discussion, contracts, and referrals.

I met with Charlie, VP Adv. Board. He sounded unusually negative – out of character. He is very concerned that "I don't know what I am doing." I need to speak with a consultant to analyze a plan and develop projections. The light bill alone can run up to $16,000/month. I became upset. Here is a man with no money, who purchased a building for $235,000 and says his rent is $2,475, not $16,000. If you don't have $2,475 – what difference does it make? He has renters – but if one does not pay, he will be in a tight spot. I don't like being told what I cannot do! Why? Hasn't God done it all? Has God shown His presence and power, His favor to FDSA and me? Why doubt Him now?

Lord, keep me focused, faithful, and fearless! I went to the movies to relax, and be alone. I watched "Block Dog" by Kevin Hooks and Spike Lee.

As I walked to my car I pondered, Lord, did I make a mistake on this car? Did I move too quickly? No. No doubting God. I waited. He delivered. Linda, don't become fearful of the unknown. God will guide your path to a new location. Hasn't He always taken care of you? Has He ever left your side? Did He not feed you, clothe you, and carry you? All is yes. Why would He stop now? Have you changed?

Do you trust in Him? Yes! Yes, "I can do all things through Christ Jesus."

I spoke with Pam Jackson. She informed me that Debbie, the secretary, quit at the end of the day. Reasons are sufficient. She, Debbie, did have Theresa sit in on the exit interview — reasons unclear. I feel indifferent. No fear or panic. I'll hire another.

I focus on our need to know how to pull funds down, how to track students in Theresa's absence. God continues to prepare us. I take all as marginal process growth.

Cherry and I talked; she is informed of Debbie's decision. Conclusion, God is opening doors. Pam, as usual, made business plans, projections, hired a new secretary. Discuss LVN needs, 4D needs; meet with Pam and Theresa to discuss managerial process and support of management decisions. Well Lord, tomorrow is a new day. Thanks for today.

Tired, but glad.

5/6/98 ~ 7:00 a.m.

Although yesterday had some news of gloom, today I feel like 'I shall mount my wings and fly. I shall run and not get weary.' God is my transportation.

Focus and drive forward. The doors will open. God's windows in heaven are pouring out abundantly wonderful blessings. I am the recipient of it all, for I am the child of I AM. There is joy in knowing I AM.

5/6/98 ~ 1:15 p.m.

I sit in front of 1450 Mt. Vernon, my old house, my home.

The old rusted clothesline remains erect in its cement base to the west of the yard. The yard has scattered grass, weeds sprouting here and there. The other cement base leans forward as though it is being pulled by the clothesline. I remember hanging tons of clothes with wooden clothespins. I see the sheets, shirts, and pants. The sun is bright and hot, there is a light breeze. I remember when we played the game, King of the Hill. The hill of dirt along the sidewalk seems awfully small now; years of rain and weather has bent the hill down.

The kids of today have no clue of the fun of the King of the Hills. Boys pushing one another off the slope, little girls screaming and laughing. Fun to me, yes, fun. I glance over my right shoulder, looking out of the back passenger window to the corner of the hill. There once sat a little girl. Lonely she covered herself with dust, trying to disappear. Wondering how could she be so alone and who would miss her. The old oak tree stands – like the Bible – it is strong, never to be replaced. A fence has replaced the brick wall. Clothes now lay across it, drying in the afternoon sun. The garage port no longer stands. The rose bush underneath my dining room is gone. I would imagine so are the vines and rose bushes outside the bathroom. I see each room, each closet. The clothes, my closet, the closet daddy used to pray in. I miss him so. Gracies (a local neighborhood Mexican restaurant) closed years ago. It is now a Church. The neighbor family has changed, but the homes of the yards, the pleasant feeling, feels the same. Although I have moved far beyond 1450 Mt. Vernon, I can still find that little girl sitting on the hill, unable to become invisible – shielded by God.

5/10/98 ~ 9:04 p.m.

Happy Mother's Day to all mothers! Well this morning, I rose with great anticipation. What gifts do I have from my loved ones? I slipped down the stairs, walked through the kitchen, into the dining room. There sat the most beautiful, bright, red roses I have ever seen. I thought they were silk roses, but no they were real and fresh! Full blossomed, green leaves. Absolutely beautiful, they were from Tahira. Next to the flowers was a box. Inside – my Hawaii set. Ernell, my husband, had purchased a shirt and pants set with a white blouse. I showed every tooth I had. I smiled, thinking that on July 12th, we will celebrate 23 years in Hawaii. I quickly returned to our bedroom, looking for the gift providers. He was in the closet selecting a shirt for Church. Tahira was in her bed, asleep. I woke her up to say thank you with a kiss. All I could do with Ernell was show my teeth, a big smile of joy.

We attended the 7:30 service at Loveland, returned home, then I went to my mother's Church. It was wonderful seeing her. She was delighted to see me! She greeted me with a kiss! An actual, affectionate, kiss on the lips. Lord, thank You. Donnie was there. During the invitation, I turned and asked if he had accepted Jesus into his life. He said yes. I asked if he had joined the Church. He replied yes. I felt good that I had asked, for if he had not, I was to inquire if he wanted to walk the aisle. I keep him and the others lifted in prayer.

Donnie has been staying at momma's house. She understands we depart with love. I travel to Mama Vivian's for dinner, laughter, and good company. Mama Julie is calling us all FAT. We eat and enjoy.

Aisha gave the greatest gift, a license plate holder that says, "Psalm 119:100. A light unto my feet, a light unto my path." I scream with joy.

I returned home and guess what? Tahira has another gift. She hands me a card and a ring box. I must read the card first to understand the ring. The card is an expression of love, friendship, respect, gratitude, and admiration. Thankfulness for my child! She seals her words with a friendship ring. I am dumbfounded – a friendship ring. I tell her how much I appreciate being her mother and her friend. I am honored that she would think so highly of me to give me a ring of love. My daughter, my friend. I show it to Ernell and remind him of my request to replace my wedding set. I removed it on August 5, 1997, never to wear it again. My life has taken a new twist. I desire a new ring of love. He smiles and says he actually has looked. There is hope. Cherry and I will not be able to make the trip to Boston – Martha's Vineyard. Her father, Arthor, is quite sick. Bleeding ulcers, edematous lower extremities, etc. The family thinks he must go into a nursing home. Arthur may surprise them all. Yes, he is 81, but seems quite determined to stay here. He is alert and can hold a conversation. He wants to go home. Martha, you will have to wait.

I have gained quite a lot of weight. I know I must lose it. Tonight, I laid out tennis shoes and sweats. Tomorrow, I will run around my backyard. Something is better than nothing. Lord, thank You for a cheerful and beautifully blessed Mother's Day. I lift Cherry and her family up in prayer. I pray for peace, oneness, love, and understanding. I pray for Arthor's comfort in you.

5/13/98 ~ 7:10 a.m.

It is raining steadily. Is God crying or is He happy with tears of joy? I lay in bed praying for the safe travel of those on the road. I pray that there are no accidents; drivers would be careful and slow down. There were 83 accidents in the South Land yesterday. I think of Arthor and Cherry and I pray for his comfort, his healing, and his peace. I pray his family is around him, expressing their love. As children, we seldom know the personal lives/relationship between our parents. He never missed one of his children's graduations, and was a proud father. There is much to do at work. Staff, focus. Shellie finally gave me Sadiq's book to review. She has not done anything in the last 3-4 weeks. It has thrown me off. Scheduled appointments with school representatives have been delayed. My window of opportunity is closing before the Summer Break. I must move on this.

Lord, thank You for this day. Thank You for Your love. I pray this day for Sadiq's release. I know You can change hearts. I pray the members of the review board release him upon his hearing. They may not know why. You changed their hearts. I pray he receives his kids with love, relocates from San Bernardino, and starts a new, blessed, productive, love-the-Lord life.

My prayer this day to my Lord and Savior.

5/15/98 ~ 7:50 a.m.

Good morning, Lord. Yesterday, I began to think of how my entrees reflect what I am going through, my thoughts, and actions. I met with Rob Steel, Economic Development Administration (EDA) Colton. I am seeking guidance and assistance for future relocation of Four-D Success Academy. He seems friendly and informative. As we talked, he began to share important information. I will talk to Dr. Fisher about possible occupation of their new site, my County Hospital. Doors open, I will walk.

I am happy at home, I am happy with my marriage and my kids. Lord, guide me, guide 4D. Bless us with the SB Co. Contract Pharmacy Program, Medical Building, Health Claims Examiners, etc. Move me into high gear.

5/14/98 ~ 7:34 a.m.

Yesterday, Chris, the young African-American male in the Pharmacy Technician Class, was arrested for Grand Theft. He stole $570 from a classmate. When I was called by 911, I knew it was serious. Pam explained the situation. How Michelle left the classroom to retrieve something from her car. The instructor was in the copying room. Chris was left in the class. The other students returned to find her coupons on her desk and the money gone.

I spoke with Chris via telephone in the presence of Pam. I suggested that if he had the money to return it. He insisted he was not a thief. I suggested the student file a police report.

Well, low and behold, the instructor found the money in the male bathroom. Police present. Chris is gone. I went to the Library to obtain info for Sadiq's book. That's where I was when the call came. A young man who had applied for the CNA Program was on hold until he received state clearance for felony charges.

The young man spoke to me and reminded me of our meeting in the parking lot at the academy. I question proceedings with the state. In some detail, he explained his conviction centered around his attempt to get his daughter from the estranged girlfriend and her boyfriend.

The outcome: he was arrested for receiving or selling state property he took from her. Sentenced, but later received custody of his 3-year-old daughter. He and her live alone. He works in Ontario daily, and his goal is to raise his daughter. He rides his bike to the bus stop, and then takes four buses to work in Ontario. He has never been late! He expressed the last of a better life, the inability to obtain a good job. He is experienced and certified in several areas. But employees see felony history and choose not to hire him. He said the cloud will follow him forever. That same cloud now will follow Chris. I am truly sorry for each of these young men. There is always a better choice. Pray for guidance.

Talk to Jesus.

5/17/98 ~ 9:10 p.m.

As I stood in my bathroom combing my hair, I began to think of the progress of Four-D. I had a personal goal to achieve the Outstanding School by the SB County JTPA. I was thrilled, but now we were selected as the School of the Year by the SB County JTPA. Followed by more accolades. The personal awards I have taken seriously, yet lightly. Although Cherry, the scholarly writer, submitted info on me for nomination, it was the selection of many judges that found me worthy of the honors.

It has been said when you believe in all that is said or written about you, you lose sight of yourself. I've not dwelt on the award. Although quite surprised, I have not told many of the positive outcomes. Each award is more spectacular than the last. The Lifetime Achievement Award almost caused me to faint. I never felt so weak in my legs. I actually had to sit down to gain my balance, supply O_2 to my brain, and realize what had occurred. Today, I am still secretly moved. I won the recognition, Lord, me! Tuesday, May 19th, we will meet Ms. Elizabeth Genne for whom the award is named, and I am excited.

Today, Tahira and I spent the afternoon at Cabazon shopping for Ernell's Hawaii trip. We had a pleasant time. She purchased tennis shoes and jeans. Aisha returned home from a fun weekend in Laughlin with friends from Christ Crusaders. It's good to have her home. I wonder where God will take Four-D next. I must remain calm, focused, and yet aggressive in action. Be smart, plan wisely.

This week SB CO JTPA will notify us of the '98-'99 contract year. I pray for a contract. I take nothing for granted.

Thank You, Lord, for this day.

5/18/98 ~ 7:26 p.m.

Awakened with thoughts of Four-D at 5:30 a.m. What direction should we go? Who do I call? Dr. Fisher? Lead me. Michael Williams came in for the interview/discussion for the Health Claims Examine/Medical Billing Program. He lives in Baldwin Hills, but is willing to take the train to Colton. He will start the week of May 26. Michael will develop and submit the program. I am excited.

I interview a young lady from a registry for the secretary position. After agreeing that she would be a good fit, she was given a tour and introduced to staff. Back inside my office, she informed me she was scheduled for surgery on the 1st week of June, and then was taking a vacation. She would be available June 25th. The agency called me and said she was scheduled for another interview. I informed them that too much of my time was taken/wasted on their interview process. I would seek my own secretary.

Cris Rodgers, Placement Coordinator, called Pam at home and resigned. Thursday is her last day. I feel greatly peaceful and content. I wish her well. Cris is not as skilled as she may have promoted herself to be. But that's for the new employer to find out.

As I sat, I thought, Lord, where is Vicki's number? She may be able to perform. Within 30 minutes, Vicki called. She will be in tomorrow at 12:00. Khaled, the computer person from up North, called Cherry and me. He actually sent the program over a month ago. He will resubmit it for review. Lord, thank You. I placed a call to Dr. Fisher. Is there space/possibility for Four-D at the new Colton site next to the SB Co. Hospital? Lord, place us where we need to be. I called my mother just to say, "I love you". She told me she told someone she loves her son-in-law best, can't stand her daughter. We laughed. I am glad she likes Ernell.

My day ended with my meeting Ms. Elizabeth Genne for whom the Lifetime Achievement Award is named. I was thrilled, we were interviewed, pictures were taken, and we laughed a while. After Pat left, Ms. Genne and I visited until 5:30 p.m. I will return soon.

What a day. Thank You, Lord.

5/21/98 ~ 10:15 p.m.

How can Four-D Success Academy go from being the Outstanding Service Provider with the SB CoJTPA to not receiving an IR Contract in 30 days? After six years, we have been denied two contracts, the IR and Full Service Contract. I don't feel anxious when one door closes. God will open another and it will be bigger and wider. I know He has a bright lamp guiding us. We must plan, focus, produce, and move forward.

I informed Cherry of the outcome. She will complete the grant next week. Theresa and Michael will focus on outside Marketing. David will focus on Rehab and increasing enrollment for Pharmacy Tech. Theresa is to check into the STAR Program and recruit for Service Training, State Rehab certification. I will focus on ETP and Veteran's Program. God is our provider. I will submit the City Proposal on Tuesday May 26th. Attend Riverside JTPA Training Friday 5/22. Get a feel of staff and projections for the upcoming fiscal year.

Today was Cris Rodgers' last day. She tried to pretend to cry. I told her all was well and wished her the best. Three-day notice, not eligible for rehire. I hired a new person who will start on June 3, 1996. I expect a great improvement in performance skill level. I sit here numb, yet calm and peaceful. This is not the calm before the storm. As I was at work earlier, I read the message written 9/15/95 on the board. I ask God to use my hands and my feet. Speak to my heart Lord. If You can do anything, You can use me. I look at my father's antique chair, the Lord's Prayer draped over the edge. I hold back my tears and smile. I know all will be all right for Daddy told me so.

Momma called and left a message. She knows where her rings are. I called her back. Well, as we expected, Zach called home, told her he sold one to the liquor store for $10. That was a $1,100 ring. The other, he sold for $20. That was an $800 ring. $1,900 value for $30, all for the love of getting a hit on coke. How ironic! She tells of him selling her clothes, shoes, all rings, and other jewelry. The boy takes anything not locked down. Sold the Church checks, his brothers' shoes and suits, food from the refrigerator. But upon release, he will return to his safe haven, his mother's home. God, keep her.

I am tired, my eyes hurt, back center point feels heavy, and my face is drooping. I desire energy. I must produce more for Four-D Success. A good night's sleep will do me good. Tomorrow is a new day with new opportunities. Goodnight, Lord.

Plant a seed. Four-D Success will exceed $2.5 million by 12/31/98.

Now go to work!

5/23/98 ~ 6:15 a.m.

I awaken at 5:30 with the thought of, 'To the utmost – Jesus Saves!' What to do if no contract with SB Co.? Create team to market Insurance Agency for Training in Molina, HMO, HFP. Possibly Helen Moddeno and Veronica Becko. I am encouraged ever more. As to ETP – must locate info and apply ASAP. Now it is time to increase productivity. God is good!

5/25/98 ~ 7:49 a.m.

God is always good. Last evening, Ernell and I attended Ernest Dowdy's 7th anniversary as Pastor of Church of the Living God. It was a wonderful evening. I got to greet Bishop and Sister Ruffin, my old Pastor who baptized me at the tender of age of 8. I knew then I loved and needed the Lord. I was on the agenda to introduce the guest speakers, Mr. Keith Lee. It was a pleasure. I told the audience of his double B.A. and his MBA, his executive administrative position with the County of San Bernardino. None of it had meaning to me. It was a resume. A resume tells the reader what the writer wants that person to know, it tells nothing of the character of the person. I wanted to speak about the character of the man I know, who knew Jesus and spoke of it openly. There I went.

Keith is a very good speaker, funny, laughs freely. His presentation was focused, lively, and specific to Ernest. After the program was over, I spoke to Keith – our IR Contract denial. He was shocked we were denied. He stated, "Consider it done. You will have an IR Contract." The full service contract I will need to appeal. He felt I had asked for too much money and our language was not as strong as some others. I am to call him on Thursday for an appointment. The appeal will go forward to the PIC on Tuesday. I call Cherry to inform her of the good news. Now, off to Church.

Thank You, Lord.

5/25/98 ~ 10:36 p.m.

Today is Memorial Day, a day to recognize the fallen heroes and those missing in action, a time to honor the veterans. Seek for peace and safety. How ambiguous. Death does not bring peace, and who is safe? The one who died? An old song – WAR – What is it good for, absolutely nothing!

Jennifer and Ashley Singleton came over yesterday to spend the night. We visited Julie and Kids. Ernell barbecued ribs and chicken, we had potato salad, Caesar salad, baked beans, corn on the cob, buttered rolls, banana pudding, sweet potato pies, strawberries and whip cream. Donna and Binki came by for a pleasant visit. It was nice being together again, talking and laughing. Aisha and Michelle are at the movies. Aisha is convicted in her heart to share the Word of God with Michelle. My advice – ask the Lord to control the thoughts you think and the words you speak! Let her find favor in your message. He will. I am so proud of her. God is using her and she accepts His guidance.

Tahira, my child, received another talk. "Be home by 2:00 a.m." I shared my father's lectures and concerns. She can't understand, but I do expect obedience. Even at 21 years of age, as she resides in my house, in my husband's house.

Today, I told Aisha how grateful I am that God woke me up. I have a good husband who takes care of me and allows me to do my work. Ernell, Honey, thank you. I love you "baby." Lord, grant us another 23 years, I have a second chance to appreciate him and love him as a friend, lover, and wife. God granted me a soul mate. My husband, my man, Ernie Smith.

My Heavenly Father, thank You.

6/3/98 ~ 6:48 a.m.

On June 1, 1998, The Reception for Lady Sala Shabazz, creator of the Black Inventions Museum, was held at the San Bernardino County Government Building. The reception was my assignment. Program, invitations, catering, guests, all went well. Approximately 215 invitations were mailed and over 150 guests attended. Lady Sala Shabazz is guided by God to present the extraordinary exhibit of hundreds of inventions by African-Americans. I am blessed to have been a part of this program. Linda Hart was the coordinator of the project and was guided by God. When God is involved, all goes right. Working on a new program. Staffing reassessments.

6/5/98 ~ 11:07 p.m.

Last evening, I hosted the dinner for Lady Sala, Linda Hart, Cecilia Lowe, and Charlie Seymour at the Hilton. Good company, good food. I made a new friend. Today, I hired Toi for the position of Community Liaison Marketing Director. I am expecting Toi to assist in promoting the Academy in a big way. I provided her with information but emphasized the importance of promoting Four-D and not me. Michael stated my humility has to change. I explained this: Four-D and I are one. I do what I do because of God's will. Four-D, me, and God... we are one, like the Trinity. God, Four-D, Me – The Father, the Son, and the Holy Spirit. I cannot be separated from them, I cannot promote me, I promote that which I am part of.

Toi was allowed to take two albums of history to review. Become familiar with Four-D and me. Boise and I discussed Sadiq's book. He will help me distribute it. I shall have copies ready for July 4, 1998. It will sell well.

Ernell has gone white water river rafting in Kern County. He will be home Sunday. Tomorrow, Ms. T and I will meet for Breakfast.

Lord, I am sleepy – thanks for this day. Goodnight.

6/9/98 ~ 12:15 a.m.

An exciting day. Toi was introduced to the Marketing team as the Community Liaison Marketing Director. A career day is scheduled for June 27th at the Academy. I explained the role and responsibility of each member present and the Chair of Command.

On the way to work, I listened to Rev. Hagee 'An Attitude of Gratitude.' It helped to focus my thoughts, spirit, appreciation, and drive. Betty Thomas prayed about gratitude prior to our meeting. On Sunday, the Minister Clairence's testimony was on First Peter 5:15 – "God resists the proud. He gives grace to the humble." He talked of his gratitude to God for his salvation, his wife who stood by him who saved his life. God is truly wonderful.

Cherry has met with the instructors in the LVN Program. I am angry and very concerned about the performance of the students and the faculty's performance. Things are going to change immediately. I will attend the VN meeting on Wednesday June 10th.

The web page Four-DDDD.com is up and going. We have secured 27 hits. The storefront should do very well. I am excited about our future.

I missed my husband on Saturday. He was on a white rafting trip, although my day was filled. Breakfast with Tamara, nail appointment, Urban League function in Riverside. That evening, I had time to reflect on our life and marriage, I missed him.

Thank You, Lord.

6/9/98 ~ 11:17

I awaken feeling disturbed in my spirit. I could get dressed. At 6:15, I told myself to turn on the TV to channel 40. Reverend Creflo Dollar was teaching about "Nurturing the Seed." Not just planting it but attending to it. I began to think of the meeting with the VN Faculty, scheduled this morning. Rev. Dollar made it so clear. My spirit was telling me to fine-tune the program. I met with Dr. Houston and the staff. I expressed myself as in the spirit of concern, love, dismay, and faith in God as I possibly could.

How can they be unaccountable for the future of their students? They need to hear the truth. I would dismiss the faculty before I dismantled the program. I left to address the next concern of yesterday – Michael, Toi, and Vikki. My decision to fire reinforced to Michael I would not work in chaos between he and the others. Frankly, we discussed the spirit of Four-D. With tears in his eyes, he clearly expressed himself. On one accord, the subject was put to rest.

Overwhelmed, I had one last issue to address. Theresa. We discussed our negative spirits, the spiritual attitudes, our commitment to Four-D and each other. Behind me was left confusion. In front of me was the clear path God had lit, brighter than before. Ron called; I'll get a report from Cherry tomorrow. I spoke with CB Commercial – the project on the corner of Mt. Vernon and San Antonio. Charlie and I talked; he referred me to an attorney. Time to go to Choir rehearsal. My day ended with this song.

'He is good. He is good. He will make everything all right. He is good. God is good. God is good. He will make everything all right. God is good.'

So True.

6/14/98 ~ 12:56 p.m.

God continues to tell me I don't need anyone else but Him. I had been contacted by Pastor West regarding my faith and tithing. Pastor Chuck had wanted to have members speak on tithing – what it has done for us. Last Sunday was cancelled. During the week, Pastor West called twice. We had discussion. I was to speak today. Oh what an opportunity to share God and to inform those present of classes and opportunity at Four-D. I purchased a new pantsuit. At Church, I was ready, but I was never called. It reminded me of the day I felt desperate and I needed students. The Church was full. I sent messages via the deacons to Pastor Chuck, "Let members know of fine education at Four-D." No announcements came forth. I was saddened, disheartened. As I left the Church, a ray of light hit me in the face. It blinded me. Jesus spoke to me, "You don't need anyone but Me." He brought us through the difficult times with no money, but with the faith of a mustard seed. Today, I am calm. I know that the future is in God's hands. I am only a vessel. He has chosen me to do this particular assignment.

Cherry has given so much of her heart to Rwanda, to its children, educational system. I have been disheartened for I was able to discern the truth -- that Claire, the young Rwandan that Cherry had taken into her home, had lied about her family outcome during the genocide. Not all were dead. Claire was sent to the U.S. by Christine, a relative. My love for Cherry and our friendship requires that I hold my peace. There was no way I could speak negatively of the situation regarding her feelings. I was not speaking against or disregarding her personal efforts.

The truth became known when Celestin landed in Rwanda. He was different in his response to Cherry. She had done so much for him... his flight to California, his dental bills, his VISA, his return home. All by her, yet he showed little regard for her effort. At the wedding, we met Innocent's Uncle. Another lie. He was not in Rwanda at the time of the genocide. Those who selected him and sent him had lied. Christine, Biruta, all had lied. Innocent supported the lies by telling of his family's death. His mother is alive and siblings in Rwanda. Claire's disrespect for Cherry and her home. The disregard for all of her financial, emotional, and spiritual support has gone unnoticed. Christine says, "Clara was the same in Rwanda." Why did they send such ungrateful members of the society to America? We have our share here.

Cherry has sent Claire to Christine's. Her future is not known. She has yet to apologize to her mother, Cherry, for her disrespect. When you have given all and it is not appreciated, it is time to move forward. I know that God has prepared Cherry for international work. Her knowledge will benefit Four-D Success when we move into the new frontier. All was not lost. Everything has a purpose in life.

The Health Claims Examiner/Medical Billing Program is off to the bureau. It will be a good program, I am praying for direction on the next building. I don't know what to do, but God does. I ask for guidance... where, how large, what do I need to move forward? He will provide. I think of my father and go listen to the video of him praying. All is all right with the Lord.

6/15/98 ~ 6:15 a.m.

The presence of the Spirit of God brings me to tears. I think of FDSA and cry. It has been a long time that I have cried for the school. The imposed suffering I have experienced has me crying for me, but today I feel as I did on July 30, 1991 at 11:05 a.m. God is speaking to me, He guides me, and I am listening. It is so wonderful to have Him in me and me in Him.

Four-D will one day be a degree granting school. The year 2000 will be a transformed period for us. God has not given me the spirit of failure or fear; He has filled me with the spirits of success and courage.

This is a new day for me.

Today is also Aisha's 20th Birthday.

Lord, I am thankful.

6/24/98 ~ 11:15 p.m.

Well, much has occurred since the last entry.

Cherry's father, Arthur Williams, has improved. We went to Pontiac Michigan to see him. He went from the ventilator to O_2 via mask, asking for water, to be turned. I think he will return to the LTC facility.

On Friday, Cherry and I met with Gary Lobster, Mayor of Saginaw. He introduced us to Councilwoman Wilmer Ham. We stayed in her home. What a treat. We laughed until we cried, attended Church...wow, the lady can sing and play the piano. She is scheduled to be here in December. We were introduced to Kareem Muhammad, a promoter. We discussed fundraising for the school. I expect a proposal for review this week. Kareem mentioned Senegal. I informed him of my contacts and communications. He put me in touch with Malik Sola who is in communication with Shok Yalya, Ada of Senegal. Shok will be in the states in two weeks. Hopefully, I will meet with him.

Gary requested our proposal to submit in the Nigeria King Igme. What a day.

Saturday, we attended a picnic at Wilmer's Church. Good people, good barbeque. Monday, we met with Stephen Zula, retail division of K-Mart. We explained our desires to be housed in the K-Mart building. He requested a proposal. After a positive weekend, I return to work. Pam and Toi had major communication over a single form. I seek wisdom. I will address other issues regarding the movement of the company.

I had a talk with my committee. I prayed to God.

I received notice I was selected to receive the one of 50 Distinguished Women in 1998 by the Press Enterprise. I drew up the first set of rough prints for the house. Ernell is positive about the change as long as I do not press moving. I go from being ecstatic to wondering what is going on. I must improve my skills to manage the business better.

Thanks, Lord.

6/26/98

Education is a key component in the development of one's ability to comprehend and implement the technical skills of modern technology and industrial growth.

The evaluation of man's thought process increases the avenues of ideas, which introduce us to technology that is awesome and provocative.

Every aspect of employment requires the components of a learned process and the application of technical skills. It is imperative that individuals take advantage of the educational and training opportunities that will lead to gainful employment and financial independence.

L Smith President/CEO, Four-D Success Academy

6/27/98 ~ 7:46 a.m.

Last night I dreamed that Julie and Mike had reconsidered their marriage. They had come to a function with the girls. All were smiling. Julie said, "I have something to tell you later." I noticed Mike was quite robust (round) in the abdomen. He looked peaceful. He had on a red long sleeve shirt with bright pinstripes. I cried and hugged all of them. I know what they had gone through. My own experience had given me insight to the feelings of loss, hurt, pain, resentment, and eventually finding peace, falling in love again, and simply wanting my man.

Last evening, Cherry informed me that Carolyn, an employee with the State Dept., had the ability to inform us government contracts for uniforms. The possibilities are enormous financially. We know that God continues to put a path for us to travel. We laugh in delight. We marvel at the unknown possibilities. Our dreams are unlimited for we know that the end is dreaming on and beyond. God has no boundaries, neither do we. The ideal is not to spread wide, but penetrate deep.

Today, we go meet with an individual and discuss manufacturing uniforms. Today will be productive.

6/29/98 ~ 8:50 p.m.

Sunday, the Minister's sermon was on "His Testimony" of how God had blessed him. After the service, I asked Ernell if he had a testimony. He said, "Yes." When I asked what it was he said, "You." A man of a few words. When asked to elaborate, he replied, "You, our marriage. That is my testimony." Such profound words simply stated. I completely understand.

Today, we had a class of 40 vocational nurse students. New faces, new desires. The day started and ended pleasantly. Cherry and faculty covered all forms with the students' rules and laid a start of a new era for Four-D Success Academy.

Toi is moving forward with marketing ideas; Michael is a ball of fire. He is in charge of Career Day. Theresa returned from a vacation. As usual, we had disagreements. Conclusion... I expressed my dislike for her tone, no tolerance, her selfish and self-centered attitude. She will either resign or I will dismiss her based on future input. I told her she seeks the 'me and my', not 'the what can I do' – only 'what can I get.' She only foresees the future for immediate gratification. Whatever the outcome, I know it will be best for all.

Information has been submitted to Gary Lobster, Malik, and Kareem. I expect a response in 2 weeks.

Me and Ernell's 23rd anniversary is July 12, '98. Hawaii, here we come.

Today, I look at where God has brought me. Last year while driving home, Aisha and I expressed God's goodness. I (we) prayed for a financial blessing. I pledged $20,000 to the God's Women's Conference. I prayed to be able to give $15,000 to the Adults and $5,000 to the young adults to help support the Administrative costs and to provide scholarships to those in need of financial support for their registration or hotel fees. God has blessed us. I will give $20,000 to GWC before the August 5th start date. God supplied all.

7/1/98 ~ 11:38 p.m.

Yesterday evening, I arrived home, feeling exhausted at 8:30 or so. I talked with Aisha as she cleaned the kitchen; I enjoyed our private time alone laughing, listening, and eating fruit.

By 9:30, I headed to bed. As I was about to enter between the sheets calling my weary body, Cherry called. She was upset over the evaluation I presented her with. She expressed anger — doesn't know if she is a partner or an employee. Why should she be evaluated? Who evaluates me? She asked and told me I didn't need to respond just then. But our relationship was such, she could freely speak. I agreed. I couldn't have responded if she had asked. I thought out her comments for as long as it took for me to turn out the lights. I fell fast asleep. No discussion from last night contents. Quite busy at work, potluck, interviews, conference calls. But bottom line is that as President, I am responsible to assess all and respond wholly and in writing.

Met Gary, who is experienced with Medical Assisting Program. He agreed to bring the curriculum to me for review. If accepted, we're in business.

Met with Thomas Winbush, a young man I am considering for computer Technical Services.

Met with Boise Jones and agreed to contract services for infrastructure development.

-Help develop page.

-Set up storefront.

-Negotiate computers deal.

-Develop Application in Computer Health Care Program.

-Set up Computer network for Uniform shop to LA Manufacturer.

-Set up infrastructure for distance learning.

Sadiq's book will be completed tomorrow! He will be pleased.

Received two letters from Sadiq. He is saddened at the death of a dear brother (inmate). It drives home the reality of where he is and the separation from his family. How lonely to die away from family. They are on lockdown; therefore, the inmates can't comfort each other or offer a goodbye to a dear friend. God will bring him home. I know he will breathe air outside of the prison walls and walk the streets with his kids. All claim victory in Christ Jesus.

This is a blessed day. Spoke with Kareem Mohammad and Brad Randall about the concert. They will discuss the issue. I know that this is God's work. Amazing how things continue to flow in a strong, positive stream.

Lord, I am now sleepy – 5:30 a.m. will be here soon. Goodnight.

7/2/98 ~ 6:22 a.m.

I rose at 6 a.m., showered, thought about yesterday – a productive day. Prepared for work, and then decided to stretch across the bed and rest my head on Ernell's chest. I relaxed a few minutes, thinking about God's blessing. How grateful I am. Last year on June 30th I struggled to meet a 4:30 deadline to deposit money, which would make the school qualify for Financial Aid. Today, I reflect on the daily cost to operate and the amount of checks I sign each month. As I think of the cost of operation, the growth, and the blessing, I pause to write.

THANK YOU, LORD, FOR THE OPPORTUNITY TO MAKE A DIFFERENCE IN SOMEONE'S LIFE. THANK YOU FOR MAKING A DIFFERENCE IN ME. BLESS ALL THAT COME TO ME. REMOVE ALL BARRIERS AND PEOPLE WHO SEEK TO HINDER. YOUR GRACE AND MERCY HAVE BROUGHT ME THROUGH. THANK YOU FOR THE TEARS OF JOY. THANK YOU FOR THE STRUGGLE. VICTORY IS MINE AND VICTORY IS SWEET.

THERE ARE NO BOUNDARIES I CAN'T EXCEED. NO HEIGHT WE CAN'T JUMP. OUR LIMITATION IS THE HORIZON CREST, A DISTANCE I CANNOT MEASURE. MY GOD IS MY BANKER. HIS FUNDS ARE LIMITLESS. HE PROVIDES ALL, ALL, ALL OUR NEEDS. HE GUIDES OUR PATH. HE SENDS OUR HELPERS. HE KNOWS OUR HEARTS AND THE KNOWLEDGE OF OUR MINDS. HE CONTINUALLY PREPARES US FOR EACH STEP WE TAKE.

ALMIGHTY GOD – HOW I LOVE THEE. YOUR CHILD, LINDA

7/5/98 ~ 10:00 p.m.

Yesterday, Ernell and I journeyed to Pasadena with Cherry and Catherine. We visited Paul Nzambebha, the artist. Paul had friends over in honor of Christine and Jimmy.

It was nice to see our Rwandan friends, Bon and Pam, Bill. I think of God's goodness, Four-D, my marriage, my family – Mother, brothers. I think of Immanuel's response to "God is good" – "No matter what."

I have been thinking of Ernell and my conversation on the house – no pool. He said he is in control with the house as it is. I began to think, 'Should I want to move or change our house?' At Church, a young couple spoke of God's blessing to bless with a new home and renters for their home. I ask Ernell and Aisha to pray for 1) Ernell to tithe and give – God will bless him too and that his clientele and salary increase to make him comfortable with a move. 3) God blesses with a new home and renters for their home. I believe God will provide through our prayer.

I pray Ernell is able to pray for himself and he believes in God's blessings and power.

I spoke with Sadiq yesterday. He is feeling better. I shared the letter info he will be receiving. Lord, I am sleepy. I have done little work these last 3 days. I enjoyed my home, Aisha, and my husband.

Lord, thank You.

7/8/98 ~ 11:36 p.m.

Well, Aisha is here, whining about her need for money. Why can't we pay her $150 month to subsidize her needs? She beats me down to avoid going to her father. He won't discuss money. I pay for her truck, which she kept for 2 years! $255 a month. I pay for her auto expenses. She has never looked at the monthly gas bill – up to $60 a month. I donate $55 or so in cash for her to purchase clothes, especially when she gets that long whining cry and face. Last time, she shed several tears. It broke my heart. I felt better after spending the day with her and spending $200. She was okay for 2 weeks. Then, she needed more clothing and shoes. About $100 took care of that.

Now does this seem like a mother who doesn't care? I don't think so!!!

Now about work! She decides when and how often she will work at FDSA for $7.50 hour. Never satisfied 2-3-4 days a week. Needs more money. Refused to work full-time at FDSA. Refused. So she took a job 20 hours a week with Robinsons May Co. NOW she is unhappy. Why? She has to work Sat/Sun 4-8 hours each day. What is this child to do? Wear out my nerves? Ask for a permanent donation to take care of her needs, as she asks why at age 20 do I have to work? *I need time to study. I need a vacation, like other kids with parents who are well off.* (She thinks we are!) *Take care of their kids* (Grown up). Well, I can't. She must be accountable for something. She will start at R May or die by getting sick of my mouth. I am in debt for two car insurances. I can't take anymore. Maybe as she reads this, she will finally understand. I am not rich, neither is dad. We had to work to provide the best. One day she will not only understand, but she will be satisfied and appreciate our efforts. Thank You, Lord. Linda

I addressed Toi today for her language and conduct at the Marketing Meeting. She cannot represent FDSA nor me in a private or a public form.

The office was busy and pleasant. Kareem, the promoter, called to say he spoke with Brad Randall at the Orange Show. He will aid us in our endeavor to do fundraisers. Cherry submitted the proposal to Stephen Zula K-Mart Corp. I sent off the financial package to One Union Bank – SBA Arrowhead. God is good!

Virgil Norby died this past weekend. I cried upon hearing the news. I thought of the 1st meeting at the coffee shop in Covina. His smile, the coffee, our discussion of the knee surgery, his cane, Michelle, the rough draft of the Brochure for Four-D Success Academy. Now he is gone. Michelle is gone. I was truly saddened. I spoke to Bob, his brother, and requested the cane. He will ask the Minister if I can have it. Thank you for your friendship, service, smile, and love in Christ.

Aisha is still here! Goodnight.

Virgil's funeral is tomorrow, July 9, 1998 @ 10:00 a.m. Trinity Lutheran Church West Covina.

7/9/98 ~ 9:35 a.m.

Cherry's dad, Arthur, died last night. I am so grateful to God that she and I went to see him several weeks ago. I think of my dad, and I am not sad. Time heals. Virgil Norby's funeral was today. I attended and received his cane, the cane my dear friend Michelle Daisy had given him. Virgil had bilateral knee surgery and Michelle, an Occupational therapist, provided the cane in 1992. The cane is the bond among the three of us. I submitted the financial package to SBA Arrowhead requesting $1 million and Union Bank for $300,000 – with the goal to expand FDSA. Received letter of support from Congressman Brown and Keith Lee. K-Mart is ours.

7/11/98 ~ 11:15

Today was the 1st CAREER DAY at Four-D Success. And it was a success. Staff participated and 9 people showed up. The numbers may have been small but the word is out. 2 were interested in the LVN Program, 1 the pharmacy tech the other parents interested in programs for their children. I am pleased. This evening at 6:00 p.m., we had the capping and pinning ceremony at SB Com. Hospital, it was very good. The guest speakers were Ellen Riley, Matthew's Mother, and Roy Nolan, the manager of Education at the Hospital. She was inspiring. She spoke on what success is. The audience was very good. I am so proud of the faculty and students. I thank God for the blessings He has given me. I sit here in my bed, tired, sleepy, and tired. Tomorrow is the 23rd wedding anniversary of Mr. Ernell and Linda L. Smith. Lord, we made it. Thank You. We are traveling to Hawaii. My honeymoon.

I will have a wonderful time, and so will he. Lord, thank You for keeping us together. I look forward to the next 23 years.

Well, goodnight all.

Sunday ~ 7/12/98

Today is Ernell and my 23rd Anniversary. Lord, thank You for blessing us through the trials. We love each other and we are happy. Hawaii, here we come!

7/12/98 ~ 9:50 California Time/6:50 Hawaii

We are here. Our flight was delayed by one hour. It was a pleasant trip. I read 14 chapters of Patti Labelle's book **Don't Block my Blessing**. I look out of the window to the sky and ground below. I pray to God, giving thanks for this day. My husband is by my side. It is time to unload and enjoy the evening.

Monday 7/13/98 ~ 7:30 a.m.

I awake at 5:45, raising my head I looked out of the glass door to the vast ocean. It was breathtaking. I was here with my MAN. God had protected us through the battles of silence and physical and emotional separation. He had brought us together – stronger than ever. I LOVE ERNELL and HE LOVES ME. Lovemaking here is refreshing, renewing 23 years captured in a moment in time. Life is good for me.

We called the girls. They are doing fine. Having breakfast looking at the ocean, blue islands off to the left and right with gray clouds hovering above them, soft music playing in the background, sparrows flying about, chirping. I have total joy and peace. Four-D Success Academy is in God's hands. I know it is secure.

We are about to journey to the volcano and sightsee the island.

7/13/98 ~ 1:03 p.m.

Traveling the road to the volcano, I look out at 8,000 ft. I look above the clouds and just say all that is needed – God – blue sky – white clouds of clusters. He separated the Heaven from the Earth – Only God.

THE HALEA KALA LANDSCAPE.

Tuesday ~ 7/14/98 8:05 a.m.

Last night, we attended the Luau at the Hyatt Regency. Great food and entertainment. The Hotel is breath taking, with a grand entrance and its three huge chandeliers. Fantastic! It reminded us of a Las Vegas mall. It was a long day from volcano craters to nightlife, eating fabulous food and walking, fire eating, entertainment.

Well, today we are off to HANA for sightseeing, a black sand beach, and who knows what else. See ya. Oh yeah, while eating breakfast, a colorful rainbow reached across the sky.

9:05 p.m.

What a day! We traveled from West Maui to Hana. We traveled 30 to 380 Kahului to 36 to 360, reconnected to the 36 up the 31 to 37 N. 365-380 to 30. We traveled 40 miles of wandering roads along magnificent share line at 15-20 miles per hour, stopping to take pictures, take in God's beauty. Kaibca, Keanae, Wailua, down to black sand beach at Hana Bay State Park. We had lunch - veggie burger, Maui fish sandwich cool drinks, fresh juicy pineapples, and chips. The sand is black. I gathered some for Mary Salim in my Sobe bottle. We returned to our journey, the sky blue, the ocean blue, rainbows, forestry thick, waterfalls, narrow bridges, and single lanes. The temperature ranged from 68 degrees to 90 degrees. We journeyed on to Kakio, Waba Falls, Oheo Salih – seven pools, Haleakala National Park, on to Kipahulu. Here the road ended. Now 40 miles of dirt road on the return home. The scenery has been breathtaking. How amazing how it changes. On the backside of Haleakala, the mountain is barren. Ocean with black sand beaches, weather at 70 degrees. We stopped at Kaupo store and spoke with Lupe Cruz. He and Anna and kids live in Rancho Cucamonga. We exchanged greetings at Seven Pools a couple of hours earlier. We exchange greetings, shook hands, and shared business info. He owns a management business. I thought of Donna Bostic. He and Ernell spoke of insurance coverage. Ernell was to call him soon. We continued our journey along the shoreline through Ulupalakua,

Kula, Waiakoa, Pulihu, Kukaloni, Pumene, back to Kahului through Mauloea, Olowalu back to Lahaina. We stopped for dinner after the (10:30-7:30) day trip at Smokehouse Bar, BBQ and Grill. I tell you, between the fresh, juicy pineapple, smokehouse baby back pork ribs, the ocean crashing against the shore and my Long Island Ice Tea, I told Ernell I was ready to have an orgasm. That's how good my day was going. Great, deliciously great. Now back at our room, we have a message to call the Airport. Well, good news. Our flight is overbooked. We agreed to a later flight @ 9:30 p.m. and received $300 vouchers each. Next trip – how about Jamaica?

I am tired, rest for a new day. I have eaten, been loved, had spirits, and am happy here with my honey. I have been reading Patti Labelle and relaxing. Oh yes, Lord, thank You.

Wednesday ~ 7/15/98 8:25

The Dells – oh what a night – to love you dear. Oh what a night to hold you dear. Yes what a night. In my white trimmed burgundy baby doll lace nightgown, spaghetti strap, burgundy-laced panties, my man found me delightful. He suggested I wear such nightwear more often. Our time together has been ours, no one and nothing else. I have no desire to call home or work. God has given us a second chance and we are taking it. We bathe in sex, love, and happiness. I am secure in his strong, muscular, chocolate arms. We are headed to West Maui Honolulu Bay to Parasail. This morning, I sat on the terrace, sipping O.J., reading my book, and gazing at the ocean.

Today is Arthur's funeral. Cherry's dad's home going. My thoughts and prayers go to the family and friends. I thank God that He allowed our paths to cross. My loving relationship with my dad gave significance to my desire for Cherry to have positive and loving closure with her dad. There is no pain and agony worse than being unable to say, "I love you" to the departed with a heart that is heavily burdened. Cherry's heart is light!

4:55 p.m.

Back in the room 9030 after a full day. Traveled West through – Kapolua, Honolulu Bay, Honokahua 30 West. The sights are beautiful, Lover Mountains, some rain, traveled along the coastline to Kahakuloa Bay. Now this was breathtaking, the beauty of the white tip blue waves crashing against me, rugged edge of the island of Maui. We stopped to take pictures. I found myself walking down to the edge of the cliff. Ernell called out to me. I felt as though the sea was calling me. I wanted to get closer, I wanted to touch it, I wanted to caress it. Ernell called again. I could hear but I felt mesmerized by the sea, what an emotional passionate urge to go to the limit. Ernell called, "Linda, where are you going?" I stopped at the edge. He warned of the high winds, he came closer to me. I requested pictures of the glory of God's beauty. I wanted a picture of me standing, bathing in its beauty. We moved on to a narrow single lane road, to a roadside stand where we purchased delicious, fresh banana bread for $4. Down Kahakili Highway_ South to Waihee, we stopped at Wahice Beach – a gravesite that marked the water edge said RASTA MAN – empty beer cans, necklaces, trinkets placed about the gravestone. We journeyed to Wacehu Beach – Waliluku city, the last city on our 5-hour trip. Parasailing up to 1,100 feet for Ernell and about 700 for me. Seeing the world below, a little fear that dissipated quickly, nowhere to go but down. Might as well relax and enjoy. The tiny boat below, blue water, I could see the coral reef below. Back in the room, I showered, put on my robe, and relaxed. Tomorrow at 7 a.m. we go snorkeling on a glass bottom boat.

Thursday ~ 7/16/98

Up at 5:30 a.m. have to get ready to hang with Big E. Parasailing yesterday – what a blast. Snorkeling today off Malokini. Traveled by The Four Winds II with Captain John. The sea is beautiful, colorful fish, corral, and blue water. 1 – 1 ½ hour out, we put on our gear and jumped into the water. Salty water, kicking about with my fins. Mask with breathing hose. Oh yes, my yellow float belt, afraid of sinking – heck I had to remember to breathe through my mouth – not my nose. We had a lunch of burgers, chicken, hot dogs, veggie burgers, chips, sodas, beer, and water. Great crew cooking and feeding about 149 people. The trip was videotaped and I asked Jane (crew member) to announce our 23rd Anniversary on tape. We bought the tape and shirt for Ernell.

On the way home, a song came on – Ernell took my hand and began to sing – I think it was ***Stand by Me*** by Ben E King. I forgot but I remembered I felt a rush of love. Ernell has always stood by me. He has given me 'my space' to operate. Now, I will stand by him with devoted love and appreciation. We sung together ***Darling, stand by me.*** We have a wonderful life.

Lord, thank You so much. We have given each other our undivided attention. NO calls to the office, one call home, message left, Aisha called to request the use of Sterling. Tahira's car battery died. She said all was well at home and office. Well, my honey is asleep. He made dinner reservations at the 'Waterfront'. Highly recommended for 6:45. Time to read.

Friday, 7-17-98 ~ 7:42

Good morning to the sound of the ocean waves coming to shore. Yesterday, I read in Patti's book and how she was hypnotized by pool water. She felt it calling her; I feel like that each time I hear the waves crashing. I shared this fantasy with Ernell.

Today we check out by noon, tour and shop, return the car by 7. On our flight home by 9:28 p.m. arrive to LAX at 5:40 a.m. Saturday. This has been the most wonderful vacation of my life. I have spent the last 5 days alone with my husband. We have totally reconnected. I can't stop praising the Lord, giving thanks. Ernell and I made it through the storm. We both are looking forward to the next 23 years. Time to get up and get going.

7/17/98 ~ 10:55 a.m.

We leave Kaanapali Resort for the last time. I say goodbye to Room 9030. We give well wishes to the guests on the elevator, we say goodbye to the assistants. I gave a sad wave bye-bye to the lady at the booth exit gate. Mountains to my left, the ocean of blue to my right, Ernell said we will come again. Lahaina, the place where I renewed my devotion and love to my husband. God has granted us another chance and we took it.

Off to Makena along the South East coast (31 Hwy) to shop and sight see.

5:55 p.m.

We traveled to Makena, walked the mall, then headed North. The weather is cooler, but the day is beautiful. I read and chatted with Ernell and took it all in. We went to Front Street to window shop, buy T-Shirts and moo-moo's for Momma. Now sitting on top of a small hill in Kahului I finished reading Patti Labelle's ***Don't Block the Blessings.*** I enjoyed every line. I got a glimpse of the lady I adore for her love expressed on stage, in song, and personality. I've always thought about what it would be like to spend a day with Patti in her kitchen, talking girl talk?

7:07 p.m.

We re-enter the Kahului Airport. Sunset Reggae music has been blasting all week on 103.7. We will miss this – back to Dollar to return car rental.

9:42 p.m.

On time, seated in 17 D and E over the wing. The American Airlines; flight 14 757 heads down the run way for the 4:52 minutes of flight to LAX. We fly on the wings of God. Landed safely at 5:45 a.m. LAX time. Collect bags and go home.

7/18/98 ~ 12:27 a.m.

We arrived home safely, unloaded the truck, and were greeted by Aisha. Tahira was at work until 7:30 a.m. Ernell and I were tired, I lay in the bed, he's in the den. Tahira arrived. She was surprised we were lying down. She said, "Aren't we going to IHOP?"

I asked, "For what?"

She said, "You don't know the meaning of IHOP – think! You and daddy went there after you got married. We were going to take you and daddy out for breakfast and present you a dozen roses!" I smiled wearily and said, "Tomorrow." She told me to wake her up at 2:00 before I left for my hair appointment. She was working the 3-11 shift at Indian Hill Convalescent Hospital. She worked a double. She/Tahira received notice on a position open in Lancaster; I think she will take it.

Aisha and I talked about her truck, desires, remodeling the house. She wants Tahira's room when she leaves. Well, Ernell and I are inquiring where we should go next. Cancun, Jamaica, New Orleans. We got $300 vouchers each. I suggest Labor Day – Cancun. It's been a great week with my honey, Ernell. Well it's nighttime.

7/20/98 ~ 7:28 a.m.

I had a horrible night last night. I tossed and turned from the moment Ernell said, "The vacation is over." Everything went through my head. I began to feel the stress of running the school. I thought to myself, so this is what it feels like. I had perfect peace while I was away with Ernell. Perfect peace.

I almost don't want to go in today, to face the business motion – but I must. I've had my carrot juice and completed my stretches. Even my left small toe is healed. It's going to be a warm day.

I enjoyed yesterday with Ernell and the girls. After eating, we went to look at trucks. He must get something he is comfortable with.

7/21/98 ~ 11:00 p.m.

Today, I received emotional and physical freedom. Unable to explain in words, but there is exceeding joy. I spoke with my mother-in-law and shared the wonderful time Ernell and I had at Maui. She understood my joy and she was joyful. She said something about it's okay to go through the upheaval to find the tracks. Sometimes you have to go through stuff to get it right.

Alive and in love with my man, Ernell.

My mothers are good to us and love us.

I give Cherry her gift from Hawaii. It is a Kuru Angel with a large heart. When I saw it, I immediately thought of her. Her spirit, love for life, friendship, her aura. She cares so much for others. The Kura Angel made me think of her father, her kindness, her love of expression, how she returned home to clean his home while he was in the hospital.

She sheltered him in ways she may not even understand. Arthur knew each of his children. He knew who he would call upon for closure and completion. He knew who he would need to take care of his death. Cherry and Eloise. How odd the one child who needed him the most for a basic need – shelter – showed the most (in my opinion) affection toward him. I shared words of sincerity as I handed her the angel.

Cherry is God's angel. She is not a disappointment to Him.

He is proud of her. She is blessed.

My friend, I sincerely love you. Your joy, personality, laughter, and friendship mean a great deal. Thanks for being there!

7/23/98 ~ 6:55 a.m.

Yesterday, I met with Judy White, Assistant Sup. of SB City Schools. We reviewed Sadiq's book. She was very impressed. She ordered 60 for the principles and will distribute and encourage them to order. She will add books to the Children's Project/grant this August, and she will inform the Teen Diversity Coordinator of it. I have an appointment today to see Dr. D. DeBruhl of Rio Vista Elementary Schools and an appointment next Tuesday to see Nancy of SB County School. I felt so overwhelmed with the possibilities, so joyful of the Lord, the things with Four-D. As I was returning to the office, I was praying. I looked at the K-Mart Building and drove to it. I parked and prayed to God. I just thanked Him for everything. Charles talked to me about the Medical Society Building – inquired about purchase. I did. And what do you know, Linda, the building manager, was open to discussion and said she would present it to the Board on Monday. The building is 22,000 sq. ft., three acres, and a possible sale for $1 million. The seed was planted. God only knows the outcome. He is the path to our future.

7/25/98 ~ 11:56

The beginning of a new home! Jeff and Otis and another young man came over to examine the house and discuss new plans for reconstruction. Jeff will do the blueprints and Otis will do the construction. This is so exciting. A new house! Ernell is talking – that's good! He stresses "cost effectiveness," but he is open to recommendations and the big change.

Foyer, columns in and out, extended living, formal dining room, new kitchen, increase family room, service area for washer and dryer, increase garage to 3-car, change stairs, increase ceiling, walk through closets for Ernell, sitting room and large bathroom with mirrors and lights, fireplace in master bedroom, French doors to balcony. The new house is going to be lovely. Oh yes, an office for me.

7/28/98 ~ 7:21 a.m.

Yesterday I signed the IR Contract with S.B. Co. I am preparing the contract for the City of San Bernardino. Riverside Contract will roll over. Hired a new secretary; I expect good things. A new class of CNA will be starting on July 1st, a class of 6-10. Things are a little slow. But I am expecting great volumes in the next 2-3 months. Have a good day. From, The Lord

7/29/98 ~ 7:15 p.m.

Greg Sheets CPA called to say the Financial reports look good. Exceed 1:1 ratio. Net income: either $45,000 or $55,000 with adjustments. All I heard was no negatives. Rossina at Union Bank called, the application looks good, possible $250,000 line of credit or loan. To schedule appointment, discuss plans. Funds came in for Payroll. I will not need to transfer from the Federal Account. We will know for sure by Friday.

Staff is working and the environment is pleasant and wonderful. Cherry is off to Hawaii without the laptop! She left Tuesday and will return Monday. I know she is having a good, relaxing time. The Pharmacy Regulations changed. Students cannot do hands on. We have discussion and began to implement changes. Develop schedule for night class, set up lab, and advertise. God is good!

Oh yes, the Press (Business) featured a wonderful Business Profile on Four-D Success Academy. I am marketing Sadiq's book. Friday, I have an appointment with Dr. D. DeBruhl and Nancy Norton. I know God is guiding this project.

Time to work on the budget for '98/'99. I expect $4 million. Now, let's get there.

7/30/98 ~ 11:58 p.m.

Today, I met with Nancy Norton, Colton School District – Sadiq's book. She will discuss it with a group of principals. She will call me next Friday on the 7th of August – My Birthday. I told her I was interested in partnering with The District offering our classes for Career Path. She became excited, gave me the name of Bonnie Hunt and Rosemary. They were in her office earlier speaking about their idea of Career Path. I called to leave a message at 5:20 on Bonnie's machine and she picked up! I have an appointment for August 17th at 11:00. Greg Sheet and Jim Jones met in my office to discuss the program for tracking students. I am excited about the future.

Yesterday at the staff meeting, I shared my poems 'My Enemy' and 'Old House, My Home'. They were able to see another side of me. Betty Thomas was moved by 'Old House, My home'. She lives in her grandfather's house. I sit here thinking about so many things. My house, my desire to remodel it, my life with Ernell, my children, their future, Four-D, and my relationship with God. God keeps me together.

I have felt peaceful for some time. Since I took control of me, no fear. Payroll, me, staff productivity, life is good. I am excited about the God's Women's Conference. Mary Salim and Betty Thomas are coming for Thursday and Friday. This will be a blessed time in the Lord.

Donnie turned 47 on July 24th. I pray all is well with him.

7/31/98 ~ 11:15 p.m.

I spent the weekend in Las Vegas with my honey, Ernell. We stayed at the Golden Nugget. Nice room. Visited several new casinos. We had a light discussion on purchasing a new Expedition for Ernell. I was treated well all the way around.

Tomorrow is the Black Inventions Museum Reception. I expect it to go well. I feel very low key at this moment. There is much to do. The Nursing Board Consultant will recommend 30 students. Adjustments required. Goodnight, Lord. Thanks for a safe, loving weekend.

8/6/98 ~ 11:14

Oh what a better blessing at the God's Women's Conference. Betty and Mary are here receiving their blessing. Last year, after the Conference I prayed to God. I asked for His grace and mercy. Save my marriage, save the school. Heal me and allow me to give a spiritual blessing to the GWC. All on FDSA to be financially sound to donate a love offering of $10,000. On my way here, I had thoughts of, *'I got bills to pay. Four-D funds may seem low.'* Now I know what the Lord God has done. I could feel the battle beginning to take place. Well, Lord, You won. Thank You, Jesus. I wrote a note to Sister Charlyn and indicated my love offering from Four-D. I know the Lord will multiply the school finances. He will continue to care for his children and his bills. I have been blessed. My marriage is solid. Ernell and I are happy. Four-D Success Academy is getting ready for an expression.

I inquired about purchasing the building. Linda asked the President of the Board – He wants a BID. She had said $1-1.2 million. I had put in a financial request for $1 million to the Arrowhead SBA and $300,000 to Union Bank. I know the Lord is preparing me. I don't ask how I am going to pay for it, I know He is. Four-D will be able to minister to others as He guides us. Next year, more staff will attend. All who chose to come will be here, the Lord will provide.

Heavenly Father, I thank You for the many messages of blessings. I thank you for the songs of praise; I thank You for my joy, my peace, and my love. I thank You. Your Child, Linda

8/7/ (52) 98 ~ 7:09

Today is my birthday. I am 46 years old. Thank You, Lord, for another day.

8/8/98 ~ 12:33 a.m.

Oh what a blessing this evening was. I worked the tape booth until I couldn't stand. I sat for the evening seminar at 5:45. Shirley Oveal asked women to come forward if they had something to say. I went forth. I said, "Last year at the conference, I was going through a divorce. Last July, I celebrated my 23rd Anniversary." I thanked Jesus. I began to shout and leap with joy. I felt as though I jumped 10 feet high, over and over, waving my hands, praising the Lord. My right knee buckled as I left the stage. The pain was a good pain. I limped back to my seat, praising the Lord.

I was assisted to the tape booth by Bonita. But unable to stand and be of service, I had to be excused. Barbara assisted me to my car. I called Ernell to express my love for him and God's grace and mercy towards us. I couldn't explain how I felt. He said some things can't be explained – MY MAN!

Well hopefully, I will be asleep before the others arrive. Betty and Mary are having a blessed time. Lord, thank You.

8/9/98 ~ 7:25 a.m.

I was blessed by Pastor Showell. She taught on your portion – being holy, accepting your portion. I heard her tell me it's okay to receive my portion. To stand in the GAP as the GAP is filled, I receive my portion.

I was so moved. God was giving me my portion, through my marriage and Four-D. I was no longer afraid of the portion He was giving me, the child that was told she was poor because her home had no carpet. I didn't know what a washer machine was, and my daddy was a garbage man. But I was rich in spirit. My daddy read the Bible to us every night. God told me to give $10,000 to GWC. He had answered my prayer of a saved marriage and a saved business. He will continue to protect us both. I informed the conference of God's word to me. The $10,000 check was coming from Four-D Success Academy to GWC. Not from Linda to Charlyn, as we are only facilitators of the assignment He has given us. I am so blessed to be obedient to the word of God.

Lord, thank You for your Word. Thank You for allowing me to work for You. I thank You for my fear to be reverent to You. Thank You for loving me. Thank You for the financial blessings Four-D was able to give. Thank You for the past blessing and the future blessing.

Your Child, Linda

8/9/98 ~ 10:00 a.m.

I pull off my bra and feel a pain, a bump in my right breast about 10:00 position. Feels the size of a neat round by long 1/2" x 1/4"? The more I palpate, the less prominent it feels. I check my left breast. It feels soft. Nothing unusual. Maybe I will get a mammogram. I had a baseline done at the age of 35. Well, my right knee is slightly better. I go to Church with the knee brace on. Tomorrow, I limp around work with it on.

Lord, thank You for this blessed day. Love Your Child, Linda

8/11/98 ~ 3:53

I made an appointment for a mammogram tomorrow at 1:30 at the Women's wellness center in Chino Hills. The lump is located near the axillary. As I exam and compare both breasts, I definitely feel something on the right side. I feel peaceful. I pray to God, thanking Him for this day, for my husband and children, for our joy. I thank Him for allowing me to awake into this new day. I am joyful for life, my work, my family. I ask that my body not sustain a moment of illness that would affect the work that I do. I receive such joy in serving Four-D Success. I pray for my family. I have no fear. I thought of death earlier and I would highly recommend the word Death be replaced with Transformed or Transcended. The Bible states that we are renewed and transformed. Death is not the end. It is a higher level of transformation, from physical to spiritual. How strange it is that we look forward to being in the presence of God, but ask to stay on this earth a little while longer. What do we expect to miss that would exceed the blessings of being in God's presence? My father, Walter Russ, and Great Grandmother, M.W. Godspeed, never feared death. They always said, "I am waiting upon the Lord." Grandmamma would wake up and say, "He did not come last night." She was prepared. Daddy had told his surgeon, "If I don't wake up, I will be in God's presence." Man, what is there for me to worry about? Nothing, absolutely nothing.

Jeff came out to revisit the plans for remodeling and to take measurements. I am excited about our new house to come. I think by Christmas, it will be done. I am so excited!

Well, time to cook dinner for my honey and kids!

Lord, I truly thank You for my spirit of peace and joy.

Love You.

8/13/98 ~ 11:51 p.m.

I calmly went to my appointment for a 'secret' mammography. I was told the fee would be $55, but after completing the health questionnaire and revealing my history of breast biopsy, I was told the cost would be $155. I hadn't shared my findings with Ernell up to this point; I wanted to know the results before talking with him. But after the financial delay and since I have health insurance, I needed to inform my husband. I cancelled the appointment and headed home to talk with Ernell.

Upon his arrival, I took off my top and bra, called him to our room, and laid on our bed. I told him I found a lump on Sunday. I wanted him to feel the lump. As I guided his hand and instructed him to palpate softly, I studied his face. My man's face was focused on my right breast. He felt the lump. He asked why I had waited to tell him. I explained. I told him I had an appointment with Blue Cross Friendly Hills in Rancho Cucamonga at 8:15 on Thursday. He asked, "If it's positive, are you going to do the right thing?" I said, "Yes. I asked if surgery was the right thing." He replied, "Yes."

We both were thinking of Michelle Blackburn Daisy. Six years, ago she refused surgery for her breast cancer until it was too late. After two years of self-treatment, she accepted having a mastectomy about four months before her death. She died October 16, 1992.

Tomorrow, I will be on time.

Today, I delivered the $10,000 donation to GWC. I am so blessed by God. I read a letter Grey Sheets wrote regarding our 1997-1998 year-end at Four-D Success Academy, approximately gross sales was $1,084,000, over $1 million. He said the net profit would be around $40,000. Lord, thank You for bringing us through.

I must now prepare for Robert Rochelle's one-dollar plan. His prayers and support have brought us through. His faith and love of God and in Four-D. Robert, thank you. Lord, thank You. I am tired, so goodnight.

8/15/98 ~ 6:00 p.m.

Well, I went for the breast exam. Shirley Gettings, RNP did the exam. She felt the lump. I discussed/informed Shirley of my previous surgery at Kaiser. I had had a biopsy and lumpectomy done. The abnormal tissue removed and the results of the biopsy were negative. Shirley asked if I had a mammogram or ultra sound of my breast. My answer raised eyebrows. She ordered both. I stated my husband wanted the exam ASAP. Due to the lengthy time frame at the clinic, she was or is going to schedule directly with the hospital. I was told I would receive a call early next week.

I informed Ernell. He said, "If you don't hear by Tuesday, we will go to a private clinic for the exam." I know he is very concerned about my health. I am okay. I haven't thought about the exam until now.

I met Donald Brown, a Jamaican sculptor. He has extraordinary pieces. I will purchase – Home of Passage? Michael set up our booth. We are ready to go.

I had lunch with Cherry and Vernon at the Double Tree. Vernon is a very pleasant man, comfortable in conversations, and he laughs. I like him. He and Cherry are a handsome couple.

They both laugh easily.

8/16/98 ~ 8:19 a.m.

I, Michael Williams, Mary Salim, and Misty attended the June 10th event in Ontario. It was not as I expected in setup, with the music so loud, but as Michael would say, "One stop, one success." We got recognition. Last evening, Cherry, Ernell, and I went to Claremont College to see the Emotions. A pleasant evening. As they sung a spiritual song, Ernell touched my left leg. I became teary.

I didn't feel sorrow, nor worry. I listened to the word and thought of Jesus. His grace and mercy. I wanted to whisper to Cherry that I had found a lump in my right breast. But what purpose would it serve, in that environment? What would I expect her to do or say? I held my words in, let the tears flow silently. I thank God for the day. This morning, I awakened by the embrace of my husband, caressing me tenderly. I am secure in his arms. He asked/discussed the breast exam. Should I make an appointment without the doctor? Can wait, I assure him.

I will call the Clinic Monday a.m. and inquire when/how soon my appointments will be made? Time is of the essence.

Time to rise for Church. Peace, joy, love, with the Lord.

I appreciate what I have. Your Child, Linda

8/17/98 ~ 8:30

The lump feels smaller, or I am not able to clearly outline it as I was earlier. I expect to hear from the clinic for my appointment.

My husband was looking at me yesterday as I limped through the kitchen. I hope he doesn't think his wife is breaking down. I doubt it. He is concerned about my health.

Ernell doesn't say much but the look, the silence, the face says a lot. I know he is praying silently as I am. Well, today is going to be a great day. I'll tell you about it later. Bye for now.

8/17/98 ~ 11:47 p.m.

Well, I met with Rosemary and Bonnie at the Colton School District Office in Bloomington. We discussed the possible referral of Seniors to FDSA for Career Development. Possibilities! I was given the name of 3 other principles. I followed up on my appointment with Friendly Hills. Good thing I finally made contact with the Clinic radiology Department at 4:22 p.m. (Office closes at 4:35) I have an appointment for Thursday at 12:45 p.m. I don't feel I was very productive today. There is a sublingual thought that slowly travels across my mind.

I feel my breast and think the lump is gone. No – it is still there. Did it shrink with my period? Maybe, but there it is still at 10:00 – not painful, but there. I feel the left breast, soft, no lumps no pain. The left subclavin area has felt hot, heavy, sometimes tired. I contribute it to weakness - poor conditioning, poor posture – like now. I straighten up, the pain lessens.

I called Ernell and told him of the appointment. He felt that Thursday was too far away. I told him it was only two days and going elsewhere would take much longer. His eagerness expresses his concern.

God knew I would need him. He kept us together. What would I do without Ernell? Lord, thank You. Your Child, Linda

8/19/98 ~ 11:53 p.m.

Well yesterday, Cherry asked what was wrong with me; she had sensed my mood swing several days ago. I told her I would stop by her house after work.

Well I did. I shared my finding, discussed my concerns and thoughts of my family, FDSA, and her family, as well as my lack of fear and Ernell's silence and strength. She is a great support. We talked and laughed. I felt better. It is good to have a friend you can talk with. We then shifted to business. Her work on the grant is coming along well. I left feeling better than I arrived.

Today was busy – 8 a.m. JTPA Meeting, 10:00 Mike Ballard, 1:00 Marcia with Penny Savers, 3:00 Marketing Placement meeting. 4:30 Review/complete/revise business plan, budget corrections. Answer the phone, talk with clients, review Wendy's folder, and talk with Cherry – Grant. Left the office at 9:45 p.m.

Arrived home, had a glass of O.J. and a toasted bagel (first and only food today). Reviewed Sadiq's book and tagged corrections, talked with Aisha, greeted Ernell, showered, and here I sit ready for bed.

I plan to rise early and be at work by 6:30/at least before 7 a.m. I have an 8:30 appointment with Jackson/ Mary Kay – 9:30 with Joan Roberts loan application, 12:45 Clinic tomorrow for the mammography and bilateral ultrasound. 3:00 Mike Ballard for bid on building.

Home, pack, prepare for trip. Rise at 4:00 a.m. and get into the van. I will enjoy this trip with my honey!

Lord, I know You have decided on the outcome. I need not worry, but if I do worry, know it's not because I don't want to be in Your presence.

It's just I love what You have given me here!

8/20/98 ~ 8:05 p.m.

I turned in the application to Joann Roberts. She requested I submit newspaper articles of Four-D Success and me. I will deliver on Monday. I had the mammography and ultrasound done at US Family Care, Montclair. The mammography is painful. The squeeze is tremendous to me. It takes my breath away. Four pictures, what do they show? The ultrasound was done by Maurice. He carefully moved the scanner across my left breast, sliding the screen and focused on the upper outer left area, moving slowly. He had a female present. She talked almost constantly. I prayed for silence. Let him focus. He seemed focused.

He moved to the right breast, frequently jelling the scanner. I told him where the lump was, and he targeted in, moving slowly, re-jelling, moving slowly. Silently, he focused. No comments, no expression to give me a clue. What does he see in the many views? I ask a few questions, where he was educated? – USC. How long? – 3 years training in Ultra Sound. Upper and lower areas of the body, MRI X-ray. He had been working since 2 a.m. First at Kaiser, then on to US Family Care. He was tired, but it did not show.

The preliminary results will be reported tomorrow to Shirley. I go to my car and sit. I look at the purple tip flowers. I think of the color purple. I watch the kids ride their bikes. I feel so peaceful. I go home, talk with Tahira.

She asked if she can go to Las Vegas on Sunday with Tommie. At 21, she still seeks permission. My child and I talk. The choice is hers. I have raised my child. I share a parent's love.

Ernell comes home; I give the outcome of the test. We pack for our Camping trip. Us and the Petes. Ernell and I... Thank You, Lord.

8/22/98 ~ Approx. 12 noon

No watch. I don't want the time. I left my watch at home. Yesterday was nice; we left home at 6:30 a.m. and arrived by 11 a.m. Located 2 campsites, set up the tents, relaxed. Cheryl and Rodger came by with friends. They are 20 minutes away. We are at the edge of the Los

Robles River. Jet skis and boats zoom pass. The campground is full, but not crowded to me.

We had Chinese beef barbeque. I seldom eat beef. Didn't sleep too well until I evacuated the bowels. Listen to my body. Beef doesn't do my body good!

Feeling better, I returned to sleep. I look at the stars and pray. God placed each star. He surely can take care of His child.

I fall back to sleep.

Well, we are now heading out to play. See ya!

8/23/98 ~ 11-12 a.m.

The results of the mammogram and ultra sound came back negative. The cause of the lump that had shrunk in size was unknown. No surgery was needed. I should do routine monthly breast exams and will receive annual mammograms.

Last night, as I looked out of the tent to the heaven, I prayed to God. The sky, the stars, He placed each star by hand. He heals all. I know of His grace. I stare beyond the stars, the galaxy; I see Him, His marvelous powers, and His strength. Only God could have created this perfect place.

I am His perfect child whole, no ill parts. His creation. He provides, takes care, feeds, and loves me. How could I be ill, sick in body? His word says to ask and have faith. I process both the ability to seek and believe. I am so fearless, so peaceful. I thank Him for my family. I pray for Sadiq, his release from prison, his 8th year. I claim his freedom through God. I believe totally in Him. All is well with the Lord and me!

8/23/98 ~ 10:32 p.m.

We arrived home safely. Some things never change. As we drive home, I read a book and Ernell listens to music. After two hours of silence, I thought of the old days with no conversation. I guess this is the way it is to be. He would make a comment about the scenery, I would look, reply, and continue to read. I asked if he ever dreamed of doing something, going somewhere. Yellowstone National Park. Me? Europe, Africa, China, other states. I think about Washington D.C., New Orleans, Canada, Niagara Falls, Sacramento, Texas, and San Francisco – places I have traveled without Ernell.

I reflect on my recent weight gain, and can't help but wonder how it affects our relationship. I may have to do more. I am silently angry at our decreased intimacy. Is it my weight that turns him off, or can it be his exerted energy in multiple sports activities? I know we love each other and we need to do more. I will lose weight, but it will be for me and me alone. Lord, thank You for that.

9/23/98 ~ 7:26 a.m.

Last night, I dreamed... *I was attending a function in which Oprah Winfrey was the guest. After the show, she ran off stage past security. She was sprinting around a corner. Determined to meet her, I walked up to the security person and without a word, he opened the path for me to pass through. I looked directly into his eyes. I belonged. As I passed through, I followed her trail, turning the corner and up some stairs to a room with thick pink carpet, wide halls that were very bright. The rooms covered two floors. I walked up and down looking for a clue — where did she go? I returned to the second floor. A gentleman was vacuuming the floor. As I was about to descend the stairs, I asked, "Which room is Oprah's?" He indicated he could not say.*

But another person was entering into the room directly across from us. As the door opened, the first person nodded to the door. As I walked to the door, Oprah was there washing her face! The sink was by the entrance of the door. I saw the side of her face and her hair. I know it was her.

I stopped and said hello. I told her I had to meet her and that I had a story to tell – Four-D Success. As I stayed in this dream, I began to think, "This can't be real." She appeared too real. I must wake up to go to the office. I had wanted to be there by 6:00 a.m.

I opened my eyes and looked at the clock. I was late; it was 5:42 a.m. I rose, showered, put on my lime green pantsuit and left for work. I was done by 6:17 a.m. and arrived at Four-D Success at 6:45 a.m. I began a full day of work with a positive attitude. Lord, we need a building.

Guide us.

Sadiq sent his 1st book of Poetry, *Walls of Gender* — 1st poem dedicated to me, "Umuhoza" Comforter of the people. Thanks, Sadiq.

Looking Back …

- I realize the Lord has been with me from the beginning of time. No one but God can place a dream in your heart as a child, and stick with you your whole life to see it come to pass. If it had not been for the Lord on my side, truly, where would I be!

- Buried treasure is just that — buried treasure. Obtaining the prize is like searching for buried treasure. It requires you to reach further than you have ever dreamed possible, to press forward with a sense of urgency. It requires you to filter through 'things'… 'stuff'… and 'people' as you move ahead in life. Excavating buried treasure is hard work, yet be encouraged that the results of your efforts will indeed pay off. Your faithfulness to the vision in your heart will yield immeasurable satisfaction as to a job well done.

- Don't be a hermit; make your purpose visible. I have always made sure I utilized the angels God has placed in my life. It's His vision working through me, and He knows who I need to assist me along the way. You cannot be shy about seeking expertise from those that have the knowledge and the answer to what you need.

- Anticipation is good; it keeps me looking forward to another day!

- I am so very grateful for my journey in life, and for those special ones the Lord has placed in my life – people like my husband who reminds me of his love for me by supporting me every day. And, my girls who let me know they have found a role model in Mom.

The way may get a bit tedious at times, yet the faces continue to change throughout the course of life. For me, it's the new faces that keep me going. The new minds that seek the knowledge our team of experts has to offer, the new hearts that are inspired to explore the possibilities, the courageous that see themselves functioning and producing at a higher level in life. Monotony has no place among an active and energized spirit that seeks to impart the positives in life.

Business by Faith

Journal 5

Begins: September 29, 1998 ~ 9:00 p.m.

Ends: June 29, 1999 ~ 11:31 p.m.

9/29/98 ~ 9:00 p.m.

I must purchase a new diary. I have been seeking a building for the move in 2000. Charlie Seymour, President of the Board, has been looking for a site. This week, we toured the State of California Transportation vacant for buildings. It is huge. When I first drove towards it, I began to have heart palpations. How am I going to do this? How? How many students do I need to fill it? Money to pay for it? The building consists of a basement, ground level, six floors, and a full cafeteria and two auditoriums. What a place. The potential is great. Space for faculty and staff, large classrooms, conference room, special events, and graduations.

10/2/98 ~ 8:26

I must purchase a new diary.

Mama, Anwar, Jaise, and Donnie went to see Gregory. My baby brother Greg got 25 years for something. He told Momma the judge was wrong in his instructions to the jury. His attorney will appeal. How sad he knew the outcome before he committed the act.

The state called Mike – The HCI/MB program is being reviewed. We will have the program going in 30 days. I will seek space to accommodate two classes. I need to write two proposals for SB County.

We closed our Riverside County site. Last year placement: 83%.

Well, off to work.

10/11/98 ~ 11:25 p.m.

Today, at Riverside Community Hospital, class four of the Vocational Nurse Program graduated, and over 250 guests attended. Mr. Charles Benneett, President of the Board of Vocational Nurse and Psychiatrics Examiners, was the guest speaker. A moving and spiritual occasion, tears flowed, applauding from the audience, and prayers. The Walter Russ Sr. scholarship went to Marquita Young. The Arthur Williams Sr. Award went to Jorge. Both students were surprised and grateful.

God continues to bless me. I awoke at 2:00 a.m. I lay in bed praying, giving thanks to God, and crying, joyful over what He has given me. A heart full of love, peace, joy, and compassion. Me, His child, as I strive to advance the school, I sometimes become overwhelmed. It is not for me to worry about. I simply must walk through the doors of opportunity.

Mr. Bennett informed me of the Dept. of Corrections requirement for nurses to wear colored uniforms. I will follow his lead and walk through the open door. Union Bank approved us for $150,000 loan and $125,000 line of credit. God always sends the money on time. We (I and Charlie) are looking at a 130,000 sq. ft. six story building. State Department of Transportation. God will provide. The seed is planted and I will grow like an oak tree. Deep base, shallow root, limbs strong, reaching through the sky. I sit in amazement of God's love. Sadiq has completed another book, ***Walls of Gender***. Excellent poetry. I have so much work to do. God, increase my skills; make me focus on time management.

10/15/98 ~ 9:30 a.m.

Time goes on.

Well the State Department of Transportation building was bid on. So I will continue to seek God's path. Friday, I will look at the closed 1st Interstate Bank building. Ironically its parking lot was the one I was viewing for additional space for the state building. I keep looking. I know there is a new home for FDSA. Union Bank wants our rental property as collateral. Only problem they will tie it up since it is part of our line of credit loan. We would not be able to borrow on it, if needed. So I went to Wells Fargo. The school may qualify for $100,000 line of Credit. We currently have $55,000. I requested $45,000. I will call B of A for line of Credit. Well, I did. I stopped and called, and 'a chick' took the application over the telephone. I requested $100,000 and should know by Tuesday. I spoke with James White of United International. He has submitted a request for $1.5 million loan. Payment would be $16,000/month for 30 years.

The future is bright. I so desire a child care — need space. Closed Riverside. Only 1 referral this fiscal year, July – Nov.

Spoke with ABHES MB Program. We should be approved very soon. Seeking space for classes.

Proposals to be submitted to SB Co JTPA on the 19th and 21st. A lot of work, good team. Success is written all over the place.

Lord, thank You,

Momma and kids are well. I am trying to work on contracts with schools for training/receiving students.

10/19/98

It seems like it has been a long time since I made an entry. But it has only been four days. I had a busy weekend. Friday night, Cherry and I got dressed to kill to attend the Union League Dinner — could not find it. The paper said it was held in Ontario, but it was in Riverside. After calling 4-5 hotels, we went to dinner, enjoyed the evening, and went home. Saturday, I attended the NCNW Bethune

Annual luncheon in Orange Co. It was nice, from 11:30 – 3:00. I left there to attend the Black Infant Health Dinner in San Bernardino from 6:00 – 10:00. A long evening went wonderfully. The group has done wonderful things to focus on the black infant mortality rate. God protects us as a people. They have reduced the rate in SB CO from 24 per 1,000 to 19 per 1,000, and the goal is 11 per 1000.

Sunday, I spent time with Ernell. It's so nice to be alone with him. I love to walk and hold his hand. Sunday afternoon, I attended the Women to State for Joe Baca at the SB Hilton. 100 plus women participated. After the luncheon when Charlyn Singleton, Barbara Boca spoke, I had the opportunity to speak with Mayor Valles. I seek for assistance to relocate to San Bernardino. Mike, Charlie, and I toured the Bank across from the City Hall. I informed the mayor, and she said she would have someone call me.

Last night, Cherry and I talked. She told me a friend of Christine Umatoni was here to help us. He writes grants for MTI for millions. He wants to write for us.

Lord, keep our blessings coming. Well, I must go to work and have a blessed day.

Lord, thank You for all.

10/22/98 ~ 7:35 a.m.

Well yesterday, the Welfare to Work proposal to SB Co. was turned in. I prayed to my heavenly Father for a continued blessing. Lord, grant us a positive outcome. Grant us the number of participants desired. The modified contract for the Medical Billing was submitted 1/19/98. We await outcome.

Riverside General Hospital has not returned our calls or submitted the facility agreement. Lord, You know our situation. We are in need of a facility. Open the hearts of the nursing directors. Provide a way for Four-D Success Academy, Inc. We are in need of a large blessing. Protect us, guide us. Give us wisdom, patience, continued love, and understanding.

I pray for the financial blessing to continue to share Your word. Lord, thank You for all You have given us. Keep us safe.

Tahira was offered a job at $14 an hour at Upland Convalescent. She interviewed at Pomona Valley. She is taking ACLS classes to increase her knowledge and promotional opportunities.

Aisha is doing well in school. She announced she wants to earn a Master's in Education. Lord, thank You for protecting my babies.

10/22/98 ~ 11:45 p.m.

I awake with the song of *Holy* by Vanetta on my mind. I fell asleep with prayers on my lips. I awake the same way. I sang and prayed to work. I took the tape to my office and continued to listen and to sing the song *Holy*. God's blessings are already done. We must go through the process of belief today.

Theresa Conley, Director of Nurses at Riverside County Hospital, signed the facility agreement. Tomorrow, Nancy Johnston will attend the orientation. Naomi called from ETP Four-D Success Academy and was approved for the ETP program. We have an appointment for November 2 at 9:00 to begin the process and site review. Mike Ballard and I talked about the Union Bank D St. building for sale. I know God will guide our process and will place us in the building we will need. Mary Salim and I prayed together for our new home and future.

I expect the state to issue approval by the end of next week. The program will be mailed to ABHES.

I signed the proposal agreement for the Cooley space.

The LVN Faculty has not been keeping up its documentation. I am concerned and furious. I let Cherry know it. They will either comply or be replaced. We can't lose it all at a state or Federal Survey. We (I) must have total quality assurance.

Mike Ballard announced his engagement to me at the end of our business conversation. He and Pam will be married in the future.

God bless all.

Tomorrow, my baby brother Greg Simmons will be sentenced for his 3rd felony. He may be facing more than 10 years from what I have heard.

God, be with him. God, protect my mother. I pray.

10/26/98

Well today, we were blessed to receive a $75,000 line of credit from Bank of America. Wells Fargo denied our request to increase our line by $15,000. It will remain at $55,000. I informed Union Bank of my decision after I had signed the agreement with B of A. Rosina and Raul were disappointed, but I expressed the need to make decisions in the best financial interest of the school, further negotiations were stopped.

I was installed as the new President of the NCNW Inland Chapter. We will have a strong board. Pricilla Brown 1st Vice President, Wanda Green 2nd V.P, Malinda M. was correspondent Sect, Christine was secretary and Effie Sharp was treasurer. The focus will be on reciting the legacy and pledge, support the Bethune Center, and develop an in-depth community youth program.

Lord, guide us.

Riverside General Hospital Facility Agreement will be at Four-D by next Friday. Sacramento too will send the approval for the HCE/MB (Health Claim Examining Medical Billing) Programs. The future is very bright.

10/28/98 ~ 11:42 p.m.

Well, what a day. I called my Momma regarding Gregory's sentencing. It has been postponed for 30 days. Not clear as to why.

I met with Doris Daniels at the S.B. EDA office to discuss Rehabilitation Funds for the new building. The proposals are due November 16, 1998. Met with Greg Sheet regarding profit vs. non-profit vs. direct ownership. Received a call from Linda Jenkins asking if I would participate in a conference call from the White House with Ben Johnson, Director of Public Affairs.

Ms. Roche called from the White House. I had been recommended by Dr. Juanita Scott. I accepted. On November 29th at 2:18, I am to call Washington to participate in the conference call.

Spoke with Theresa, Director of Nurses at Riverside General Hospital. The person in charge of signing the contract had us on hold. Another school had come on the scene. Now, he wanted to be fair. It was questioned, how long we had been in business, etc. I requested an appointment ASAP.

Cherry met with the Faculty, heartfelt discussion. Orientated at Riverside General. Excellent rapport with Kermit Sims. Lord, You know our enemy. I went to Choir rehearsal and shared this heavy burden. They reminded me of the armor of God, not quitting, fasting, and prayer. Heavenly Father, You have given us much. We are always at Your mercy and seek Your grace.

I went to Cherry, we talked, I cried, and she prayed. The load is heavy but I know that God is carrying me. All that is good comes from the Lord. It is already done.

Thank You, Jesus.

10/29/98 ~ 6:19 a.m.

I awake with a prayer in my heart and on my mind. God is all. All is God. I am God's child. God takes care of His child.

I hear my father saying, "Baby, it is going to be all right."

Words of Faith.

10/31/98 ~ 12:15 a.m.

Jeanne Templeman seems to be striking back. I requested a change in consultants. Jeanne has requested much of Cherry. Weary, but strong, I stress we must take a stand and fight. We fight in spirit with truth and love, God's grace, and shield of armor.

After brainstorming with faculty members, Cherry called Riverside Community and spoke with Pearle Lee. She requested and received the okay to take students in our M/T PM slot. Problem solved. Jeanne notified. We continue to move forward.

I stop to reflect on my heart/mind. I think of the ungrateful student that wrote the letter to the Nursing Board. Stupidity runs deep. Only a fool will burn his house down with nowhere to go. I have an appointment to meet Gary Andary, Dept. for Social Services, and

Child Services at the D St. building. I want a Child Center. I must start on the City Block Grant.

Ernell is at the Men's Advance with other Loveland men. Last night he called and sounded disappointed. He said it appeared to be for men who wanted to go into The Ministry. His voice told me much. I almost apologized for signing him up. I was so sleepy when he called at 11:00 but I became lucid enough to say, "Enjoy yourself." I have not heard from him since. I guess the sessions are long and he is busy. I know he is in God's great hands. All is well. Tomorrow, Cherry and I will meet Stephen at FDSA for a tour. I expect him to assist us in our development.

Lord, thanks for all the love, progress, and protection. I know Riverside General will let us in.

10/31/98 ~ 9:57 p.m.

I miss my honey. Last night, I stayed up until 12 midnight waiting for him to call. I know he was in session at the Men's Advance, so I retired. I woke up about 2:30 a.m. to turn the heater off. Tahira was downstairs, in from her date. We chatted for a short time. I had to excuse myself, early to rise. Met Cherry and Stephen at the office.

She had given him a tour prior to my arrival. We discussed international business and Four-D growth in terms of students and finances. Stephen is currently employed with ITT. His focus is on financial growth through grants, C-SAC, marketing analysis. We discussed him joining the Academy. He agrees. In two weeks, we'll start him full-time. I passed out the Block Grants from the City and County. We will meet on next Friday. The week ended great. I called home at 12:30 and my honey was home. I could not wait to see him. I missed him.

I took the twins to the City of San Bernardino, Court Street Fair for kids. They were interviewed by the Sun Telegram. Burger King for lunch and fun. Then back to Grandma Russ' house by 5:00 p.m. They wore me out. Momma is 75 and young, Lord.

Tomorrow, I sing praises unto the Lord. Goodnight.

11/2/98 ~ 12:00

Well today, I signed the proposal for $2.2 million to purchase the building. God knows the outcome. I shall soon.

We completed the City Block Grant to San Bernardino.

Ernell and the fellows left this evening for their annual bass fishing trip to Lake Mead. I know they are going to have a ball.

Tomorrow, I leave for Kansas City for ABHES Workshop. I will return home Tuesday night.

Lord, grant us a financial blessing and a building blessing.

11/3/98 ~ 11:28 p.m.

Received the Program agreement for the Bureau for the HCE MS/MB Programs. Tomorrow, they will be mailed to ABHES. Cost $1800+$1500= $3,300. Call received from Kareem Muhammad – The Promoter. He has been working on our behalf to bring entertainment to SB – Sponsored by Four-D Success Academy. Vickie Winans is showing interest – I am so tired.

Kareem also informed me of the Africa Summit in May in Phoenix. He will provide the entertainment and a great opportunity to speak about international health care services.

Lord, goodnight.

11/5/98 ~ 11:44 p.m.

I was late for my 9:00 a.m. appointment in Al Twines office. I started not to go in after I had parked. It was 9:19, 5 minutes to get in. Oh well I thought – there is something in there for me. I talked to Al about the building I am looking at.

The meeting for The Black Inventors Museum had been cancelled. Al and I talked. As we discussed the building, he brought Joe Rodriguez in. Joe knows the owner of the building, Jordan Grinke. A lunch appointment is scheduled for the same day. I called Mike Ballard. We all met, Mike, me, Joe Larry and Jordan. This is my introduction to get acquainted with Jordan. He and his family own the building in a family trust. Jordon asked about the Four-D Success story. He understands trials, God's grace, and he listens. He inquires if we are non-profit. I explain both companies. He likes what he hears. I discuss the Child Care. He refers me to O C Smith, Director of Child Care. I will call him tomorrow. Gary of Social Services did not show up. I will reschedule. I have a meeting Monday with Delores Armstead. Seeking funds for construction or relocation.

I took Daddy's $1,000 bond to Temple Church today. He had purchased it prior to his death. It matures in 1/99. Daddy wished for the bond to go to his Church. Even in death, he continues to support Temple.

Four-D Success is going forward in spite of the negative comments from others. I know God will protect and provide.

Tahira will start at Pomona Valley Medical Center on Monday. She told me she is ready to move into her own place. I immediately said, "I think the first of the year is a great time." I laughed and said,

"Many parents would want their 22 year old out of the house." I told her, "I'm not most parents." Besides, she could not leave before Christmas. I expect her to comply with my wishes.

My writing is so sloppy. I am physically and emotionally tired.

I pray to be absolutely refreshed in the a.m.

Lord, thank You for ALL that is and is to come.

Thank You.

11/8/98 ~ 8:29 a.m.

I awaken with prayer in my mind. Praying for the school, the students. I am consumed with God and Four-D Success Academy. I lay next to my husband, arms embraced. We fell asleep holding hands, our fingers intertwined.

I think of Vincent Pearle's Book, ***Think Positive.*** One has to pray, visualize, energize, and actualize their thoughts. Make things happen. I see the new Academy. The halls are bursting with faculty, students, God's Business growing. I rise and go to Tahira's room to exercise. I walk the treadmill while listening/watching Gospel Hour. As Pastor Chuck is going on the air on Channel 9, there follows a quick 20-second commercial about a Gospel Concert coming to Pasadena with Vickie Winans. I place a call to Kareem Muhammad in Detroit, the promoter. It would be great to have Vikki do the FDSA non-profit promotion before the Pasadena Event. God is in control.

Standing by my bed, I look out of the window. I gaze upon Daddy's flowers. I instantly feel him - everything is going to be okay. Friday, I hired a Financial Development Analyst – Stephen. We discussed a list of projects, which should begin on the 15th of November. God is directing my path.

I am learning to be a better administrator of my duties and responsibilities.

Lord, protect us from all enemies. Open doors that are closed. Give sight to the blind. Let them see us and our good work. Let no man or woman speak against us for fear of Your wrath. Those that don't fear You are a fool. Raise us up. Set us in a new building. I see myself in a meeting with Jordan Grinke and someone I can't clearly picture. He tells me he has financially made a way for Four-D Success Academy to occupy the Union Bank Annex and own The Tower. I sit here overwhelmed; tears swell up in my eyes. This is real. I hold his hand and cry bringing thanks to God. I see, I believe, I receive.

Faith is the substance unseen, that which I stand. Faith in God, my Lord, Jesus Christ.

I see the Academy as it will be, as God has it. Daddy's flowers blooming on this Sunday morning.

Peace is within. I place a seed of love and it grows.

11/8/98 ~ 10:21

Watching T.V. Gospel Channel 9 KCAL. I see Vickie Winans is coming to Pasadena. I call Kareem, he and I just got off the telephone. Lord, Lord, Lord.

Vickie Winans is available; the Mississippi Mass Choir is available. He mentioned two other groups. We discuss local talent. I am so excited. He is researching scouting. I explain my desire to bring entertainment to San Bernardino. The Mayor Judy Valles is Hispanic. She supports the Black Inventors Museum. Kareem said, "You know Gloria Estaban would do well there."

I screamed, "You are absolutely right."

I have to get the name of the local artist – have to talk to Aisha. Kareem and I will talk on Tuesday the 10th. I can't express my thoughts and joy. We got off the phone, and I ran to the family room screaming and talking and jumping in front of Ernell. My husband doesn't know what to do with me sometimes. I ran upstairs and called Cherry's house. It takes two calls to leave my exuberant (happy) message. I'm going to the spa outside. I want to feel this cool air against the warm water and my skin.

Lord, thank You.

11/11/98 ~ 11:03 p.m.

I was too tired to make an entry yesterday evening. Well "Principal for a Day" I was assigned to Sierra High School, Lorie Jacobsen Principal. Exposed to classes, faculty, students, great opportunity to promote Four-D. I will return to Sierra as a mentor.

Mike and I talked about the building. He will submit for $2.2 million tomorrow. The city block grant will be submitted tomorrow. I have an appointment with the fire and building inspectors, the Children Services, and Mike on the 19th at 2:00. I met with Mayor Valles at 10:00 a.m.

We got a new copier – all is happy. Received a call from the Wellness Foundation requesting we submit the Child Care info for approval of $70,000 over a two-year period. Lord, the door is opening.

I parked in front of the facility. I envisioned the arrival/business of the business students, faculty, the Child Care Center. I counted out the spaces in the front for the name of the school. I thanked God and prayed.

Tomorrow, Ernell is taking off for his annual bass fishing trip. Have a ball.

11/13/98 ~ 11:25 a.m.

Flying on America West to Kansas City Missouri. I reflect on God's blessings. I have grown to be a successful businesswoman. Successful in planting a seed, praying, and following the path lit by God.

As I reflect on my life, I see success. Not being afraid to try, not being afraid to pursue goals, not being afraid to dream, dreams to reality.

I fly on business matters, I meet on business issues, I conference on business concerns. As I was reading the Black Enterprise, I focused in on the Editor's message. As a business, I must focus on quality of product, excellence in service, and promotion of profit. A businessperson goes into business for the sake of business. A merchant goes into business to make a profit. I will be the merchant. The profit will assist Four-D Success to excel in services, grow the business. I think of the Child Care Center. Mike B. is right I will need the 5,000 square feet for the children. I think out of the box. I see the whole services – babies, toddlers, and kids. Parents secure in knowing their child is safe. They are able to go to work. Employees are satisfied – no call off due to, "My baby is sick. I don't have a babysitter." Reading the Business Press, I think of ways to market the school KCXX 1039. Contact Physician Group for Placement Contact the San Manuel Indian Mission students to train.

Lord, guide my path. Let the seed flourish into strong trees with the community. Let partnership spring up. Let Four-D Success Academy RISE above to show all.

11/15/98 ~ 8:00 a.m.

In Kansas City, Missouri. I came here on Friday, arriving at 1:30 p.m. I was pleased to see no snow. The snow boots would not come out of the suitcase!

I was tired on Friday. I arrived to my room knowing I would not venture out into the lobby, not to mention outside. Yesterday, I attended the Accreditation Workshop, mandatory for all schools due for their review. I learned that since we had received our self-evaluation, Four-D would be reviewed during the 1st quarter of '99. We would be prepared. I also attended the Evaluators Workshop. I am interested in assisting with the review of other schools. It is important that I become more active and known by the review team and commissioners. Not for any favors for Four-D, as we stand on our own performance, but for name recognition and service. I did become acquainted with Andy, one of the commissioners.

While on a break, standing in the hall by the telephone, eating a big cookie, a young man spoke to me. I responded as usual with a pleasant hello and smile. He was attending the ACCET workshop down the hall. I was in the ABHES Workshop. I returned to class. At the end of my day he was by the telephone, preparing to call out. He asked if I like music, Jazz, and I said, "Yes." He told me of a place, walking distance, but I responded, "Oh I would not walk around here at night. I don't know the area."

He responded, "I'll walk with you. We can have dinner and listen to Jazz."

"Fine with me." We met in the lobby at 8:00 p.m. What a pleasant evening. We talked and walked 3 blocks. I could see the red neon sign from the top of the sloped hill. We talked about the workshops,

Florida, California. We had dinner at The Spaghetti Factory. We talked so much, I did not finish my dinner or the bread. Now you know I can kill some bread. Des and I talked about international affairs. He teaches English to foreign students. He was seeking accreditation to enhance his enrollment via INS. His student would come to Florida for 2-4 weeks for study. They had to return to the country with the possibility of extended stay. He is seeking to qualify for student visa status.

Des is from South Africa. He shared his views of apartheid, Mandela, the power of the Zulu, tribal war, the Church (Dutch), the English, the Church teaching before apartheid: Whites were created superior over non-whites by God. The Church acknowledges their mistake prior to Mandela's release. Imagine the Church's role in suppression around the world. Slavery of so many races, murder of people through actively being deceitful like the situation in Rwanda. The Catholic Church and living priest assisted in the murder of thousands of Rwandans.

From the Spaghetti Factory, we moved next door to listen to Jazz, more conversation over a glass of wine. Good music, good company. We talked about our families, lines of work. I know this would be a person I would want to keep in contact with. He felt and expressed the same. Back at the hotel lobby, I received his business card. I will call or e-mail. We said goodnight with a smile and a friendly hug. Des the South African – a white man, a new friend. Des asked me what I thought of white people. I told him of Tamara, other experiences in my life. Bottom line, he and they are children of God. I saw him as another child of God. God chose His children to be the color they are. I don't know why – but He did. That's all. Well its 8:34 and my class starts at 9:00. I had better get moving.

I called Ernell's room, but he had checked out. It was 6:00 or 7:00 a.m. in Arizona. He must be on the lake, trying to catch bass, the big fish. I'll talk with him tonight.

Amazing Grace – this song will be on my heart today.

11/16/98 ~ 1:45 a.m.

I was ready to go home! I called the airport and changed my return flight home. Home today – can't wait until tomorrow. I had received the most valuable information. The rest in exhibits and presentation. I saved $107! Not charged $15 for exchange. Ernell will pick me up at the airport. I have not seen him since Thursday. He and the fellows left for their annual fish trip.

Last night, I had dinner with Dr. Will Kimmons, VP and Dean of Student Studies at Lawson University Alabama. We went to Gates for barbeque. Conversation sounded like an assessment to me: what/why attributes were, what I thought of myself, etc. I informed Willis of my happy life with hubby, beautiful girls, love, my work. He wanted to give a friendly kiss. I warded that off. "No, Buddy. Not here. Go to that box you said you had in your room." Willie and I had a laughing time. I enjoyed his company.

Preparing for bed, I counted 2 more days. But this morning I said, "To heck with this, I am going home. I miss home, Ernell, and the kids."

I will arrive at 4:51.

Oh yeah, I called Cherry yesterday regarding Stephen. I felt uneasy regarding his request to increase his pay from $20 to $22. He said he had to pray over my offer, he had loans to pay off, bills, he had a roommate, and wanted to move. He needed financial independence.

He needed to save money. This occurred after I had informed him a written letter of employment would be mailed by Wednesday. It was after 5:00 p.m. He and I were alone in the school. I told Stephen I would not increase his starting pay to $22. FDSA was not responsible for his debt and I suggested he pray on it. With or without him, the school would move forward.

I asked what did he want in his revisit to the wages $24-25 per hour. My position stood. We departed the school building. I felt uneasy.

In my conversation with Cherry, she was aware of what he had done. He had informed her of his discussion to ask for more money after accepting the initial offer. She advised against it, but he proceeded.

I request a letter to rescind the offer. Cherry will follow through in the best interest of the Academy. It is best we continue without Stephen. I will return to work on Wednesday. All is well.

Love, homebound Linda.

11/16/98 ~ 8:00 p.m.

I arrived at 4:41 p.m. California time. Ernell was there to pick me up. I was thrilled to see him. It was good to be home. There is no place like home. It took 2 seconds to feel the coolness in the house. Now at 8:00 I am in bed with my heating pad on high. Ernell says it's not cool. I look at the temperature control, and it is set at 66 degrees. I fuss a little and say I can get warmer in bed. I leave downstairs and turn the heater on, the blanket to high. Ernell turns the heater on. I get in bed. It is good to be home – in spite of the indoor frost.

11/18/98 ~ 11:10 p.m.

Today, Cherry, Stephen, and I met. We cleared the air and came to an understanding. He will start December 1st, 1998. Margie and I did her review. She was increased to $11/ per hour. We discussed the negative influence of another employee. Not on Margie's performance, but the sadness it brings to her heart. I truly appreciate Margie's support.

Happy note = I was an active participant in the City of San Bernardino Readers Program. I read the book, ***Splash, Splash*** by Jeff Sheppard to 2nd graders from Thompson Elementary School. There was a good response and participation from the kids. The show will air on Channel 3 in the near future. Four-D Success Academy is a sponsor of the Reader's program.

Cherry told me today that she is making herself Vice President. She clearly sees her role in research/development of programs and grant writing. All I can do is laugh and hug her. Title or not, she works to improve the school.

Lord, goodnight.

11/20/98 ~ 11:40 p.m.

Well, today Cherry and I flew to Sacramento to attend the LVN Board Meeting. Four-D Success had requested 45 students for the November 23rd start date. We were approved. The Consultant, Jeanne's report indicated the student's complaint, but failed to acknowledge the findings and the truth. Supporting documentation, her investigation. But Cherry represented the school well, publicly expressed the truth, acknowledged the complaints, and explained the 16% attrition (2 students dismissed for fighting both with A-B grades). Mrs. Theresa Bello-Jones mentioned the dismissal due to the fight prior to Cherry speaking. Although the consultant's report left much to question, God took care of us. Cherry called the office with God's good news. All were happy.

I explained my desire to expand to another state, Oregon or Arizona. Cherry laughed and said when I die my tombstone is going to say "stupid". I don't know when to quit. Now, that sounds good to me! Why quit when God's got my back? Tomorrow, I'll attend the Child Care Summit in San Bernardino. Cherry may go to the Riverside County Fair. Norm Martin will be there. We have an appointment with him on December at 8:00 p.m. He is the President CEO of Parkview General Hospital.

Lord, thank You and goodnight.

Oh yeah, I am inserting the date, day, time, and names of the birth of Eula Mae Russ' seven children. On November 10, 1998 at 7:45 p.m. I was sitting in Momma's kitchen. We were talking about something and she started talking about one of the boy's birth. She stated the day of the week and time of the birth. I was again astonished. She recalled clearly the date, day, time, and weather conditions of each birth.

I have trouble remembering the specifics of my children's births.

1. Ronald Lorland Morris dob 11/5/49 @ 2:45 a.m.
2. Donald Lorland Morris dob 7/24/51 @ 1:28 p.m.
3. Linda Lee Russ dob 8/7/52 @ 9:50 a.m.
4. Walter Russ, Jr. dob 6/6/54 @ 5:15 p.m.
5. Wilbert Dale Russ dob 2/17/59 @ 2:57 p.m.
6. Zachary Horace Russ dob 9/10/60 @ 5:15 p.m.
7. Gregory Allen Simmons dob 11/10/63 @ 6:45 a.m.

God Bless us all!

11/22/98 ~ 12:27 a.m.

Saturday, the Child Care Summit held in San Bernardino and sponsored by the Mayor's office was GREAT. I made so many contacts. I was tired and exhausted. Gary Audary, the Child Care Services Advocate spoke early into the program. He acknowledged my presence and informed the crowd that in twenty years he had seen something new; all the players at the table at the same time. I had EDA, Sr. City Planner, Planner Asst. Fire Marshall, The inspector, Child Services, and a Realtor all at the table. With Collins' help, a miracle had occurred. Even Collins has said it never had happened before. He set up the appointment.

I spoke with John Michaelson, SB County Finances. Faith Michaelson (his wife). Supervisor Eaves Asst's. Teri and Juanita, Linda - Mayor Valles Asst. Linda, Jane Adams, and I marketed Four-D Child Care Center. It is going to happen. God knows it is.

I'm excited.

11/23/98 ~ 7:22 a.m.

There is no challenge I cannot overcome. I awaken with THESE words on my conscious mind. God has already taken care of the challenges. He has removed the enemy. He has changed hearts. He has cleared the path. God directs my path. He directs my footsteps.

I just praise the Lord for this day. I feel so blessed to be in Ernell's arms. God has shown our blessing. We have each other.

The girls are doing well. I saw Momma Saturday evening at the Taylors home. She was dressed to kill, black and gold and gold heels. Eula Mae Russ can dress. Tonight, she and the twins are going to Texas for a vacation. God, deliver them to safe setting.

There is no challenge I cannot overcome. Lord, thank You for the message.

11/24/98 ~ 10:44 p.m.

Wendy and I are working on the self-evaluation for ABHES Accreditation. It will be completed by 11/30.

I received a call from Al Twine. He has spoken with Gerry Eaves about the Academy's move to SB. I asked him to speak with the head of EDA. Tomorrow that conversation will take place. He has spoken with Delores Armstead. I met with James White. Gave him pictures of the building. He will forward financial package book for review. I informed him the bid was for $2.9 million. I will come back at $2.7 million. James will speak with another investor on our behalf.

Mike informed me Larry has a counter offer. We should receive it tomorrow. God, bring it all together. Sitting in the bathroom, I closed my eyes and envisioned the lamp, the Marquee placed at the corner of 3rd and D Street. The lamp lights up at dusk.

I hear you, Lord.

12/1/98 ~10:52

Yesterday, Mike and I viewed the building with Don and Reta. Sprinklers will/may need to be put in. Jordon said his feelings were hurt. The offer was an insult. Mike and I apologized. But an offer had to be put in and they came with $2.9 million. Tomorrow, Mike and I will counter with discussion of $2.7 million.

I write this knowing God is my banker. I surely don't have $3 million. But what do my limited funds have to do with God's account? He will make a way. If not this building, then a better one.

The future is exciting and bright. Today Stephen started in Financial Aid Department. He has identified areas for improvement. We made payroll. God is good.

The Pre-Evaluation for Accreditation was mailed/picked up last night at 10:00 p.m. I was late getting to the Fed Ex office so I had to fly it there for today's arrival. The cost increased from $12 to $239. The price I paid for missing Fed Ex, but it did arrive between 12-1 p.m. That's all that matters. Not the service.

I am working on 2 grants for the Child Care and MB/HCE Program. Good support from the County.

The City EDA approved the HCE/MB Program will receive students. Oh yeah!

Ernell and I leased a 1999 Black Suburban 4x4 on 11/30/98. I am so happy for him. I had to encourage him to get what he wanted, not what he would settle for. This morning, he thanked me for supporting him. He would have done the same for me. Well, I am tired.

I prayed for Sadiq's release. I prayed for Jennifer and Julie. God knows all. Goodnight!

12/6/98 ~ 10:55

The day of reckoning.

Coming to awareness. I was wrong in the words I spoke, filled with anger as Cherry told me of Jones' actions. She was letting the students leave at 1:00 p.m. instead of 3:30. 2 students were coming to work-study at 1:00 instead of 3. I could not believe what I was hearing. Paula was (is) putting our program in jeopardy. She attended the NAACP Annual Dinner where the guest speaker for the evening spoke of "What would Jesus Do?" As we face obstacles, valleys, issues of immorality. What would Jesus do? We are in the right place. He has placed us here to do good.

Today, at Church Evangelist, Chris Joy taught the word 'Our place in time.' As we pass through time from where we have come to where we are going – we are in a place of travel, our past to our future. God knows where we are and where we are going. Are we going to stay in the path of light, God's blessing? I listen, knowing the message was for me. I am passing through time on my way towards heaven. Goal is with God.

Therefore, I do for I am His child and Fathers take care of their children. What He has, He will give as I need it. I must stay focused, unafraid, pressing forward toward the success of Four-D Success Academy. My success in life is also associated with my marriage. Ernell and I are in love. Happiness fills our hearts and home. Our children are happy and blessed. Lord, I am unbelievably thankful to You for saving us. I can't imagine what I would be doing without him and my kids.

My mother returned a week early. I have not called her. I thought she would call me or she just needed a break. Zach is in a group home. Donnie stole a turkey from her freezer while she was in Texas. Life goes on.

Well it's bedtime. Goodnight Lord.

12/7/98 ~7:30 a.m.

Today, is Ernell's Birthday. 49 blessed years. I awaken feeling blessed, having slept well. Received a call from Pam. ABHES had approved the Medical Billing/Health Claims Examiner Program. We will start today or tomorrow.

12/9/98 ~ 10:54 p.m.

Oh what a day! Well first yesterday, Otis sent 3 guys to inspect the building. Although they were unable to give me a quote, I felt comfortable with their input and examination of the building. I will call Otis tomorrow to say thanks. Once I obtain the architectural designs for the tenet improvements, the contractor, Otis, will be able to give me a quote. Today, I had a meeting with the 5th District Councilman for San Bernardino. He and Orhay had received the info submitted, talked with Ernest Dowdy, and received great reviews for Four-D and me. We discussed the Academy and our move to the city and the Child Care Center. I was invited to the upcoming meeting at the EDA office to discuss Child Care. I left the meeting feeling very positive. I called James White; he said Four-D qualified for $2 million. He had some innovative ideas to cover the cost of the purchase of the building. I referred him to Mike. I called Mike, I felt so excited with my meeting with the councilman. Mike informed me that Larry Walter had called and asked if we would pay $2.7 million. Mike said no, but he felt they are looking seriously at our offer. He expected to close the deal soon. God, this is too exciting. Four-D Success owning a building, a Child Care Center. My, my, my.

Momma and I talked yesterday. Zack is at a home. It's hard for her to say he can't come back. I felt sad, but I know he shouldn't. She will lose money, but gain peace of mind. I will pay the $150 for the twin's skates. Life is good. Goodnight, Lord.

12/16/98 ~ 10:51 p.m.

Home after 5 days. Steven and I left Friday. I stopped to be with my husband. Now back to the writing.

12/17/98 ~ 11:15 p.m.

This past week has been busy. I signed for the building – preliminary – $2,781,000. Mike submitted for counter. I met with Delores Armstead and submitted financial reports. I am seeking financial support for the SB Downtown building. I met with George Collins and Steve Wilson, Supervisors Chief of Assistance.

Greg, CPA, reports numbers that do not support the move for Four-D. I immediately went to God in my thoughts; I know He sees the clearer path. I must NOT (never) think 'I cannot' when I know GOD can!

I tell Greg I must present the course of action. I cannot act or react out of fear!

Steve and I attended the CASFAA conference in San Diego. We learned what we needed.

This evening NCNW had our Annual Kwanzaa meeting at Malinda's home in Grand Terrace. Approximately 24 members and guests attended a wonderful event.

Tomorrow, I will respond to the city grant. Pray for success and continue to move forward. Ernest Dowdy and I met today and discussed business and prayer. We do help each other spiritually. God, send us what we need.

The Completion of the Masters 12/18/98 ~ 5:45 a.m.

What the mind conceives, the mind believes. What the mind believes, the mind conceives.

We are taught failure.

Sitting in the Financial Management for the non-financial manager class, I realize that the process was to determine the safety nets. Is it affordable, what will it cost, will I receive a benefit, a profit, what is the cost per production, what is the cost of the product? All of the safety nets were the guides to stop or move forward. It was there and my mind began to question, ***Can I afford to move and will I have enough money?*** I don't have $2.7 – $3 million. I, I, I... I shook myself free.

Sitting back looking at the page of members, categories, I realized I had to be removed, and God stepped in. I don't care to learn such details. Replace the "I can't" with GOD CAN.

Yesterday, as Greg Sheets CPA talked, his numbers showed I couldn't move forward...not enough safety nets...I smiled and thought of the class! I chose to move forward. GOD CAN.

Faithfulness

12/19/98 ~ 3:30 p.m.

An expression of Love.

Last evening, Four-D Success Academy, Inc. held its annual Christmas Party at the Marriott in Ontario, it was grand. Wendy and her assistants put together a great memorable evening. The dinners of salmon and Cornish hen with side dishes were delicious. Staff participation and guests totaled about 60.

I had fun. Conversation, dancing, laughing, gifts, and hugs.

After the party at about 11-11:30, Ernell went home and I joined Cherry, Demala, Steven, and his guest for more conversation and coffee at Applebee's in Montclair. Scholarly topic of international subjects. We parted about 2:00 a.m. I slept well. Lord, thank You for bringing us another year.

Today, Ernell and Aisha are out skiing. Tahira is sleep. I cleaned my house, decorated the Christmas tree, and washed clothes. Standing in the shower, I began to think of what God has given me. I praised Him, crying, releasing tears of joy. I released more tears than the shower released water. My mind envisioned the Child Care Center. I see children, all ethnic groups. I see a child in a wheelchair, I see the nursery, I see the sick rooms, I see children in the open area. I see Margie walking the hall of Admissions Department. I see students. I see the non-profit office. I see Four-D, I see PASS OVER written over the door. I see God's protection, I see the City Council Member and the County Board of Supervisors come together to assist Four-D Success Academy's move to San Bernardino. I see the approval of funds and calling Greg with joy and laughter. I see the $2,781,000 is covered. The papers are signed for $750,000 and $540,000. The bank approved us for $2.2 million dollars. WE CAN AFFORD TO MOVE. GOD CAN.

I just cried with joy. All I could say is LORD, THANK YOU, THANK YOU, THANK YOU until I held myself still. I stood in the shower, the temperature changing from cool to warm. My mind flooded with praises for God. I believe what my heart conceives. I believe in faithfulness.

Lord, thank You.

12/25/98 ~ 9:45 p.m.

Merry Jesus Christmas. What a lovely day. My man and I embraced with love, kisses, and caressing, all so goooood. Up by 9:00 a.m., we reminisce about our girls. There was once a time they would be knocking and calling us to get up at 6:00 a.m. As they got older, the knocks came later and later. Last year, the knock was at 8:30 a.m. "Time to get up," Aisha and Tahira calling out. Today, we called them. Pictures were taken and gifts exchanged. Tahira and Aisha had a disagreement several days ago. Tension filled the air yesterday. I spoke to each of them separately about forgiveness. They exchanged gifts today. Aisha gave Tahira boots and a sweater. Tahira gave Aisha a $150 certificate. Ernell got socks, sweaters, and a $300 certificate for a ski body suit. I got perfume and undergarments. We visited family, had a gift exchange, hugs, kisses, laughs, and love. I thank God for this day. His gift to us, our gift to Him, our love for one another.

Lord, thank You for my family.

Last night, Ernell and I had dinner at Cherry's home with her guests, Stephen, Christine, Claire, Pam, and daughter, Innocent, Catherine, Justine, Catherine's male guest, and Amanda. Dinner was lovely.

Cherry is a great hostess. We exchanged gifts. She gave a photo of her and me with a message of God's love, sisterhood – I gave her a set of earrings.

Earlier in the week, Stephen had the staff to help with the audit on financial reports. He found significant errors made by Theresa. It is questionable if she had altered or removed info from student's financial files. The purpose of her actions, I guess, was to harm me. But Four-D, staff, and students should not be paralyzed for the purposeful action to cause harm. We will prevail. God will guide us through.

I stood in the lobby of Four-D Success Academy on December 24 at 2:35 p.m. I prayed and cried, thanking God for another year. What we have come through has prepared us for the future. I know He will carry us through troubled waters.

I began to envision the school, students, programs, and staff. The signing of a contract affordable to use. All was well. I know God will provide. I know we will continue – no matter what, God is good – all the time. Through God, all things are possible. My banker is God. He has endless funds. I am His child, heir to His funds and bank. He provides as I need. I ask as I believe. I fear not, I stay close to His heart. My daddy Walter would say, "All is right with God, Baby, don't worry." I worry not, for God gives all.

Lord, thank You for what is to come.

Thank You for what has been.

I love You.

12/26/98 ~ 8:00 a.m.

The day after. Now Aisha and I are going shopping.

12/28/98 ~ 10:15 p.m.

Well Steve and I discussed his view of Four-D problems and identified how to address them. We entered in the Management meeting to address the issues. The Financial Aid problems created by Theresa were discussed. I believed she intentionally sabotaged the Academy to affect me, not caring about the staff. I tried to impress upon them the position she intended to put us in and she was not hurting the Academy, but them as well. Her negativity affected the attitude of others, how they related to each other, assisted one another. We, once again, dressed the attendance procedure, policy, re-entry of student's documentation. WE are getting it right – moving on. Cherry received a call from Riverside General Hospital. We were awarded the facility agreement to train the LVN students. Nursing Programs selected were Loma Linda and Riverside Community College, Four-D Success Academy.

Lord, thank You.

Visit from P. Stranger, program manager with the City of San Bernardino. He was given a brief history, introduced to staff, and given a tour. He was impressed. He thought we were a two-room school. He could clearly see how much larger and how packed we were. I pray for their support.

1/1/99 ~11:30 p.m.

1999 A new year for a new beginning. 1998 ended with a positive note.

-My husband and I reunited our love and marriage. I have felt like a newlywed. My heart was right.

-My mother's health is good. She and the boys are doing much better. Momma and I took a cruise to St. Thomas for her 75th Birthday.

-Ernell turned 49 years old. Aisha, 20, and Tahira, 22. I am 46.

-Four-D Success was blessed with another year. The Financial Aid Audit brought concerns, but we will correct them.

-Riverside General Hospital granted the LVN Program an agreement for clinical training.

-I placed a bid on a building in San Bernardino 26,000 sq. ft. God will provide.

-Cherry and I attended Dr. Height's gala celebration hosted by Susan Taylor. We met Susan – trying to promote the Academy. Letters to Susan Taylor Essence and Laura Randolph Ebony.

-I was selected for the Women of Achievement award.

-I received the Elizabeth Genne Lifetime Achievement Award.

-One of 50 Influential Women.

-Businessperson of the Year by the Black Chamber of Commerce.

-Four-D Success Academy donated $10,000 to the God's Women Conference.

-The copier was donated to Adopt-a-Bike.

-The Riverside Training Site was closed due to lack of students.

-The Academy did not receive the Welfare to Work contract. The future is bright.

-The Pharmacy Tech Program is doing well.

-Approval received for the Medical Biller/Health Claims Examiner Program.

-Words can't express my joy in my marriage being saved by God.

-Sadiq is doing well. He has come full circle in his life. I know God will grant him his freedom one day.

-Donnie and Gregory are in jail. Gregory is in San Diego. Donnie is in SB. Donnie is expecting a child.

-Walter and I are doing fine. My daddy – he is still watching me, "Baby, everything is going to be all right. God is good."

Lord, I thank You for 1998. Keep me focused, keep me humble, kind, and considerate. Grant my prayer to help others. Fill me with abundant love – to share and fill others with. Protect my home, family, Four-D Success Academy. Give Sadiq his freedom. Protect all of my brothers. Free their body and spirits of alcohol/drugs. Open their eyes to You, Lord. Keep Momma healthy. Keep Ernell and me together. This morning, he said, "The troubled times are over." I believe him. Thank You, thank You, thank You.

Love Your Child, Linda

1/5/99 ~ 9:50 p.m.

When I think about God's goodness, I cry. As overwhelmed as I may be, and sometimes saddened, when I think about God's goodness, I cry. There is no pressure I can't handle; there is no sadness that can steal my joy. When I think about God's goodness, I cry.

I have been carried through the valleys so low. I have been placed on the mountain crest so high. No storms or winds stop my path, for the Creator created both and me. When I think of God's goodness to me, I cry.

I stood in the shower thinking about Maria and Barbara, the first class of two students of Four-D Success Academy Certified Nurse Assistant Program. They have, long ago moved on, and so has the school. I think of God's goodness and I cry.

A time when $3,000 in debt with $56 in checking. I think about God's goodness and I cry. $1,000,000 for 1997-1998. I think of God's goodness and I cry. Trouble ahead, storms to rage, winds high, I know of God's goodness and I cry. Words of thank you are not enough. But that's all I can say, as I cry tears of joy.

1/9/99 ~ 10:15 p.m.

Friday 1/8/99 was my mother, Eula Mae Russ's, 75th birthday. She had a birthday party. SHE cooked chicken, greens, black-eyed peas, hot water cornbread, chitterlings, potato salad, German chocolate cake, and sweet potato pies. She invited the usher board and guests. They had a good time. It was wonderful to see the love she received. Walter, Genie, kids, Betty, Yolanda, Kathy, Ernell, and I were there. She has been blessed.

Work was draining. I had asked Mike to hold a meeting to discuss the meeting objectives with team members. But it turned into an unprofessional, rude, unproductive mess. I stepped in and calmly addressed my concerns. After, words were provided. As I prayed, I asked God to remove anyone who could not or would not work for the positive growth of FDSA. I asked that He pull the team together with respect, support, etc. I found myself overwhelmed with tears as I spoke. But the words were from my heart.

Today was a day of rest. I washed a few loads of clothes and got my hair done by Evette. Ernell cooked dinner – fried fish – and washed my car. Tomorrow is a new day.

Oh yes, Charlie brought Linda Randolph MD MPA to the school. She is very involved in Child Health issues. A wonderful contact for us, Cherry and I will work with Linda for Friend's of Four-D Success project.

Life is challenging. All things come together for good.

1/11/98 ~ 11:45 p.m.

Today, I hired Alicia Pace as the new Pharmacy Tech. The Smart System is being implemented. Stephen is working on our financial problems. I am working on the CSAC Program. Cherry is delirious about the "Friends" side of the business. Ernell and I are packing for the ski trip to Canada. God is good. We will continue to move forward. Lord, thanks for another day.

1/16/99 ~ 11:00 a.m.

Happy Birthday Dr. Martin Luther King. Thank you for your dedication to my life and the lives of all.

Today, I am in Vancouver Canada with Ernell and the National Brother Land Ski Club. The view from the room is breathtaking. Snow covered the tree branches as far as the eyes could see. Valleys run between mountains. Large clouds hovering, caressing the base of the mountains and setting into the crest of the valley gorge. The sky embodied the view, and I think of God's creation. Snowflakes pass the window, fallen from the sky to the ground below, no two alike. God's creation. The stillness in the room, a passing car along the road below, no birds in the sky, no noise, calmness, peace.

I sit and give thanks to God. PEACE and calmness. I pray and give thanks. The clouds are low, the mountains and valley are now hidden behind the blanket of snow. Visibility less than ¼ mile. Snowflakes falling in a steady stream of white soft flakes, each different in size and shape. Quietly falling from God's clouds. I sit, become self-centered, and think about my life. How strange it is... the different facts of our life, the tosses and turns, the emotions and needs, the desires of our heart, secrets, personal secrets. I sit and think, thankful for outcomes as they are. The snow continues to fall. My life continues in Vancouver, Canada.

1/18/99 ~ 4:00 p.m.

Here I sit in the Vancouver, Canada Airport, awaiting the flight back to Los Angeles Airport. These past four days have proven to be quite interesting. I found myself skiing on Friday. I took a lesson in the a.m. In the p.m., I skied the beginner's slopes. At the end of the day, I could feel the pull behind my right knee. It is still weak from the praise jump in August. I stayed in Saturday. Reading, having a quiet day to myself. Ernell and friends skied up a storm. Dinner in the evening with him was quite quiet. We attended the evening function. We danced once and left. Sunday, we attended a comedy show. Tommy Davidson was the top act. Dance after the show, again, I asked Ernell to dance. The look on his face was so disappointing. He had had a great time doing his thing. Having a good ole time, but the second I asked to dance his face dropped – and so did my heart. I didn't want to stay another second. He knew I was hurt. He couldn't recover. He said, "Let's dance," with such hesitance. I stayed calm, controlled. I ask to leave and we left. I had nothing to say after that. We walked in silence. I thought of all the places I have been without him, the fun I have had. As I don't make his fun, he should not be required to make mine. We are different. We do enjoy different things. We need different attention. Life is funny. Then quickly I felt empty, and lonely, again. Sitting here in the airport writing, Ernell is with his friends. Where do I go from here?

1/18/99 ~ 11:15 p.m.

Home, unpacked, the girls are here. It is good to see them. Aisha asked her father if he had a good time. He lit up like a Christmas tree, teeth showing, big smile. That is what disappointed me yesterday at the dance. His look was totally opposite.

I must choose my own fun. What pleasure makes me happy? It is not skiing. I look forward to Boston in March.

My life keeps taking emotional twists and turns.

1/20/99 ~ 10:35 p.m.

Well, Ernell and I had a pleasant conversation about our love life. I am not quite sure what was resolved. I shared my desires to get involved in an activity. I enjoy movement of my body. I expressed how disappointed I was about the dance scene at Vancouver. I know he understood.

This morning, we embraced.

Today, Mike, Greg, and I discussed the plan to meet with Wells Fargo Bank. Ernell has offered the $190,000 on the house to be used for the purchase of the building. God is working things out.

Walter Jr. called this a.m. Greg received 25 years plus 3 for his third felony crime. He would not take his situation serious. I tried praying for him. I asked him to accept Jesus. He broke away from me, sweating, saying he had a headache and was dizzy — Satan was whooping his butt. He refused to accept Jesus, for within a week or two, he was hooked on the street and back in jail. At the young age of 14 is when his criminal activity began. Now at 35, he will be locked up for 28 years, so be his choice. He is at home. Tomorrow, I will attend the Child Care Workshop in Riverside. It will go well. God is good.

Thank You, Lord.

I will call Momma tomorrow. I know her heartaches, but she at least will know where her son is.

I signed Union Bank of California papers for $125,000 loan.

Times have changed.

Next week, I should sign for $100,000 loan – total $225,000. Growth taking place.

1/21/99 ~ 11:15 p.m.

I blew up today!

Yesterday, I was informed that Pam (Office Manager) had the attendance sheets I had been looking for to complete the audit. I have questioned the work of everyone – Staff – instructors said they had turned the sheets in repeatedly. Margie personally went into the office, looked through the books, and found the attendance sheets. While in a meeting with licensed staff, and Pam, the office manager, and, Margie, a program department employee, Pam walked out of the meeting. She has not assisted with the SMART system. Today, I left the office at 8:30. I returned at 10:28. As I was entering the building, I decided to go to the HCE/MB class. As I was turning the corner, I saw Pam and Vikki going south on Mt. Vernon. I was livid. They had gone to lunch and they returned with fast food.

Pam couldn't see what the big deal was. Vikki was more concerned and apologetic. Pam approached Margie. They left the office, and she did not return. I must make a move to replace her position. She cannot function as a manager.

Lord, make me better.

1/26/98 ~ 12:05 a.m.

A day for change. Lord I am better. Saturday, I removed Pam from the Office Manager position. It was a teary-eyed process for her! I took all keys. I had enough issues concerning her attitude. She continued to display unprofessional conduct in her actions, walking out of meetings, not assisting in the Smart Project. The time has come.

Vikki was replaced/terminated due to the 'down-sizing'. She had informed me that a student had cried and reported to her sexual harassment from/by another instructor. She had passed this info to Pam. I had spoken with the student's mother earlier in the day. There was no mention/concern of her child being mistreated.

I know I had to operate on good ground, professional business, and judgment. Reshape the organized chart.

Pam- Placement/Fed Work Study Coordinator.

Wendy- Adm. Assistant/Registrar

Stephen- Coordinator, our Placement Registrar, Business Admissions.

I feel so much better.

EDA City cancelled my interview regarding the grant proposal. I was informed my application was so thorough the interview was not required. Lord, let this be good news.

Thank You, Jesus.

Oh yes, on Friday the 22nd at the Nursing Board meeting, the Consultant gave a report filled with such negative twists that it was obvious her goal was to discredit us. We were approved with Contingencies to enroll 30 students. I spoke briefly during the comment period. I know God will protect and guide our path.

1/26/99 ~ 11:45 p.m.

Oh what a day!

1) I spoke with Dorion from Essence Magazine. She called to inform me that I would be featured in June's issue! I had a 1.5-hour interview (9-10:28 p.m.). It was great; I have so much in me about the journey traveled in the development of Four-D Success Academy. I talked and talked. She asked questions and typed.
2) We signed our contract with Riverside General Medical Center after 4 months. Lord, thank You.
3) I spoke with Al Twine. He mentioned, "You never know what is in God's plan." I thanked him for his and Joe's assistance. Tomorrow, I meet the Wells Fargo Bank Rep about the sale of the building. Lord, let them find favor in us. Provide us the finances to service the debt.

I sit here reflecting on my life. Sunday while driving home with Ernell I began to cry and thank God. I could not find the words to express to Ernell how God was working. I know that the Lord is going to make a way for the building. The spirit touched me.

Goodnight. Love You.

1/27/99 ~ 10:14

Well, today was the day! Mike Ballard, Greg Sheets, and I met with Larry and Jack (Wells Fargo Bank) to discuss the loan on the new building. I was also interviewed. Jack needed to see me. Who/what was I. I answered questions. We laughed easily. Mike opened the conversation congratulating me when I inquired about what he mentioned in the interview. I elaborated on Dr. Height/Clinton. The

Essence/Taylor meetings and the interview call for the feature article in June. The tone was set. After the meeting (1:15-3:00), Greg said, "I thought he was going to have you sign the papers." He felt confident that the meeting had gone quite well. He indicated that these guys would not have stayed in the meeting that long if they were not interested. He felt good about the process.

I felt great. Lord, thank You for bringing us this far.

Goodnight, Lord.

1/30/99 ~ 8:52

Friday after work, Stephen and I attended Senator Joe Baca's celebration (birthday). Well-attended by 600 persons, Pastor Chuck Singleton was the guest speaker. I introduced Stephen to several people. Ms. Francis Grice asked me to fill out an application for consideration for a Commissioned position by Governor Davis. I will submit the application by Tuesday.

Thanks, Lord.

2/1/99 ~ 9:00 a.m.

I forgot to mention, Tahira put $1,000 down on a $119,000 Condo. 1605 sq. ft. in Rancho Park, Rancho Cucamonga. Three bedrooms and 2.5 baths. My baby, the homeowner – we are all going to Church. Thank You, Lord.

2/1/99

I think of my life, and the school. I marvel at God's love for me. I think of the school's new location. Am I confident in the occurrences trusting in God, or am I sure of me and the contacts I have made? I sit and listen to my heart, my soul, my God. I know that I am not full of myself. I think if I prepare myself for a disappointment, then

I am the one that failed. But this is God's plan. I cannot fail, nor can He. Whatever trail I am on, God lights the path.

After the event on Friday, Stephen and I sat in my car. We shared our desires, dreams of the future, Four-D, and our lives. There are no accidents with God. My path is destined to do good for others. Lord, thank You!

2/1/99 ~ 10:28 p.m.

Today, I submitted a letter for support from Senator Joe Baca. The Senator will submit the letters to Gary Van Osel, City EDA Director, and Tom Laurin, Executive Director of Economic Com and Development.

I spoke with Daris Daniels.

Interview cancelled due to completeness of application. She would not say what the outcome would be, but did say things were being processed to the next level. She could not say what amount – things would change. Lord, I don't know what to feel. Confident or anxious, but I am not cocky. I am relying on the Lord.

Lead me. Guide me.

Along the way for if You lead me, I cannot stray. Lord, let me walk each day with thee. Lead me, oh Lord, lead me.

2/3/99 ~ 9:53

Visit today from Ann Sherman, Esther Estrada, Board member and Jeanne Templeman Consultant. Site review of facilities and school. The only 'finding' was some miscommunication with management over schedule. I noted verbally that since 1996, we were never informed of a 'communication' issue with any hospital. Cherry provided clear detail in our relations with the Hospital. We gave them a tour of the facility, they met with LVN students, discussed the Child Care Center. We visited the Uniform shop. End result? We were told we are "Innovative." We will receive the draft report for the April Board Meeting.

Senator Joe Baca signed the letter of support to the EDA SB City Department.

Received a call from Faith Michelson, Jerry Eave's office – Child Care, status of the new process – after discussion, she informed me of Mayor Valle's meeting tomorrow at 10:00 a.m. I will be present.

Lord, Thanks.

Oh yes, Tahira is a homeowner, $119,990. SOLD. My girl, my lady.

2/8/99 ~ 11:50 p.m.

Well, Ann submitted a letter to Cherry requesting information for a 'search'. She is having Cherry retrieve info from class 4, 5, and 6. She has it. But I know we need God's protection against the enemy and smiling faces. I guess when the truth is sought, it sure makes Satan pissed, but I know we are protected by God. Today, Jenkins, Assistant to the Mayor of San Bernardino, visited. She arrived at 8:00 and left at 10:30. What a visit, we shared the city's view of revitalization, Four-D's relocation, the Child Care Center, and computer lab. We found the facility. She was very impressed with us. She stated her support and she would inform the Mayor of our need for support.

I know she followed through. She informed Charlie Seymour of her visit. Cherry and I had lunch with Betty from Assemblyman John Longville's office. The Mayor was having lunch with a gentleman. I wonder if they were discussing FDSA.

I am progressing slowly on the ETP. I wait patiently on the Wells Fargo announcement, EDA, and Federal Demonstration Partnership (FDP).

Guide my steps, Lord. Thanks.

2/13/99 ~ 11:14

What a day yesterday was. We received the letter from the County for the grant, moved to the next deal. I requested $104,000 for training. I will know by/on March 20th, 1999. I submitted my package/application to Senator Baca and Governor Davis for consideration for appointment as a Commissioner – four areas.

-Education

-Education Post Secondary

-Health Care Development Plans

-Equal Housing and Employment

Sleepy. Goodnight.

2/14/99 ~ 10:46 a.m.

Today is Sunday, Valentine's Day. My husband's gift is small loop gold earrings and a bracelet with 24 hearts and diamonds.

Today, I change my life. I have control of my size and weight. I weigh 185 lbs., and I will reduce to a weight I am proud of. God, grant me strength. Heighten continuous desire to achieve. I want to weigh 140 lbs. I will weigh 140 lbs. by my 47th Birthday. I have the 4 D's to succeed.

My husband is mopping the floor; I am getting ready to go shopping with Tahira for the wedding. (Mike and Pam)

Ernell's gift, a pretty wife.

10:06 p.m.

Well, it's done. Mike and Pam are married. When it is all said and done, Mike is happy again. At the end of the evening while dancing with him, I could see the sparkle in his eyes. He motioned toward the ring on his left third finger and smiled. I complemented him on this disposition. His response, "I have my girls, family, and friends here with me. I am happy." God, thank You.

I thought about Julie, as well as did others. Good times we had together, vacations, children growing up, times passing. I pray that she is okay. I could not call. What would I say? I thought about her this week, but I didn't want any discussion on Mike or their divorce. Pam looked lovely in her white beaded gown. Smiling, kissing, dancing, and greeting guests. A bride, a wife, a mother. God bless this union. Keep it together.

I pray today – different. My mind is full of thanks, my request are many for my heart to hold. God, grant me my heart's desire. Empower me with wisdom, growth, love, and self-assurance.

I submitted my package to the Governor and Senator Joe Baca.

Tuesday, I took pictures for Essence – June issue. How I did it with Four-D Success Academy, Inc.

Lord, thank You for all the many blessings.

2/19/99 ~ 11:02 p.m.

Yesterday, I picked up my letter of support from Assemblyman, John Longville. The support letter was strongly written, supporting an appointment to the commission for Health Care Services or Post Secondary Education. I am honored to receive such love and support.

Stephen informed me we were approved for the Cal Grant. We will know the amount in April. Today, Gary Lobster, Mayor of Saginaw Michigan, came to town to visit and take care of business. He, Cherry, Ernell, and I had dinner at the Crescent City. Great dinner and Jazz. He will be here until tomorrow or Sunday a.m.

The 5 LVN class graduation is tomorrow. We have been tested and tried. Lord, we survived. We pray for our future protection.

Thank You.

2/24/99 ~ 8:20 p.m.

I am always thinking of what I should be doing to assist Four-D in its movement forward. Everyone does not operate as I do. I have no boundaries in my job duties or title. Whatever that must be done, I try to make time for it. I try to assist other departments to help carry the load. This may not be healthy for personal growth of the staff. It becomes a codependent situation. I spoke with a rep from B of A regarding an SBA Loan. Chris sounded hopeful. I will submit the usual paper work by Friday. I should have an answer by 2 weeks. (3/12/99)

ABHES is coming on 3/1 and 3/2. Wendy is preparing for the site visit. She is carrying her load. I have spoken with Pricilla – bank teller training through ETP. She is doing her research, spoke with John - dental training for Arizona, California.

Cherry is looking at a Surgical Tech Program. I am looking for a great writer.

I spoke with Davion – Fundraiser. I want more info, resume, and contacts to review so we can move forward. Linda Jenkins is working with me – funding with City of SB for the school and meeting scheduled for March 4th to discuss the Child Care Center.

Lord, guide my path.

2/25/99 ~ 11:30 p.m.

Well Betty Thomas, RN Coordinator was selected as the Employer of the Year for 1998. She received $300, a letter of appreciation, and her name placed on the wall plaque. I met with the evaluator regarding the ETP Program. Things sounded and looked positive. They are considering 60 students for a year.

Stephen and I had dinner and discussed staff positions, requirements, growth of the company, his father's illness, his brothers, his cultural responsibilities as the head son, God's presence, our path, the light, goals, and faith.

Through God, all is possible. Stephen's father has a fragment of metal near his heart. Surgery is needed to sustain his life, even for a year – 5 years. He feels obligated to do something. God will prevail. I believe God has a plan for me in this but I don't know quite what.

Follow the path.

2/26/99 ~ 9:40 p.m.

Today, much occurred. In preparing for the accreditation on Monday, I asked Wendy if everyone had turned in their tests, book, etc. She informed me Nancy was turning in the test on Monday. I spoke to Cherry. She thought it was done. My response to Wendy, "Like hell, I want those tests here by 3:00 p.m. Call Nancy now!" I left for my 11:00 a.m. appointment.

Dolores was out. I needed to calm down. I went and had my nails done. Arriving back to the office at 1:00 p.m., I ate a big bowl of oatmeal. Calm, I went to work. Nancy came in. Everyone got it together. Computer in, telephone in, program label laid out on the table for the ABHES visit.

Sal/Margie and Wendy are going in tomorrow to check charts and files. I am going in after my 5:00 p.m. hair appointment. Call received from Naomi – ETP Consultant. She is working with me. Our goal is to have an approval for the March Board Meeting. We discussed the number to start with: 20-60 students. I learned more about the program. Following her call, I received a call from Caroline Braswell. Jean definitely wanted the program; even wants me to consider Poway. They (Braswell) want a minimum of 60 students. We may have a contract for 80 slots $320,000. Lord, bless us.

I spoke with Councilwoman, Susan Lein; she is pleased that I will attend the meeting at the Mayor's office for Child Care. We will discuss available property on Gilbert St. We also discussed the conversation I had with Ann. Ann was not as welcoming as the Manager of Main Street. Susan said she would call Gary Van Osdel – Head of EDD. She asked me not to be discouraged. The door was not closed. I have her support. Lord, thank You.

2/28/99 ~ 11:24 p.m.

A blessed day at Church, and a teaching on God's grace, Isaiah 30:15. Covered by grace, we are blessed beyond words. We continue to journey into the light of God's love. He creates situations to remind us of His greatness. So often, I am at awe of all that comes together like a puzzle. So many pieces, but one big picture. Tomorrow, the ABHES team will be at the Academy for the recertification for accreditation. I know all is well. The team has done that which is necessary.

Aisha is back from the Campus Crusade Trip. Tomorrow I will get the details. Tahira is busily looking for furniture. She and I visited a couple of stores, had lunch at Marie Calendars', and then arrived home at 4:30 p.m. A pleasant evening at home with my husband and kids. Lord, thank You.

The Child Care Center – a good name = My Child's Care Center.

Goodnight, Lord. Thanks.

3/2/99 ~ 8:20 p.m.

Yesterday, ABHES Monitor arrived for the accreditation visit. Findings were addressed by the staff and me. Changes needed for the catalog, lack documented inservices for faculty. I stayed to address the preliminary report. Today, we had a visit from Delores Armstead from the County EDA. She toured the school, saw the need. We discussed the loan application process. She said she would make a call to Gary Van Osdel. She said, "Don't give up." Our application is still alive.

I met with Margaret, a staff member at SBCSU. She is a grant writer. We discussed grant non-profit vs. profit set up. She and Cherry will meet for this discussion.

I was so exhausted at the end of the day. I am in bed and will be asleep by 9:30.

Lord, sing me through it. Thanks.

3/6/99 ~ 7:11 p.m.

Saturday evening, my hair is rolled up and I am in bed relaxing, checking out the TV, and reading *Ebony*. I think of my mother's concern about her house taxes. I tell her not to worry; I will take care of them. It's good. $220 due March, $400 due in April. At times, I feel her passing important things my way again. I have always been the most resourceful and responsible child. God has prepared me.

I have had a relaxing day. Up at 8:45 a.m., Ernell was on the slopes skiing. Watched a little TV as I prepared waffles for Aisha. To the car wash at 10:30, gas, bank, and grocery store. Home at 1:30, cooked dinner. Ernell was home by 4:30.

The girls are about. Aisha is cleaning and Tahira is resting. Aisha jokes about Tahira. She says Tahira turns over and I get excited! I think of my work, where we are, where we are going, bonus for staff marketing, the Child Care Center, the non-profit organization.

My life is good, getting better. Ernell, Linda, Tahira, and Aisha Smith. My life is blessed by God. Thanks.

3/9/99 ~ 7:56 a.m.

Unable to sleep soundly on 3/6/99, I was awakened with thoughts of the building in San Bernardino. I see the building renovated on the north first floor. I feel it is being sold to another party. I feel anxious. I must take charge. Lord, who do I call? Who must I see?

Yesterday, I shared my thoughts with Mike. I had not received the signed counter offer from Jordan. Could he enter into negotiation with another? Yes – What!

I called Larry Taylor yesterday. What is really going on? I have no signed contract. He thought I had? Unlikely – he is the agent! He said Wells is working the numbers. Can we afford the note?

I called Gary Van Osdel, Director of EDA. We talked; I explained FDSA's status and needs for the City to come to the table with the County for the loan to move forward. He noted the name Delores Armstead. He will call her and get back to me by Friday. For the first time, I felt a real breakthrough. Only Susan Lien, Councilwoman, had called on my behalf. Delores, Linda, and Collin had not made any calls as promised.

Sometimes, it is better to represent yourself. This is what I told Gary, and he agreed.

I worked on the Child Care budget on Saturday, and lost it all on Monday. It didn't save on disk, not on C Drive. Oh well, start over.

Lord, thank You for Your love.

I paid my mother's property taxes. She will rest better.

Sadiq called – he is writing a letter to Oprah and Susan Taylor. Thanks, Sadiq.

3/10/99 ~ 11:38 p.m.

A day of rejoicing.

I arrived home at 9:00 p.m., checked the mail, and noticed an envelope from La Salle University. Now, I had thoughts earlier in the week, *I feel smarter.* Laughing to myself, I thought, *The MBA is coming.* Well, the letter of congratulations arrived. I received my MBA from La Salle University. I called Cherry, and she screamed.

She wants us to celebrate, tell the world. The girl is hilarious sometimes, but I do thank her for her support.

Ernell and Tahira are going over her papers. She is attentive. Later as I enter into her room, she smiles and the tears flow. "Mommy, my escrow closes tomorrow." My baby is a homeowner at 22. We embraced. I kissed her cheeks. I am so very proud. She tells me her dad also has said the magical words, "I am proud of you."

Aisha was tearful (earlier), questioning if we are proud of her. She is 20, living at home, in college. "Is she a 'parasite'?" we tease her, etc. She needs TLC. I hug and kiss her and express words of praise. She is going to New Jersey for Campus Crusades to witness to others; she is working and attending college. I am pleased with her progress. We discuss God's path, doing our best at our assignments, productivity, and the future. She is happy.

As I sit in Tahira's room, talking and laughing with my girls, I realize that all of our lives are changing. My children are grown women, making decisions for their lives, planning their future. Preparing to leave home. I am so very grateful to God for our family unit, our life. It has been good. There is much joy at the Smith's residence. Ernell quietly (light snore) sleeps on the couch. I know he is happy. He doesn't say much, but after 23 years, I know. Ernell, I love you.

Thanks.

3/14/99 ~ 9:33 p.m.

I received a call from the YMCA. Cherry has been selected as a Woman of Achievement for 1999. When they called her, she cried. I am so very proud of her and her acknowledgments. She is doing a good job. I am scheduled to be out of town. I must change my plans. I shared with Ernell my decision to relieve Pam Jackson of her duties at Four-D Success Academy. She informed me she was not qualified for the position of Placement Coordinator. She has had many opportunities to flourish, yet she is her own stumbling block. My chest has been heavy, pressure in my right shoulder. When I heard a speaker talking about stress shortly after that, that we need to function and that we need to control and eliminate. Stress affects our health, spirit, and attitude. My health was affected. I feel so much better, now that I have come to a decision. I share my thoughts with Ernell. He is supportive of my decision.

God speaks to us constantly. We must pray and listen. Lord, thank You for another opportunity to get it right.

The ETP Project was submitted to Sacramento. I attend a meeting on 3/26 for the outcome. God, bless it. Wells Fargo has not made a decision yet. I submitted a proposal for Child Care to Jane Adams, she has $300,000 to distribute. I met with Gary Van Osdel on last Monday. He was to call Delores. I will follow up this week. Lord, bless all transactions.

3/15/99 ~ 9:56 p.m.

I arrived to work at 8:20 a.m. Let me back up. The message at Church eased my discomfort of having to face the morning. 1st Kings 20: 1-6. The message for me was God is always there. Through the trials, there is triumph. Last night at 11:45, tired, sleepy, while sitting at my computer desk, I picked up a magazine. The covered topic of the magazine dealt with firing staff. I read each word, understanding how I must follow through, reminders of proper process, courage, and closure. I thank God for the message.

Now at 8:20 I asked Juanita for Pam's term check and 3 week severance pay. Four-D will cover her medical insurance through April 1999. We cancelled the loan of $2,100 due. Betty Thomas sat in as we processed the termination, and all went smoothly. I received the keys. Pam left with only her belongings. Betty and I talked, prayed, and cried. It was the best thing for Four-D Success. The rest of the day was quiet. I submitted the memo to the staff. Malinda (NCNW) and I arrived for the board meeting. Only she and I were there. We stood in the cool air and talked. I stated I needed counseling. We talked, I talked, and she listened and responded. We prayed. I felt better; I needed to express my sorrow and loss. I want to express my love for Pam, but I felt she had abused my kindness. I had been pushed across the line of tolerance. Malinda told me to close that chapter of my life, that Satan will try to harbor in my mind but, 'Greater is He that is within me than he that is within the world.' Words I need to hear.

Lord, bless Pam. I pray she finds comfort in You. Bless her with a better job. A job she will put forth great endeavors to be successful and assist in the growth of the place of hire.

Protect her family: safe, secure, and together. I pray for her father's health and his family. Lord, thank You for this day.

3/18/99 ~ 9:36 p.m.

God's blessing abounds. I had an interview with a gentleman, a retired pharmacist. James had been referred to me by Tony Jackson, Pharmacist at SB Com. Hospital. James accepted the full-time teaching position – he only wants $800 per month. I sat in awe. Is this real? A highly experienced, retired office of the armed forces accepted a position with us.

He will start April 5th. I am moving Alicia to Externship/Placement, Veronica Beckas to ETP Coordinator. I was full of delight. I talked with Charlie about his celebration. His birthday is Saturday. He will be a young 80! On Thursday, March 26th he is having a golf tournament and dinner. Four-D purchased a table.

Steve and I had dinner. His father is ill with bullet shrapnel near his heart and lungs. He needs to have surgery. Steve is burdened with raising the funds. He requested $35,000. I felt my vessels close. God, help me talk through this. Four-D does not have $35,000, nor do I, but God does.

Home in bed. Ernell arrives, starts packing for the fun weekend trip to Laughlin — Mom, Earl, Ernell, and I. FUN!

Lord beside us all!

3/20/99 ~ 5:40 – 6.25 a.m.

Lord, thank You for the tears of joy. Last week, I prayed to God to show me how to keep His word in Four-D Success Academy. I had been feeling upset, anxious over the last month. Concerned about the lack of spiritual support and openly praying with students, I felt that the focus was shifting. The religious beliefs or lack of belief in God was going to penetrate the very fiber of the Academy's foundation. I ask God to guide me. The faculty in the LVN program do not express themselves as the instructors in the CNA program, the days of 'old'... Betty, Mary, Shirley, Lanell. I knew these ladies prayed for the students and with the students of Four-D Success Academy. Now, I was feeling a loss.

I had expressed my concerns to Cherry. Her response shocked me. Using Federal Dollars to train, I had to be careful about this 'prayer stuff.' My God! Now it's 'prayer stuff.' I could not respond. I prayed silently to God, "Lord make a way. The foundation was built on prayer."

Several days later, I expressed my thoughts and concerns with Cherry. I knew she understood. I believe she felt anxious over some of her faculty's concerns. Not a process or belief as I do. Would they be driven away if the 'requirement' was to pray? It was not stated in the policy of the school. Satan is always busy. But my God never sleeps. My prayers never cease. Lord, show me a way. Last Sunday at the 7:30 a.m. service, sister Singleton taught. As she spoke, I could feel my body relaxing, her words were for me. My prayers are answered.

A couple of months ago, I had prayed to remove that which did not belong to Four-D. The termination of Pam Jackson lifted the spirit of the school.

The following day, all staff went about doing their work. I could see staff laughing and talking to each other, not one person asked me about her. After seven years of working, supporting, praying for her and with her, I had come to see her. Pam played on my kindness and love for her; she could never truly appreciate my goodness and her blessings from God. I extended an invitation for her to accept Jesus in my office. Head lowered, she would not speak. Finally, she said she was afraid her husband would not support her, etc. As I spoke to her, I realized it was not her husband, but her. She used the situations of others to remove the light from herself. She chose to walk in darkness. Yesterday, Helen Madden came into my office to present a picture and tape from a workshop she had attended. The picture was a nurse and doctor standing along the bed of a patient. Touching the patient was Jesus. The picture said all I needed to share with anyone entering the doors of the Academy. It reflected the philosophy of the school, the caring, kindness, and compassion of the holistic man. I shared the picture with Cherry, and she lit up with delight. I requested that she frame it to be hung in the school hall. A gift from Helen, a gift from God. Helen asked me to watch the tape and I did. As I sat and listened to this lady give her testimony to an audience of nurses and doctors. I knew, once again, God has shown me a way to incorporate His words and works into the fiber of Four-D Success. I called Cherry with enthusiasm, sharing the tape. I requested that she view it. I requested that she incorporate it into the fundamentals of nursing. Again, God showed Himself to me.

Awakened at 4:48 a.m. with the presence of God in me. I began to pray and thank Him for the many blessings. I thanked God for the school, for the finances to move, for the furniture, the staff, the students. I thank God for the Child Care Center, the equipment, and the kids. I recited the verses, 'Whatsoever in your heart, ask in His name and receive.' I believe it is mine to have. I prayed for it, I thank God for it all. The spirit filled me; I began to cry as I prayed. I know that is all done, the money is there, and God is guiding me. I believe my banker has endless funds. I cry, "Thank You, Lord." I believe and I receive. I could see the building; it is under His protection. All that enter through any door will be blessed and protected, lifted by God, love, and Grace. The word PASSOVER over every door, PASSOVER me Lord. A new day with the Lord.

3/22/99 ~ 10:30 p.m.

We received a call from Walter Jr. I was in the shower finishing up on a warm long shower when Ernell said Walter was on the phone. I knew it was for something important. I immediately thought of my mother.

On the other end, he tried to casually tell me how Momma was not herself. I could hear her mumbling in the background. I knew she had had a stroke. I told him to call the paramedics. He said she was trying to remove her clothes. *Good,* I thought. She was not paralyzed. She was moving. I could envision her mouth drooping, speech slurred. But she was moving. I relaxed. ***Think the best Linda – not the worst. The outcome has already happened. So no need to freak out.*** Tears traveled down my check. Ernell handed me a Kleenex. The Paramedics arrived, assessed Momma, and took her to Kaiser Fontana.

The twins will be fine. Quiet in the background, I know they are very concerned about their grandmother. Ernell called Earl and Mama Vivian in another room. "Get ready. Ms. Russ had a stroke. We are packing and out by 9:30 a.m."

On the road, I received a page. Dr. Nelson and Walter calling from the hospital. Momma had a slight stroke. Catscan detected old stroke. She has good strength, coordination, speech slurred. Dr. Nelson informs me of a new drug TPA. May prevent further damage – but high risk of bleeding and death. I rule NOT to give the drugs. She will be fine; I will take the slurred speech. I think of Daddy and his/our decision with the heart valves. No new treatment here.

We take mom and Earl home and head for the hospital. Momma in bed in semi fowler position. She is alert, moving her lips. Her speech is not too clear, but she is trying to talk. I greet Dr. Nelson. He is ordering speech therapy. Momma stayed in the hospital for a few days. Speech therapy. She is able to eat JELL-O without any problems. Kathy and friends, Billy and Yolanda, come by.

Momma is transferred to her room at 5:30. 8 hours later she settles into her bed. Who do you call when you are in trouble? In Heaven, God. On Earth, I first thought of Cherry. I dialed her number. Walter was on another house telephone. I could not speak. I hung up the cordless phone to talk with Walter.

Later, I called Cherry to inform her of what had occurred. She is a friend who understands. Home in bed, tired. Ronnie is at Momma's house. Tomorrow I will call my Aunt Ernestine. She must be told.

Lord, I went to You, for there was no other home I know to call on. Thank You for the comfort.

3/23/99 ~ 7:15 a.m.

Momma appears to be doing better. Her speech is affected. She must speak slowly to formulate each word. This allows her to be understood much better.

She was evaluated by the speech therapist and physical therapist. Her strength and gait are fine. No apparent loss. Her eyesight is the same.

I took the twins and Donnie to see her last evening after their baseball practice. They needed to see "Grandma," and she needed to see them. Jaise asked, "Who is going to take care of us if you are sick?"

Momma responded clearly, "I am going to take care of you, don't you worry." After a short visit, it was time to go. Ronnie is at the house with them. He said he will stay until Momma is released. We will discuss living arrangements.

Walter, Momma, and I signed forms giving me authorization to make decisions regarding her treatment.

I believe she will have full recovery.

Lord, thank You.

Erma and James Marshall stepped in to take care of the twins on Sunday and Monday. I am so grateful for her friends.

3/24/99 ~ 11:00 p.m.

Aisha and I visited Momma. She is up and about. Her speech seems to be the same. She must be reminded to speak slower and clearer. When she does, I understand her as usual. Ronnie is a trooper, cooking, cleaning, and washing, doing the senior son thing. The twins have asked Momma once again, "Who is going to take care of us?" Momma told me this with sadness. I told her, she and her kids would take care of the twins.

She is so used to being in control and independent. Now she said, "I can't drive to the store, cook by myself, or talk clearly." I informed her I understand all she said. With a little time, she would be in full swing.

I spoke with the twins and asked that they not make such statements. I explained why, and they agreed. Aisha and I left at 9:30 p.m., walking out of the door laughing. God is good, all the time.

I spoke with Delores. She received the "go ahead ASAP" on my loan applications. She will present it to Supervisor Jerry Eaves. With his approval, it will go to the full board for rate. I am requesting $1 million in loan. Jack Baker is still trying to work my member. With the $1 million loan, the school's first year deficit is $117,000. I know we can make it. I told him not to close the book on us.

This Friday, I go before the ETP Panel Board. I know God has worked it out. Tomorrow is Charlie's Golf Tournament and dinner. I know it will be a sunny blessed day for him and his children at Adopt a Bike/ Computer Golf Academy. God's continued blessing to you.

3/29/99 12:01

Received a called from Teressa Conley, Riverside General VP Adm. Complained of students not performing and Instructors lacking skills. I went to the hospital at 1:30, students checking on rides home.

Paula's response is unacceptable. She let the students leave because they were tired from working nights. I spoke with the Clinical Manager. E-Mailed Cherry, spoke with K H and Mary. I will not allow staff or students to interfere with our progress. Paula will be dismissed. Every instructor who does not follow policy is out.

Momma is doing just fine. She drove to the store, bank, and took the kids to softball practice. I was slightly upset with Ronnie until I sat down and talked with her. We talked from 7:00-9:45. She looked good, hair combed into a puffball, skin clear, smiling, and talking, speech improved.

The hospital called for a follow-up speech visit for my mom. She was out. Lord has continued to bless her and us.

Home again.

Saturday, I presented *Mind, Body, and Soul*. Alternative health healing, positive thinking.

I was pleased with myself. I was asked when I was going to write a book.

Lord, thank You for this day.

4/7/98 ~ 11:05 p.m.

On March 2nd, Paula gave written resignation from the Clinical Position. I spoke with her on the 1st. No excuses accepted, the company was severing professional ties. She gave verbal resignation followed by letter on Tuesday. I had a meeting with the faculty and requested written responses. It is clear they all understood why I was angry with no tolerance attitude. I have felt angry, edgy. Even at home. I arrived to a cool house, the temperature read 62 degrees. I told Ernell it was cold. His remarks drove me to bed. I refused to exchange words or let myself lose control. After all, I have a heated blanket. To bed I went at 8:30 p.m. x 2 nights.

Today, I was productive. The office was quiet. Cherry, Matthew, Wendy, Stephen, all faculty arrived at different times. Quiet, productive.

Yesterday, I attended SB Co. Contractors Meeting. Must be requested with South Bay PIC application due Monday. I will meet the deadline. I forgot what it was called. I almost drove to Long Beach today but saw it on my desk 75% completed. So much to do. The Cooley set will be ready for the LVN on April 19th.

The ETP Program is underway. Veronica is energetic to do well. I expect 80+ students.

Momma is doing fine, up and about, no restriction on physical alertness or movement, speech still muddled. Appointment at the end of the month with Speech Therapist. She will be talking full force by then.

I will stay tonight and tomorrow, then home to my husband and kids.

Tahira is preparing to move out on Saturday. I will miss her. We will miss her. A new beginning for all.

Lord, thank You for all of the wonderful blessings.

4/11/99 ~ 10:50 p.m.

TAHIRA.

A tear to a mother's eye. I looked into her room. The mattresses are leaning against the wall. I see the bed frame, the floor. Reality sets in. My baby is leaving home to start a new life. Now, I had seen her new home. Ernell and I even paid for the window covering. But now the bed is up. I shed a tear. Memories of my child leap through my mind. Her smile, sensitivity, the way she holds her hands, clasped together (like me). The wonderful gifts from her, her friendship, the ring given to me on my 46th Birthday. Now the nurse, the homeowner, the woman I helped raise is starting a new life.

In the kitchen, I held her and cried. I told her I would miss her. I am proud of her and loved her. She laughed and said, "Mommy, I'm only moving to the next city."

Our lives will change. Last Saturday, the contractor came to look at the plumbing needs. I believe I will get what I desire for our home. Each time Ernell tells me we will need to 'modify,' I smile, not conceding, just praying to God. I know we can do this.

God has brought us through many trials. I am so very grateful to have my family together. How do I say thank You?

Thank You.

4/17/99 ~ 12:30 a.m.

So much has happened in the last 7 days. It seems as though it's been weeks since I last opened this diary.

I received a call on Tuesday from Jane Adam's Secretary. She asked how much money I was seeking for the Child Care Center. I was speechless. I had submitted a budget for $528,000. $400,000 would be a good start! I don't know what they will provide. I am grateful to God for my financial blessing.

I spoke with Otis Lacy Taylor and Stephen B. I had to get involved. Jordan informed me he had another buyer for the annex. I move – Larry tells Mike not to worry. I don't trust him. I am not his interest. He works for Jordan. Mike better keep an eye on the deal.

He drew up a new proposal for $1.5 million. I need $150,000 to close the deal by August 1, 1999.

Lord, guide me. Protect me. Bless me.

Remember Rwanda

4/18/99 ~ 3:45 p.m.

Today, Ernell, Stephen, and I attended the special program at the Southside Church of Christ. The special program was in remembrance of the Rwanda Genocide. It's sad, but true. Gross inhumanity against another. The killing of approximately one million Tutsi and moderate Hutus. Today was a day to remember the lost loved ones, the cause and effect.

I've never understood the conscience that can kill without regard of God's punishment. It is never worth the loss of the kingdom.

Tomorrow, we will start with 40 students. Lord let us graduate 40. Let us do all that is right and avoid the pitfalls of error. Time to write the 1999-2000 proposal to SB Co. It is due Wednesday by 4:00 p.m.

Lord, thank You. Guide us. Give me, bless me, with wisdom.

4/21/99 ~ 4:35 a.m.

Graduation of LVN, class number 5. I feel as though it is the last of the residual of class 3. We will have peace and better process from here on out. A new entrance requirement, the graduation was very nice. About 400 guests. Gary Lobster, Mayor of Saginaw, Michigan attended and gave our closing prayer.

It is now time to take him to LAX for his departure home.

This has been a good weekend. Lord, thank You.

4/22/99 ~ 6:45 a.m.

On April 20th, I received a call for 100 books from Rio Vista Elementary School. Dr. Duneen DeBuhurl placed the order. I was excited. Now I must recopy them, get prepared for more orders. I sent off and received the ISBN #. All papers have been forwarded back to BB Booker.

Sadiq's books are off the ground and his dream is a reality.

The SB Co. proposal made the deadline. Now the wait to see if it is approved. I am still working on the 293 building. I know God is guiding me. I had Carol Hatch and Stephen to walk through. And we discussed the layout. I have some ideas to share with them. I am excited.

Ernell and Aisha are off to Mammoth today for a weekend of skiing. I am going to Colorado to meet the First Lady of Uganda. Cherry, Stephen, and I, attended a fundraiser last night for Supervisor Jerry Eaves at the Kola Shana restaurant. Then, I traveled to the Hilton Hotel to hear Rosie Grier speak at the SB County Recognition for schools of excellence. Cherry, Stephen, Mike, and Alicia were to be there, but they didn't show up. I don't know what happened, but they missed a good, funny, and informative speaker.

A full day. Lord, thank You for the guidance. Love, Linda

4/23/99 ~ 9:50 p.m.

I was dumbfounded today. After all we (the school) had been through, Cherry did not get the request to start a June class in on time. The request was due the 15th. She submitted on the 19th. More significant revenue lost. She wrote a letter to Ms. Jones requesting an acceptance of the late request. I just doubt her finding favor. I feel wounded. I can't cry. I ask God for wisdom. If she denies the request, we must strive to produce the revenue to survive. I will take the charge to follow up on compliance dates on all departments. Lord, guide me. Stephen and I meet at his home to discuss a plan of action.

Home at 10:00, spoke with Ernell. He and Aisha arrived safely in Mammoth. Plans to ski Friday and Saturday, home Sunday. I know they are going to have a wonderful time.

Bedtime.

Goodnight, Lord.

4/24/99 ~ 7:30

The Nursing Board approved to place us on the June Agenda – Lord, thank You. The Women of Achievement Award was held at the

Pomona Sheraton. Cherry received recognition for Health Services. I gave the invocation. Off to Denver, Colorado to meet the First Lady of Uganda.

4/26/99 ~ 10:00 p.m.

Awestruck at the events in the last 24 hours. Emotions have run high to a calm peace within.

The First Lady spoke so well about God's vision for her. She has taken the steps to implement his works. She knows that through God, all is possible. The walls of Jesus did come down.

Today, Jordan Grinker informed me he had sold the tower and the annex on Friday. I remained calm, my mind confused. He never mentioned the tower being sold with the annex. Earlier, I had obtained estimation on the cost of fire sprinklers. About $2.00 per font, $74,000 for the bank, and $10,000 for the Annex. As Gordon tried to express, "I'm sorry," I felt calm and peaceful. I knew that all would be well. There is a building for us. Maybe God will direct us to a new building. We will continue to build and save funds for the right time.

We have about 30 students in the VN class # 9. The CNA, ETP started with 8 of 14. Students are going to Riverside for other interviews this week.

I wonder where God is going to take us next. I wonder and pray for preparation.

4/25/99 ~ 11:12 p.m.

Driving/Riding through the mountains of Denver, I feel so privileged. I have been in the presence of Miss Janet Museveni, first lady of Uganda. I heard the message of Jericho. Marching around the castle, not giving up. Had he stopped, he would not have successfully brought the walls down. God will use us, but we must not despair nor quit.

I look at the mountains, snow, and blue sky. I thank God I am so very blessed. I acknowledge to Stephen and Vincent my gratitude for encouragement and hospitality respectfully.

I am so sorry Cherry left. She missed a blessing. But all will work out. This afternoon, I will meet with Ms. Museveni's staff to discuss education and health needs of Uganda. Lord, keep my mind focused, my ears open, and my mind clear so I may receive all that I need.

5/4/99 ~ 6:30 a.m.

An emotional twist. After returning to the office, reminiscing about the meetings in Colorado, I turned my thoughts to Cherry's action. So much goes through my mind. Why she really abruptly left the Denver meeting. Was Catherine home when she arrived?

I attempted to meet with her in my office last Tuesday. After the first sentence out of my mouth, she exploded with words. I sat silently and listened. She is sick of me... I am negative, a negative spirit... Not a threat, but if she doesn't become a partner she will not be doing this for another 5 years... She has her own plans. Body language, tone of voice, all with a little head shaking and attitude. Stunned, I sat and listened to all that was said and not said.

Daddy taught me to hold my peace. I held it.

I guess, at times, it seemed I cowered but no, I held my peace.

I must get centered with my own spirit and my purpose.

No fears of losing anyone. God, protect and guide my path. Four-D's path. We are all replaceable. If she or I leave the school, would it perish? Should it?

I have talked with financial and legal advisors. I have spoken with Ernell (although I could not tell him of Cherry's actions) and expressed the need to protect the school's interest.

Today, I will talk with Cherry. I am prepared for any outcome. I called her this morning. I requested my diary, the notes of my dad, also an appointment to talk with her. I am at peace. Lord, thank You.

5/8/99 ~ 10:42

Mother's Day.

Today, Tahira took Momma Russ, Anwar, Jaise, Aisha, Ernell, and me to Wild Bill Entertainment Restaurant in Anaheim. Dinner of barley soup, biscuits, salad, corn on the cob, baked potatoes, fried chicken, ribs, vanilla ice cream, apple tarts, sodas. The entertainment was good with singers, dancers, and comedians. We returned Momma and the boys home, and stopped by Mama Vivian's for a few minutes. We arrived home by 9:00 p.m.

Yesterday, I eagerly went to work. I couldn't wait to arrive, up at 5:50, walked on the treadmill until 6:25. Showered, out by 7:30-7:45 to work.

I arrived into the parking lot. No cars to be seen in the whole block, no people. I smile. I love Four-D Success. I enter, set things down, kneel, and pray. I give thanks to God for all family, husband, kids, mother, brothers, family, the students, and Four-D. I thank God for me, my spirit. I pray for lasting faith. I pray for the new building. We need the space for growth for the Child Care, I pray. I pray. God hasn't brought us this far to stop. It has been a while since I was alone and took the time to sit still and pray. To feel God's presence, to know I walk by faith, that Four-D is protected. I pray with peace, I pray with joy, I pray to give thanks for all.

I pray for life, love, those who suffer. God hears all prayers. He hears me. He speaks to me. I listen, I pray, I am filled, I rise. I think clearly, I spend the next 6 hours thinking and writing. I strive to improve Four-D operations.

God is with me.

I spoke with Richard Nevin's attorney a couple of days ago to address Four-D's protection. Ernell will have ownership if anything should happen to me. Cherry is in line to manage day-to-day operations.

Sadiq called yesterday to say he had a lump forming in his left side. He had noticed a lump years ago, seen a doctor who told him he had a hernia. He is worried. I am not. I briefly inform him that I do understand his anxiety. I think of my breast. I am encouraging him to not think of the worst. Negative energy is draining power. We change to a lighter topic. We close with goodbyes of love.

Well it's 11:27 p.m. Time to retire next to my husband. Today, we made love and held each other so close. I tell him it was worth going through the tough times to end up here and he agrees. Our love is solid. Our touch is gentle and loving, felt to the heart. Ernell, thank you. God, thank you, you gave me what I needed. HIM! Goodnight.

5/11/99 ~ 10:48 p.m.

Essence Magazine.

How I Did It. Starting a Health Care Training Center. Four-D Success Academy received coverage – National. I received a call from St. Louis and e-Mail from back East. Hopefully, the National Coverage will promote the Academy. We received a "counter offer" on the 201 East Building. I feel blessed. God protects us.

The ETP project is going well. 14 enrolled, another 10 to start.

Saturday, I went to work, entered my office, kneeled, and prayed. I gave thanks to God for all He has provided. I pray for family, students, friends, the building, marriage, and equipment. I am so thankful, I pray and pray.

Lord, thank You.

Oh yeah, Donald had a son born today. Donald Lorland Morris, Jr.

5/19/99 ~ 8:15 p.m.

Well I feel blue for such an exciting event. Today, I signed to purchase 701 N East St. for $1,185,000. Nervous, no. Blue, yes. I guess the joy is smothered by my inability to build onto our home, Ernell, and his obstacles. The front will cost too much to change. We will save $15,000 to leave it. Delete my office, remove the kitchen island. If they change the direction of the master bathroom, we will not need to move the wall north. We demolished the plan. Then he says he does not want to be in an apartment this summer while the construction is going on. I hold myself, my peace.

I feel my spirit struggle. Not good. I work hard. I want this for me. I don't go out. If I am not working, I am at home. Ernell doesn't see the need for the changes. It's not the money; we made more than $180,000 last year.

This year, I will earn $93,000. He will earn – $120,000-130,000. I am sad the house I desire is never to be.

My energy must stay in the school. There I control what I want to build. I am tired and sad.

5/23/99 ~ 10:02 p.m.

Last evening, Ernell and I attended Pastor Dr. Ernest Dowdy, Jr.'s 8th Anniversary for the Church of the Living God. It is always a blessing to be present and be in the presence of Bishop Ruffin, the pastor who baptized me when I was a child. Keith Lee, Director of the County of San Bernardino, delivered the theme, 'God's man standing on God's promises,' Romans 4:20-21.

Today, Pastor Chuck taught on Joshua 1:1-20. "God's Promises, Knowing Who You Are." I/you know who you are; you have direction in your life. We all have a purpose. Faith is knowing God's promises. Pastor also clarified the difference between the Pavilion being a busy venture, arm of the Church. He sought support for the Cathedral building fund. I wrote, I pray to God for a $1 million dollar contract. I will contribute $100,000 to the building fund. I spoke with Pastor Chuck and informed him of my prayer. He spoke of being in the right place, knowing the right people. How he met the King of Jordan, Hussein, via Rev. Jesse Jackson. I informed him I had met with the First Lady of Uganda, and discussed healthcare for Uganda.

Lord, guide us.

Cherry and I met with Julius on Saturday at Carrow's Restaurant in Pomona. We discussed the Surgical Tech Program. I feel so revitalized, so focused, so in tune with God.

Pastor Chuck said, "Don't let anything block your blessing." For me, that meant don't slow down because others think you should slow down.

Four-D Success Academy, Inc.'s proposal to purchase 701 N E St. San Bernardino papers were taken to Church and prayed on. I ask God to close this deal to provide the finances to support it. There is a tinge of fear. I was seeking to purchase a $1,185,000 building. Seven years ago, I sought a building with free rent. I stood on faith then. My fear subsided and was replaced with joy and faith. God, in His wisdom, had brought us this far. He was planning to take us further. We were being prepared.

Lord ,guide me to be a better leader. I pray to be wise.

Lord, thank You once again.

5/25/99 ~ 11:49 p.m.

Today, Stephen, Greg, and I met with Union Bank and EDC Reps. We were analyzed personally. Our financials were reviewed closely. The meeting lasted from 2:00 p.m. to 5:00 p.m. The outcome? They will get back with us. God was with us – as always. I believe. I receive. Lord, thank You for guiding us to having the reviewers to find favor in us.

As you prepare us to move forward, I pray we always remain mindful of where we have come and to where we are going.

Lord, thank You for you are ABLE! I keep thinking of Daddy – He didn't bring you this far to leave you. I cry as I think of what God has done. We have come far on faith. There is no limit one can go on faith.

Peace and joy fill me. I will continue to do my best. I have been responding to e-mails regarding the Essence Article. I hope to be of assistance to others. Lord, goodnight.

5/30/99 ~ 9:44 a.m.

Standing in Aisha's new bedroom and Tahira's old bedroom, I began to cry. Wonderful memories of my girls flooded me. I recalled when we first moved into our two-story house. The gathering of the boxes to pack for the move. I can see the girls descending the stairs. I was worried about the stairs. Were they old enough to walk up and down the stairs safely? Aisha was three, Tahira was four. Well they took to the stairs like old pro climbers, no injuries, and no fear. Through the years, they and the Ballard girls, Michelle, Monique, and Monica, used the stairs as a play slide. Head first, thump, thump, thump to the bottom.

I see the canopy twin beds. The tailored twin dresses, the small tea table and dish set. My babies have grown to become wonderful, responsible, educated women. Their courses in life are different. Tahira owns a home at age 22. She works full-time (plus) as an LVN. Aisha is preparing to go to New Jersey – Atlantic City for summer work and missionary work with Campus Crusade for Christ. She is truly changed with God in her life. She exhibits peace, a positive attitude, and joy. God will guide her. I look towards the outcomes as they unfold. I cry and thank God for my family, for keeping us together with love. I cry with joy. My life is good. My husband and children are healthy and happy. My home is at peace. All that I have gone through has brought me to this point in my life. I am happier than I have ever been in my twenty-three years of marriage. Lord, thank You.

Friday, Cherry and I visited 701 N E St., our new school home. I inserted the key into the lock and turned. I had the key to Four-D Success Academy. God has brought us a long way. He will make a way. We will need $150,000 as our 10% down. I don't have it. God does! We must stay focused and ask God for guidance. All is good and done in Four-D Success Academy's favor.

Continue to speak to my heart, Lord. Your Child, Linda

6/4/99 ~ 11:22 p.m.

Today, I submitted the signed Escrow papers and the $20,000 money order check to Ontario Escrow. I have scheduled appointments with roofing companies and fire sprinkler installers for estimates. Otis, Lacy, and I are to meet tomorrow. We will look at the building and receive the plans for tenant improvements. He will provide an estimate ASAP.

Today, I received a call from Virginia. Ms. Roche had read the Essence article. She called me because she needed direction. She has been struggling through an R.N program for 5 years (a 2 year program). We discussed her grades in theory and clinical performance, in meeting the objectives, study habits, study groups, tutoring, skill labs, counseling services, career counseling, support from the faculty, and meeting with DON.

She stated she had given up everything. She was depressed. She had thought about quitting. I told her she had to stop talking about depression. She was going to sink herself so low she would not be able to catch the life ring when it was thrown to her. She had to set her sight on graduation for December. She has one term to do. She would do it. We exchanged telephone numbers to keep in contact.

I felt this was the highlight of my day. I had truly helped another person. I was able to take the focus off of me, the school, and problems of management. I was able to give my heart and undivided attention to another. God has given me the opportunity to make a difference one more time.

Ernell and his buddies are on their yearly river-rafting trip. Have a ball, honey.

Love you all ... Night, God.

6/6/99 ~ 7:25

Awakened at 5:55 a.m. My heart is heavy. I feel the burden of my soul. There is a split of the heart between Cherry and me. We are not of one accord. I thought the trip to Boston helped address the unknown issue. She told me she was jealous. My time was taken by Stephen, and she felt left out. I acknowledged her feelings. I made statements to reassure her of my position with her and Stephen. I explained my position regarding Four-D Success. I would not put the school in jeopardy of a partnership. The school will not be in position of a split. Maybe the position of 'partnership' has caused her to realign herself differently with me and Four-D. I had a meeting with her to address the problems of Nancy and Kaye sending students to the Acute Hospital knowing there would not be an instructor. Their lack of leadership and lack of accountability clearly indicated their lack of desire to accept responsibility for their actions, or they totally lacked understanding. While in a meeting with Nancy, Kaye, and Cherry, Cherry clearly separated herself from me. Her comments clearly stated she supported their actions and she was not in agreement with me. A more seasoned manager would not disagree with the president openly. One may not agree, but you will not go into a management disciplinary meeting on subordinates and disagree with the executive manager. I prayed to God about my heavy burden, my heart of sorrow. I sought resolution.

I called Cherry and asked her to listen in silence, and she did. I told her I had been in prayer this morning, asking God to mend our hearts. I did not know what was wrong between us, but I sought His help. I shared with her my view of her lack of management support — regarding memos to faculty held regarding office hours, compliance to the personal liability insurance for faculty. I, with a heavy heart, clearly stated my thoughts. I closed by saying, "I ask that you pray today at Church that God put our hearts in order, our friendship, not the school, but us. If I have hurt you in any way, I am sorry, for I do not know what I have done. Goodbye." My burden lifted, and God healed my heart.

6/8/99 ~ 11:09 p.m.

I have been extremely busy keeping appointments for appraisals on the 701 N E St Building. I have gone from one major project to another. The building needs a new roof, total inside improvements, exterior paint, and fire sprinklers. The initial estimate of $24,500 for the roof, $17,500 for painting, $62,500, and $81,900 for the sprinklers. Electrical air conditioner is not known. Otis, Lacy the general contractor will provide a written estimation for the total tenant improvements. The building must appraise for at least $1.5 million. God must provide a way to make it. I don't know how I do it. Doors open, I walk through, I seek information. On the way to work, I instantly thought, *Go to the building - lots of questions*. Then, negative thoughts came regarding behaviors I have experienced from others at work. I realized the deceitful interception. I changed my thoughts, stay on the road to see Colin. I prayed for focus. Met with Colin, he definitely is not pleased with the building. Bad taste of previous owners, abuse of power, and misuse of EDA funds. The building has set for a number of years. They (city SB) sold it for $800,000. The previous owner sold it for $1.1 million.

I went to City Hall and spoke with Valerie Ross, Senior planner. The building does not need retro fitting, no environment issues. She is pleasant and helpful. I felt happier when I left.

- I forwarded the asbestos report to the Air quality management office for review. Awaiting results.

- The elevator will be assessed Friday at 10:00.

- I spoke with Al Twine last week. We briefly discussed the need to I.D. African-Americans with intent for training for the political arena. I recommended that he, as a member of Westside Action Group, focus on this as an action issue. He called me today to meet with West Jefferson and him only.

I don't know where this is going? Well its 11:30 and I am very tired. Lord, I pray for positive closure on the 701 N E St. Building. I pray to become a better manager of the business. Help me improve on making sound, effective decisions. I pray for a mature, effective management team.

Lord, thank You for ALL you have given me.

6/15/99 ~ 7:10 a.m.

Today is Aisha's 21st Birthday. She is off to New Jersey for the summer. She will be working with Campus Crusade for Christ. My baby is now grown to be a beautiful loving child of God. She seeks to touch others through missionary work.

I remember talking with her when she was three and four. She would be so full of anger, crying silently. I would have her close her eyes to see color. She would tell me what she saw: red, yellow, blue, green. I would calm her spirit with gentle words, create mental pictures to relax her, guide her thoughts, streams of tears, being 'just mad'. As we would sit and talk, I attempted to guide her to an area of peace and understanding, an area of self-expression and love. Through the following years in elementary school, Aisha learned to control her anger, not to react to words and actions of others, but to act accordingly. Once her fifth grade teacher reported how well she had handled a situation in which a classmate was attempting to make her feel uncomfortable. As the only African-American child in her class, Aisha was comfortable with herself and others. She did not fear being 'the only one.' She had friends. Today she has continued on that path. She is not the only one. She has friends.

My baby is off to New Jersey until August 27, 1999. She will return more mature and grown.

Tahira is on her own. Now it truly is Ernell and me. Life has changed for the better. God has protected us as a family. Last Sunday, we presented Ernell his Father's Day gift, a gorgeous picture of him overlooking the Grand Canyon.

I am working and running, seeking the information I need for the building. Sometimes, I feel sick to my stomach. I know God is carrying the school and me. We will succeed.

I feel and hear negative comments, words of discouragement, but I must remember I am in God's protection. He knows those who will try to stand in our way. I know He will raise us above all obstacles.

The school in SB is ours; the Child Care Center is ours. God is our provider. We are a success.

Lord, thank You for ALL You have given me and my family. I love You as You love me.

Your Child, Linda

6/16/99 ~ 10:35 p.m.

Aisha arrived safely in New Jersey. She received 1 drawer for all of her belongings. She sounded happy. Today she called; she got a JOB within 24 hours of arriving. She landed a job at Peter Pizza for 30 hours a week, 11-5 p.m. My child has stepped out into the world with confidence, love, joy, and God!

Tim from Elite came back (2nd time) to evaluate the building. Thomas turned the water on and the pipe was blocked. Water splashed onto the floor, down into the drain. I am so happy I was there to witness it. Tim told me the plug prevented the water from going to the upper floor pipes. The transducers for electrical was not turned on so the electrical condition could not be assessed.

I informed Thomas and Mike I would not purchase a building listed for "Sale – as is," if the building could not pass an inspection for a city permit.. I was not going to pay to fix something to see if it worked.

Saddened over the day's events, I came home at 1:30. Had a 3:30 nail appointment. Mike left a message on my pager, the extension on the building until July 15th. The other items I will discuss tomorrow. Pam reminded me to take the papers to Church and pray over them. I have turned it over to God. He will take care of all. I needed to be reminded. Juanita also told me on Monday, "You can only do your best. God will take care of the rest." I am doing my best.

Veronica Beckos notified me of the students in the ETP CNA Program. She and the Hospital Adm. and DON had agreed to dismiss 4 students. I am quite upset. She agreed without notifying me! I must take control and assess the program to keep it moving forward. The dismissal after 7 weeks is a loss of $10,000.

Tired, sleepy, I must retire. I spoke with Gloria, a high school friend. She has breast cancer. Doctors removed lymphoids, breast tissue, and damaged some nerves. She says her arm is crippled. She still had to do radiation, which made her extremely sick. She came off of it. She said, ***"I chose not to have physical surgery."*** I don't know what I would do if my past breast biopsies were positive.

Lord, thank You

Goodnight.

When I write, it is my prayer time. Thankful time.

6/20/99 ~ 12:38 a.m.

Well Lord, I am coming to the end of another fiscal year. I am calm at this time. The next two weeks are going to be very busy. We have VN students to enroll. Currently, we have less than half of what we need. I am praying for 45 strong candidates. I trust in You, for You know all of our needs. You supply all. We have come this far by faith and grace. The building seems to be a gift from You. As I walk through it, I feel comfortable. I feel the spirit. I see the plans clearer.

As I go through the activity of research, I release the negative energy that had flowed through my mind. It is a terrible thing to forget all that God can provide and replace it with doubt and fear. If I am to believe in God and have faith in His every presence, then I must not doubt. I must not be captured and crippled by fear.

As I revisit and capture my being and God's being, I come to understand once again: I am His child with all rights and privileges as an offspring. I travel through life questioning myself only to realize that God chose me to do this work. He selected me knowing all of my limitations, but He equally knows all of my gifts. The gift to laugh, to love another, to be unselfish. He knows the sincerity of my heart. For that, I cry tears of joy – joy that lightens my heart, deepens my spirit, radiating the love of God. Four-D Success Academy has allowed me to be consistent in giving.

As I come to the end of another recording of this diary, I reflect back to Claremont. Margie Harris and I were talking about the beginning. The smaller space, fewer students, staff. We have come far. Today, there are 35-40 staff members. We are in a 10,000 plus square feet building. We are more productive and organized. God has a plan that He is unfolding daily. I have the keys to our new site. 701 N E St. San Bernardino. Lord, thank You for the new home. Your Child, Linda

6/23/99 ~ 7:05

Today, I sit in my room. Alone. Ernell and the boys are at the lake. Aisha is in New Jersey and Tahira is in her home.

The Bureau of Post Secondary visited the school on Tuesday, June 22, 1999. We were prepared and organized. Dick informed me we were one of the most organized schools of 15 he had visited. Four-D Success was the 'largest.' We discussed what small vs. large schools were. Small schools have enrollment of – 100. Four-D had 150 enrolled the day of the visit. Dick talked to me about Quality

Assurance. There are two sides, Administrative and Product. The administration areas of concern need not have an affect on the product outcome. He expressed we had a good product. His talk helped me a great deal.

We received the ABHES report back. About eight areas to address, the report is due in September. The temperament between Cherry and I has been cool. The energy is low. Although the trip to Martha's Vineyard allowed us space to talk, I do feel the lackluster energy that did not exist in past years. My focus is on Four-D Success growth, the new , and proposals. Things will revive and survive. New managers bring energy and professionalism to the school. I am pleased with the new approach.

Today, we are hosting lunch for the students and faculty, an effort to show and express appreciation. My God is always with me. He protects me. He prepares me for the future. I walk each day by faith. I know my path is guided by Jesus. He brings individuals into my life to aid the mission of Four-D Success Academy.

Lord, I truly thank You for Your love for me.

6/26/99 ~ 12:28 a.m.

I received a call from Greg, my youngest brother. I expressed my thoughts and disappointment. He is going to the law library to write his appeal.

I informed him that if his ethics and character do not change, he should stop the appeal. If he was working to get out only to be rearrested, as history tells, he should stay in and not waste his time.

I expressed my thoughts — Momma's stroke, the presence of God, and God's grace on her. End of subject.

6/27/99 ~ 10:28

Now it is a new day, I come back with a settled heart. Gregory Allen Simmons, my baby brother, made choices that put him behind bars for 28 years. Now, he states it scares him. Too little, too late. Sorry, my dear brother.

Cleaning up my home allows me to release tension, think of good things — like my husband coming home to a clean house. Washing clothes, dishes, mopping, cleaning bathroom, etc. Checked my e-mail, so on and so forth.

Lord, thank You for this day! My momma is doing fine. Resting well while the boys are out.

6/29/99 ~ 11:31 p.m.

I can't say that anxiety gripped me although I could feel my feet swelling, my body's response shifting down. I wonder if I am harming myself. The reason for such a thought.

I met with Dave today; we reviewed the final draft of the plans. I am excited. I return to the office excited and informed Cherry. She responds with how tired she is with the LVN program. She is sick of it. She has other plans for herself.

I inform her Four-D cannot pay for her and another person as DON. I tell her what I envision for her as Program Director. She has other plans. I reflect on the change. I press on.

Appointment with the Director of Nurses at Upland Convalescent Hospital. She is interested in the work-study program. A 250-bed hospital, and we could train 50-60 aides a year. Four-D Success Academy received high praises from the DON and graduate students. I left feeling good.

I spoke with Otis regarding the T.I. for the 701 North E St. Building. Bottom line, $339,000 + 141,000 = $380,000. The sale is $1,185,000+$67,000 = $1,632,000. The T.I. could be reduced by $60,000 – possibly. But as I see the numbers put before me, I swell. Otis reminded me that it is a large building. If we need the space for expansion and can service our debt, then it is a good deal. Property owner, valued property in the City of San Bernardino.

I sit and think, 'Lord, am I on the right path?' $1.6 million. Stepping out on faith. My banker has endless funds. My purpose is to help others. God knows my heart. I progress with Him as my guide. I must sit still, and listen, seek guidance. Fear will paralyze me. God will release me. My swelling feet are false evidence of unreal non-existent financial losses. Four-D Success will prevail.

I spoke with a young lady named Shirley from Chicago, Illinois. She is opening a school. She called for advice and then invited me to visit her home in Chicago or Georgia. While sharing, I thought maybe I should visit Chicago. Open a school.

Aisha called, she is doing fine. Last week, they reached out to 4,000+ citizens and discussed the 4 Spiritual Laws. She is doing fine. Her shared room is so small that two of the roommates must leave in order for others to stand. She will appreciate her room upon returning. I do miss her.

Lord, thank You for this day. Guide me, keep me free of fear.

Looking Back …

- I have never accomplished anything within my own strength, wisdom, or ability.

- Doors of opportunity always present themselves — how prepared I am to walk through determines the ultimate height of my success.

- Invite the wisdom of others. Their input could very well be the missing link you have been toiling for.

- Excellence should be demonstrated at all times in every area of business, especially with presentation and documentation. How one perceives the services you offer will be evident in their overall interest. Make sure the details are clearly defined and easily understood.

- Be direct and passionate about matters that concern you and others will feel your excitement and want to take part as well.

- I always seek to provide the highest level of learning possible, whereby remaining competitive against the giants that try to swallow me up. The 'David' within me refuses to give into the goliaths of the world. One must be sure of the call, and with that assurance, walk boldly — He won't let you fail nor be trampled upon as long as you stay on the path that lights the way.

- I keep my mind strong by reading literature that adds value to me personally, professionally, and spiritually.

- It's important to take the time necessary to regroup and reassess your objectives. Over time, your output will easily deplete your energy as you care for the demands that are placed before you. Discover ways to escape and replenish as you purpose to keep your foundation strong.

- Love is expressed in many ways. It is not rude, loud, or unforgiving. I have to choose to walk in gentleness and kindness, as that is most pleasing to the Lord.

- You cannot expect God to shower you with blessings if you don't extend yourself in ways that are pleasing to Him. So no matter what others may be doing, you must take the high road, and press beyond the silliness of the moment.

- Situations in life can cause the core of your beliefs to be questioned. You must, however, remain steadfast and unmovable in those things in which you believe and build your faith on. No matter what it looks like, no matter who falls by the wayside, God is still in control; and opposition will come in many forms, but with God, you have the last say as to how you will respond. Stand in faith in the meantime!

- I have learned how to respond to negative attitudes and recognize them as detractors. Anyone that suddenly takes away from the vision is a detractor. Anyone that thinks 'it' should be done a different way, after the standard approach has proven to be successful is a detractor. Anyone that decides to not carry his or her own weight or stops adding value to the team is a detractor and must be nullified before that cantankerous attitude filters through the workplace. Keep a keen eye for behaviors that easily drain a well-oiled machine into moments of uncertainty.

- As the leader, the final responsibility and accountability rest with you. Do not be afraid to take charge. Your strength to move forward in boldness comes from Him, and He has not given you a spirit of fear, but of power and of love and of a sound mind.

- I have no doubt that my steps have been ordered, and greater is He that is within me than he that's in this world.
- I must remind myself of my ability to ***do***. I can do this, I will do this, and I will be successful in my ***doing***.

- I seek no one's approval but the Lord's, for He is the authority upon which I manage my life and business affairs.

- People may question my approach. I may or may not have an answer. Often times, it's a simple knowing from within that I am on course and moving in the right direction.

With God, everything is bigger, much grander than we could have ever imagined for ourselves. You may not consider expansion, but feel free to embrace thoughts of growth; consider ideas that build upon that which you have already established. If you keep in mind that it is His kingdom being built on earth, and that you are just the vessel, it may be easier to wrap your mind around expansion.

As you come to terms with the idea that He has commissioned you to do that which you do, it will become effortless to receive and harness the direction as it flows to you. *"Do this... do that... go here and speak to her... go there and talk to him... start this new program... change this concept, and add this one instead...*" The expansion will start in your mind and heart first. You must believe within yourself that you are able to achieve what's been placed before you to do, then simply do it without wavering.

If you haven't already, it's time to discover the buried treasure of faith that awaits you. Opportunities for the future are ready to unfold if you would only believe in yourself and your ability to succeed in succession. May you experience faith on an intimate level is my prayer for you.

About the Author

Linda L. Smith, a Registered Nurse for 35 years, combined her love of Nursing, high standards of health care professionalism, and deep spiritual faith, and founded the first and only African-American owned, fully accredited vocational career college in California licensed to teach Vocational Nursing and other allied health care programs. The institution has been recognized as an Outstanding Business by numerous agencies.

Linda has been featured in *Essence Magazine,* is a contributor to the book *Creating Value through People,* and authored *Business by Faith, Integrating the 4D's of Success Personally and Professionally.* In October 2013 a documentary, *Linda L. Smith, A Profile In Courage,* was released and received the Accolade Award.

She was appointed Vice President Board of Trustees for the Inland Empire Loma Linda Ronald McDonald House and to the California State Assistance Fund for Enterprise, Business and Industrial Development Corporation Board of Directors by Governor Brown's Office.

As Founder of Four-D College and an inspirational speaker, she helps women and men pursue their vision with confidence.

Speaking at Colleges, Universities, Conferences, and other events designed to support those pursuing success, particularly in the Health Care Industry and Entrepreneurship/Business and Leadership, Linda teachers her 4D's of Success Personally and Professionally, imparting valuable information to help those who desire to start up a business, or progress in their current business or career path. She shows them how to overcome challenges and achieve success in business and in life.

Her experiences are soul-stirring, her message is powerful, and her delivery is profound. The way in which she shares her personal story, including struggles and adversity, is both educational and empowering.

To book Linda to speak at your event, contact her at www.lindalsmith.com or linda@lindalsmith.com.

www.ingramcontent.com/pod-product-compliance
Lightning Source LLC
Chambersburg PA
CBHW060337200326
41519CB00011BA/1964

* 9 7 8 1 9 3 4 5 5 6 7 3 3 *